INTIFADA

The Long Day of Rage

By
DAVID PRATT

CASEMATE

Philadelphia

Published in the United States by
CASEMATE

© 2006 David Pratt

ISBN 10: 1-932033-63-7
ISBN 13: 978-1-932033-63-2

First published in the United Kingdom by Sunday Herald Books,
Glasgow, Scotland.

ISBN 13: 978-1-904684-16-9

Cataloging-in-publication data is available from the
British Library and the Library of Congress.

10 9 8 7 6 5 4 3 2 1

CONTENTS

Background to the Israeli-Palestinian Conflict   1
Main Palestinian Groups   5
Foreword   7

1.   A DAY OF RAGE   11
2.   WAR OF THE STONES   17
3.   APOCOLYPSE TOMORROW   63
4.   THE BULLDOZER IN THE CHINA SHOP   81
5.   THE RESISTANCE ESCALATES   107
6.   "I HAVE A FEELING THIS IS GOING
       TO BE VERY BAD"   145
7.   ROCKET THE CASBAH   177
8.   ANOTHER BRICK IN THE WALL   205
9.   THE DEMISE OF THE ENIGMA   225
10.   THE CHANGING OF THE GUARD   239

Afterword   263
Acknowledgments   265
Notes   267
Select Bibliography   277

To my mother and father, and with love for Caron,
who put up with all the worrying absences.

'Did you want to kill him, Buck?'

'Well, I bet I did.'

'What did he do to you?'

'Him? He never done nothing to me.'

'Well, then, what did you want to kill him for?'

'Why, nothing – only it's on account of the feud.'

'What's a feud?'

'Why, where was you raised? Don't you know what a feud is?'

'Never heard of it before – tell me about it.'

'Well,' says Buck, 'a feud is this way: A man has a quarrel with another man, and kills him; then that other man's brother kills HIM; then the other brothers, on both sides, goes for one another; then the COUSINS chip in—and by and by everybody's killed off, and there ain't no more feud. But it's kind of slow, and takes a long time.'

'Has this one been going on long, Buck?'

'Well, I should RECKON! It started thirty year ago, or som'ers along there. There was trouble 'bout something, and then a lawsuit to settle it; and the suit went agin one of the men, and so he up and shot the man that won the suit—which he would naturally do, of course. Anybody would.'

'What was the trouble about, Buck?—land?'

'I reckon maybe—I don't know.'

'Well, who done the shooting? Was it a Grangerford or a Shepherdson?'

'Laws, how do I know? It was so long ago.'

'Don't anybody know?'

'Oh, yes, pa knows, I reckon, and some of the other old people; but they don't know now what the row was about in the first place.'

—*The Adventures of Huckleberry Finn*
by Mark Twain

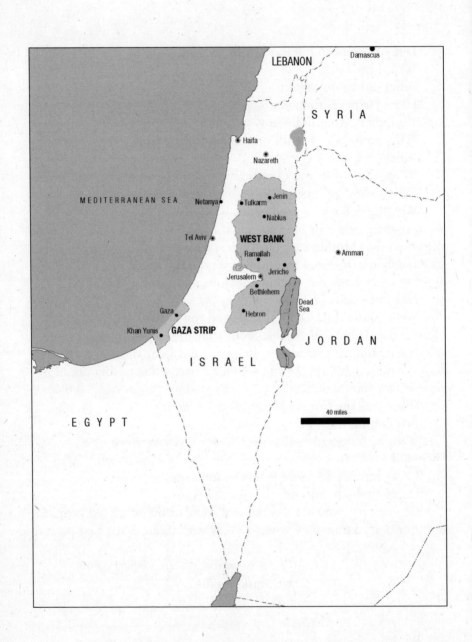

Background to the Israeli–Palestinian Conflict

1947 The British refer the 'Palestine problem' to the United Nations, which passes a resolution for the partition of Palestine.

1948 The state of Israel is declared. The result is the first Arab–Israeli war, which lasts from May until January 1949.

1956 After Egypt's nationalization of the Suez Canal, Israel invades the Sinai in league with Anglo-French forces. Due to Soviet threats to intervene and American refusal to support the action, the invading forces withdraw.

1964 The League of Arab States founds the Palestinian Liberation Organisation (PLO).

1967 The Six Day War. Egyptian, Syrian and Jordanian forces invade Israel. In response, Israel occupies the West Bank, Gaza Strip, East Jerusalem, Syrian Golan Heights and Egyptian Sinai Peninsula.

1973 The Yom Kippur War. Egypt and Syria launch attacks to try and regain land lost in the 1967 war, but fail.

1979 The Camp David Accords. Egypt signs a peace treaty with Israel, the first Arab nation to do so. Israel withdraws from Sinai but continues its occupation of Gaza.

1982 Israel invades Lebanon under the command of Ariel Sharon with the aim of destroying the PLO. Thousands of civilians are killed during the operation and the PLO flees Lebanon, dispersing to other Arab countries, with a headquarters in Tunisia.

December 1987 The first intifada begins in the Gaza Strip and spreads to the West Bank. The situation appears outside the control of the PLO, and the Islamic fundamentalist group Hamas begins to emerge as an important player.

1991 The Gulf War. The PLO backs Saddam Hussein, which results in the withdrawal of its support and funding by Arab governments.

1992 As a result of its new-found isolation and financial hardship, the PLO is forced to begin negotiations with Israel, which lead eventually to the Oslo Peace Agreement.

1994 The Oslo Peace Agreement is signed. The deal sees the PLO return to the West Bank and Gaza Strip in the form of the Palestinian Authority (PA). It is the first peace deal between the PLO and Israel. However, the agreement leaves all Final Status issues unresolved. These are:
  • The return of Palestinian refugees from 1948 to their homes
  • Where the borders of the Palestinian state will lie
  • The status of Jerusalem
  • The status of Israeli settlements on Gaza and the West Bank
A deadline of 1999 is set for the resolution of Final Status issues.

1994 Israeli troops withdraw to the edges of major Palestinian population centres, to be replaced by the Palestinian police force. The result is increased poverty and authoritarian rule administered jointly by the PA and Israel.

1999 The deadline for resolution of Final Status issues passes. There has been no change in the situation, except for increased poverty in Palestinian areas and the massive growth of Israeli settlements, which have doubled in number between 1992 and 1999. The lack of a political solution results in increased tension and outbursts of violence between Israeli troops and Palestinian stone-throwers.

2000 Bill Clinton, attempting to establish a legacy for himself during the last days of his presidency, calls a conference at Camp David. Negotiations break down and delegates return to the Middle East with tension increased still further.

2000 Ariel Sharon decides, for internal Israeli political reasons, to visit Haram al-Sharif in Jerusalem, which is Islam's third holiest site and the holiest site in Judaism. The following day Palestinian stone-throwers take to the streets in protest in Gaza and the West Bank, marking the start of the al-Aqsa intifada.

2001 Ariel Sharon defeats Ehud Barak in an election and becomes Prime Minister. Palestinian suicide bombings are matched by invasions of Palestinian cities by Israeli tanks, raids by helicopter gunships, and the placing of two million people under curfew.

2002 Israel re-occupies West Bank cities and begins building a 370-mile barrier, separating the West Bank from the rest of Israel.

2003 Attempts to revive the peace process fail. The Roadmap, a peace plan drawn up by the Quartet (United States, European Union, Russian Federation and United Nations), is signed by Palestinians and Israel, but security problems result in its early derailment.

December 2003 Israel announces a policy of 'unilateral disengagement' from the Gaza Strip.

November 11, 2004 Arafat dies. Former Palestinian Prime Minister Mahmoud Abbas replaces him as leader.

February 2005 Israeli Prime Minister Ariel Sharon and Palestinian President Mahmoud Abbas declare an informal ceasefire. Palestinian militant groups say they are not bound by the pledges made by both sides, but agree to observe a de facto truce.

August–September 2005 Israeli soldiers remove 9,000 Jewish settlers from the Gaza Strip and West Bank and formally withdraw their military bases in September, ending 38 years of occupation.

December 2005 Ariel Sharon leaves his Likud party to set up the Kadima party.

January 2006 Sharon suffers major stroke and Ehud Olmert becomes interim Prime Minister. Olmert says he will talk to the Palestinians, but only if they disarm.

January 25, 2006 Palestinians hold parliamentary elections. Hamas wins 76 seats in the 132-member Palestinian parliament, defeating President Abbas's long-dominant Fatah with 43 seats. Hamas says it wants to start talks immediately with Fatah and other Palestinian factions over the shape of a new government. The United States and European Union brand Hamas a terrorist group.

March 28, 2006 Acting Israeli Prime Minister Ehud Olmert leads the centrist Kadima party, only four months after it was founded by Ariel Sharon, to victory in general election.

June 9, 2006 Explosion thought to be from an Israeli shell kills seven members of a Palestinian family as they picnic on a Gaza beach. In response, the armed wing of Hamas calls off its 16-month-old truce.

June 25, 2006 After crossing the border from the Gaza Strip into Israel, Palestinian militants attack an Israeli army post. The militants kidnap Corporal Gilad Shalit, kill two IDF soldiers and wound four others. Israel launches Operation Summer Rain.

July 2006 Hezbollah militants cross the northern Israeli border and kidnap two IDF soldiers, killing others. Israel launches land, air and sea attacks on Lebanon, while Hezbollah fires rockets into northern Israel. After 34 days the Israelis withdraw, leaving Hezbollah unbowed.

September 2006 Violence and rivalry erupt between Fatah and Hamas in the Gaza Strip.

September 26, 2006 A UN study declares the humanitarian situation in the Gaza Strip 'intolerable,' with 75 percent of the population dependent on food aid and an estimated 80 percent of the population living below the poverty line.

Main Palestinian Groups

Hamas

Hamas, an acronym for Islamic Resistance Movement, emerged during the first intifada in the 1980s and led a suicide bombing campaign over the past decade as part of its avowed goal to destroy Israel. Hamas won the January 2006 Palestinian parliamentary elections, defeating the long dominant Fatah. Hamas gained increasing popularity among Palestinians because of a perception that it is free of corruption.

Fatah

Mainstream Palestinian nationalist movement founded in 1965 by late leader Yasser Arafat. Fatah is formally committed to negotiating with Israel to establish a Palestinian state in Gaza and the West Bank. But Fatah was accused of corrupt and inept leadership and gradually lost popularity.

Islamic Jihad

Founded in the 1970s, it shares Hamas's goal of replacing Israel with an Islamic state. But it lacks popular appeal and has not run candidates for elected office. Islamic Jihad denies Israeli charges that it is funded by the Iranian-backed Hezbollah group in Lebanon.

Al-Aqsa Martyrs' Brigades

The main militant faction within Fatah. The Brigades were formed by disaffected young men in the movement, many of them members of Palestinian security forces, after peace talks collapsed into the second intifada in 2000. In addition to fighting Israel, the Brigades have sought to oust a veteran Fatah elite seen as corrupt and autocratic in favour of a younger generation. But the Brigades have also been associated with worsening factional lawlessness.

Popular Resistance Committees

The Gaza-based PRC is a coalition of militants. Some PRC members remain on security payrolls and most are disgruntled former members of Fatah. The PRC has carried out attacks on Israelis, often in joint operations with Islamists and the al-Aqsa Brigades. It has also been linked to gang chaos.

Abu Rish Brigades

A splinter faction linked to Fatah, named after a Fatah militant commander killed by Israel. Based in southern Gaza, it carried out primarily bomb and rocket attacks on settlers and soldiers, and has also been involved in a wave of armed chaos.

Hezbollah

Arabic for the Party of God, Hezbollah is a Lebanese Shi'ite group with both political and military wings. Formed during the Israeli occupation of southern Lebanon 1982–2000, it shares much of the Palestinians' animus toward Israel and has waged similar resistance. Currently outside the Israeli-occupied territories, it has had access to military-grade weapons, as proved by the 34-day Lebanon War in summer 2006.

Foreword

'The Palestinian intifada is a war of national liberation. We Israelis enthusiastically chose to become a colonialist society, ignoring international treaties, expropriating lands, transferring settlers from Israel to the occupied territories, engaging in theft and finding justification for all these activities . . . we established an apartheid regime.'

—Michael Ben-Yair, Israeli Attorney General, 1993–96

Nothing is neutral in the Israeli–Palestinian conflict. If there is one thing as a journalist I've learned during almost twenty years of covering this story, it's the impossibility of ducking the political flak and sometimes downright vitriol that inevitably comes the way of anyone writing about this emotive issue.

As a foreign editor I can think of few other international political issues that so quickly stir emotions, fill newspaper mailbags, or generate internet blogging the way this long and bitter struggle does. For the journalist or writer who steps into the debate, it's almost a surefire certainty that they will come under ideological bombardment, and run a gauntlet of accusations that could see them denounced as anything from an 'anti-Semite' to a 'Zionist stooge.' Familiar as such accusations are to any writer or commentator, they will no doubt go on being made towards others who in the future try to wrestle with the provocative issues which lie at the heart of this political battle of wills.

For these reasons this book makes no pretence towards impartiality. First, because as I say, it would be an impossible thing to convince every reader of. Second, because the weight of evidence which as a reporter I have come across over considerable time, convinces me that the State of Israel has a case to answer for in its appalling treatment of the Palestinian people.

Already, based on that one previous paragraph I can hear the clamour of accusations. On the one side there are probably those thinking, how dare he 'recognise the State of Israel'? And on the other, how can he 'appease terrorists' and 'ignore the suffering of ordinary Israelis' at the hands of Arab suicide bombers and gunmen?

If there is another thing of which I am certain amidst all this rancour, it's that both sides, Palestinian and Israeli, have their own respective narratives of victimhood. Without doubt, each community has a story to tell, a litany of atrocities that has befallen them over the years at the hands of each other's soldiers, gunmen, bombers and assassins. Indeed, one of the greatest difficulties facing any reporter of this conflict is the extent to which these dual narratives and the bloodshed that accompanies them have a way of blurring the specifics of each individual tragedy.

Writing once about the disinformation, propaganda, charge and counter-charge, that so characterised the civil war in Lebanon and Beirut during the 1970s and 1980s, *New York Times* correspondent, Bill Farrell once summed up this burying of actuality with the remark: 'There is no truth in Beirut, only versions.'

To this day these 'versions' of the truth still bedevil any correspondent's efforts to try and get to the bottom of events in the Israeli–Palestinian conflict. That said, I remain convinced that a great injustice continues to be perpetrated against the Palestinian people. This injustice, and the responses of Palestinians – and Israelis – to it, provides the basis of this book. It is first and foremost a book of reflection and reporting based largely on dispatches, notes and diaries kept during many years of extended stays and visits to the region. In essence, it is, if you like, a series of reportage snapshots which, combined, I hope provide an accessible entry point for anyone trying to gain a better understanding of the mechanisms that lie behind the intifada and the wider events surrounding it. For that reason it is pretty much chronological, though readers may find that datelines are sometimes based on the time when any notes or diary entries were started.

I have also tried to provide some answers to those questions I'm most often asked about the intifada, such as how it started, who the main players are, what fuels the rage, and where Palestinian resistance to the occupation might be heading during these unpredictable days in the Middle East.

In June 2004, in a *Washington Post* article entitled 'Israel's Intifada Victory,' American neoconservative commentator and columnist Charles Krauthammer detailed how he thought that Israel had 'won strategically' its battle against the Palestinian intifada.

Travelling around the Gaza Strip and West Bank today and witnessing the punitive restrictions on movement and the penning in of the Palestinian population behind a network of walls, fences, checkpoints and barriers, it's possible to perceive how Krauthammer reached his conclusion.

The reality, of course, is that popular uprisings are not defeated in this way, only exacerbated, and those behind the Palestinian resistance will only find other ways to take the fight to their Israeli occupiers and enemies. As the Israeli writer Amos Elon once put it: 'In the intifada the Palestinians discovered the power of their weakness and the Israelis the weakness of their power.'

This book is my account of time spent among Palestinians and Israelis as they contest this battle and struggle to live ordinary lives in extraordinary circumstances.

DAVID PRATT
February 2007

1

A DAY OF RAGE

'God gave us the stone, it has God's will in it. It's all we have.
The stone has awakened the Arab world from the leaders to
the laymen. This is only the beginning.'

—Mohammed Mahmoud Abu Fodeh,
22-year-old Palestinian activist

City Inn Junction, Ramallah, May 2001

It's a strange feeling being shot at. It was much later before I thought about just how close the bullet had come. So close I could hear its buzz as it sped past. So close I felt its heat as it grazed the bridge of my nose. So close that the Palestinian driver of the ambulance into which it slammed, was able to bend down and pick-up the rubber-coated metal shell and hold it to his face before staring at me incredulously. *Lucky, very lucky*, his look said. I turned to a colleague and suggested it was time for a Coke and chicken sandwich at Salah's place. He agreed, and we scurried across some waste ground as another fusillade of bullets cracked against the surrounding buildings. Within minutes the cries of 'Allah o Akbar!' ('God is Great'), the acrid smell of burning tyres, and the wail of ambulances ferrying wounded from the fire-blackened street were behind us.

A 'day of rage' the Palestinians call it. Though sometimes it feels like the past years have been one long day of rage. This no longer seems like an uprising, just all-out war. Low intensity maybe, but a war nonetheless.

The usual motley mix of journalists and Palestinian *shebab* – the foot soldiers of this war – had gathered at Salah's. One youngster stinking of petrol from Molotov bombs was stuffing a pickle sandwich into his mouth. He was wearing a green Islamic headscarf with a Hamas flag tied round his neck like a cape; anywhere else, you'd take him for a football fan. Every day, boys like him dice with death, running the gauntlet of Israeli bullets and tear gas.

'The usual?' enquired Salah, in an American twang picked up during his stay in Pennsylvania. 'You been gassed today? I've got some more eau de cologne, if you're going back to the barricades.'

These days the *shebab* prefer cologne-soaked hankies to the traditional onions to alleviate the effects of tear gas. At a lunch table strewn with cameras and lenses, two Canadian photographers and another reporter, 'George the Greek,' were thirstily downing cans of Sprite, having likewise taken time out from snapping the bedlam on Ramallah's frontline.

One of the Canadians was sweating profusely under the weight of the flak jacket and Kevlar helmet his news agency insisted he wore; their concern no doubt as much to do with avoiding the need to pay compensation should he be wounded as interest in his personal safety.

George the Greek knew what it was like to be hit. As an old Middle East hand, once wounded in Beirut, he was busy telling the other younger Canadian to sharpen up his street skills, otherwise it was unlikely he would last longer than the two days he'd been on the West Bank.

'What happens if you get stuck that far forward and the stone-throwing stops and a fire fight begins? Simple, you're screwed,' he warned as the newcomer looked on sheepishly.

Even by the usual 'days of rage' standards, the last 48 hours had been especially bitter. As with Newton's third law of motion, so it is with the intifada. For every action there is an equal and opposite reaction; a continual cycle of resistance then repression then resistance again. No sooner does each side seem to have found its threshold of acceptable violence and suffering than it hardens into another bloody phase.

The day had started out quietly enough, not in Ramallah but in Jerusalem, as the *muezzin* called the faithful to prayer at al-Aqsa mosque. On the Via Dolorosa a group of tourists moved from church to synagogue to mosque, never quite sure when to cover their heads or take off their shoes.

As squads of Israeli soldiers started to muster in the narrow alleyways of the old city, the visitors looked on nervously. By the time the hack-pack of BBC and CNN camera crews arrived and strapped on bulletproof vests and helmets, the pilgrims were tugging at their tour guide's arm asking for reassurance. Much to the disappointment of the pack, only a few rocks were thrown that morning and the usual debate ensued. 'Ramallah's always a good bet,' said one impatient snapper. Another insisted it would 'go off' in Hebron that afternoon.

A three-shekel-fifty taxi ride and 20 minutes later we were in Ramallah. No rocks here either. Act I was over for now and the *shebab* had vanished. The big boys were now on stage and Act II was well underway as Palestinian snipers brought a furious response from the Israelis.

The place was like a scene from a movie except it was all too real. On the hillside opposite we watched the Israeli tank turrets swiveling menacingly before unleashing a clatter of heavy 50-calibre machine-gun fire at the buildings from which the flat *pop* of a sniper's rifle could occasionally be heard.

'No pictures, no pictures!' screamed a Palestinian Authority policeman, as one of the snipers appeared from behind a wall. His face was dirty, sweaty and grimacing with pain, his flak jacket hanging open where it had taken a bullet, at the very least breaking his ribs or damaging his lungs.

'Tanzim,' whispered a reporter crouching next to me against the thickest wall we could find. Bundled into a car, the sniper was gone in seconds. The shadowy armed wing of Fatah, the Tanzim ('organisation' in Arabic) regularly engaged the Israeli army in gun battles from inside Ramallah, despite superficial attempts by the Palestinian Authority to distance themselves from the group.

That night the Israelis struck back, their agents allegedly behind a remote-control bomb that killed a Palestinian man and three children in their home. The house was a bomb factory and the man blew himself up, claimed the Israelis; a victim of collaborators and spies, insisted the Palestinians. The only point of consensus was that the man had been a Hamas activist and was wanted by Israeli security. A three-story building had been reduced to rubble, but our hack-pack was there before the dust settled.

Amid the belongings strewn among mangled steel and concrete were children's shoes and a photograph of their grandfather. One bystander, realising an ABC TV crew was filming the scene, leaned forward and propped the portrait upright for the cameras, only to be chastised by a furious cameraman, who wanted the scene to 'be natural.'

Off we all went in search of those who had survived – the man's wife and fourth child who had been outside the building at the time. At Ramallah hospital a crowd had gathered. The funeral that afternoon, like most here, would become a political rally from which the spiral of killing would receive fresh impetus.

Along with a colleague, I was ushered into what I thought was a meeting with the survivors, only to find myself in the chill of a mortuary looking at the crushed and burned skull of the victim. As the hospital orderly pulled back the second freezer drawer and I saw what was left of the first child, I had already seen enough. 'Don't you want to take more pictures?' the puzzled orderly asked, oblivious to any explanation that no newspaper in my country would run such images.

As the *shebab* peeled off from the funeral procession and headed for the barricades of City Inn Junction to wreak revenge that afternoon, George the Greek, the Canadian photographers and assorted cameramen were not far behind.

'Today I have a passport to heaven,' declared Qassem, one of the *shebab*, loading another stone into his slingshot and strolling into full view of Israeli snipers. Instantly a bullet zinged past a few feet away, almost granting him his ticket to martyrdom.

'Allah o Akbar!' he shouted defiantly, before launching the rock at the Israeli Jeeps sitting 50 yards away in the rubble-strewn street. Seconds later there was the crack of an M-16 automatic rifle and a teenager rolling a burning tyre towards the vehicles crumpled to the ground after being shot in the face. Barely had he collapsed when two others rushed to his aid, sweeping him into an ambulance that sped forward on cue from a sidestreet.

Spurred on by the sight of their fallen comrade, hundreds of young Palestinians who had gathered surged forward, hurling rocks, Molotovs and insults. It is a ritual of attack and counter-attack, anarchy and respite. For hours I watched as more than 200 *shebab* took on Israeli soldiers in an unrelenting cat-and-mouse battle.

Here and there, the bravest and most reckless edged towards the Israeli positions, taking cover behind low walls, lampposts, anything that might stop a high-velocity bullet. Some, hiding their faces behind *kaffiyeh* scarves, openly taunted the Israeli gunners.

Throwing stones is a rite of passage for the *shebab*, and suffering wounds at the hands of Israeli soldiers is seen as a badge of honour. For the *shahid*, or martyred, instant recognition of their sacrifice comes when their faces look out hauntingly from posters plastered on cars and buildings. Some *shebab* turn up because of peer pressure; others are driven by personal grievances against Israel. Often they compete to outdo each other in acts of daring that all too often cost them their lives.

'How can we stop them when they see what happens to their friends?' a Palestinian mother who lived in a block of flats near the City Inn Junction complained to me. 'They're angry and upset and want to express themselves. This is their life. No school, no work, just stone-throwing and coming to funerals. There's nothing else for them to do.'

Amongst the *shebab*, many of whom have spent time in Israeli jails for their acts of resistance, there is also the constant fear of informers, spies or those willfully or innocently seen to be working for the Israelis.

As the riot raged, a Japanese photographer, who had been spotted crossing to the Israeli side between taking pictures of stone-throwers who asked not to be photographed, was bundled off behind a building by a group of angry *shebab*. Refusing to hand over his film the mood rapidly turned ugly and only the intervention and reassurance of colleagues finally saved the photographer from a severe beating or worse.

'Can you believe the Israelis call these non-lethal?' asked 20-year-old Nidal, as he picked up one of the scores of scattered rubber-coated bullets like the one that had narrowly missed me the day before. Part of its thin coating had been stripped away on impact, leaving a ridged, grey metal ball about half an inch in diameter and as heavy as a wristwatch. Before anyone invented high-tech machine-guns, laser-sighted rifles and tank shells, this was the kind of bullet people used when they wanted to kill each other.

'I'm sick of fighting them with rocks. Their bullets have taken so many of us now. The Stone Age is over. What we need are guns, then they will really know our will to fight,' Nidal complained angrily.

A few minutes later, as we advanced cautiously toward some overturned cars marking the forward frontline barricades, a cluster of tear gas grenades bounced over the top of the cars and landed in our midst. Huddled behind the scorched shells of the vehicles, *shebab* and journalists alike, without gas masks, were left temporarily blinded and retching. Two boys overcome by the gas were stretchered off to the ambulances that sat like delivery vans waiting to be loaded up.

To the outsider there is something absurd about this deadly ritual. Sometimes it verges on black comedy, like when one group of hungry rioters, stones in one hand and sandwiches in the other, ate and fought at the same time. Or, when a local ice-cream seller, his vending tray bedecked in Palestinian flags, turned up to offer the *shebab* other refreshments.

At the end of the day's clashes, we all head for Salah's Café to wash. For Palestinians travelling outside Ramallah and stopped at Israeli checkpoints, sooty faces from burning tyres and dirty hands guarantee arrest on suspicion of rioting. For the hack-pack, it's just an opportunity to make ourselves presentable before heading back to Jerusalem to drink beer and swap tales of derring-do in fashionable cafés. We will all be back tomorrow – the days of rage seem never ending.

2

WAR OF THE STONES

'With stones in their hands
they defy the world . . .
They burst with anger and love, and they fall.'

—'Children Bearing Rocks,'
Nizar Kabbani, December 1987

Gaza Strip, September 2004

Travelling from Tel Aviv to the Gaza Strip is a bizarre and unsettling experience. Though less than an hour's drive is between the cities, the two are worlds apart, living proof of the 'them and us' divide between Israelis and Palestinians. Only after passing the infamous high-tech 'Erez' checkpoint that marks the northern gateway to Gaza does the transformation really become complete. First though, there are the ID checks, then the heavily armed Israeli soldiers and their sniffer dogs, next the turnstile gates, razor wire, and surveillance cameras. Finally comes the long claustrophobic walk down the connecting concrete tunnel, stinking of stale urine and littered with empty plastic bottles discarded by those Palestinians who have spent hours waiting there – often in vain – for permission to enter Israel. Within minutes though, it's as if Tel Aviv's palm-lined seaside boulevards, nightclubs and hip bars were just a distant Middle Eastern mirage.

Welcome now to a land of shabby concrete city blocks, cinder-brick shanties and filthy overcrowded refugee camps, a place where open sewers criss-cross dusty alleyways and few houses have electricity or clean running water. Though barely 28 miles long and four miles wide, more than a million Palestinians cram into the Gaza Strip, one of the most densely populated places on earth. Guarded on all sides by the Israeli army, one third of them live in the squalid camps built in 1948 to hold those forced from their homes by the creation of modern-day Israel.

Those dark days are known as the *Nakba*, or 'catastrophe,' the common term by which Palestinians remember the mass expulsions and massacres that accompanied the 1948 war. Stateless since then, things have barely improved. Gaza is little more than a giant open-air prison; a human holding pen where most Palestinians have never known a single day of real freedom in their lives.

With the economy a wreck, carving out a living here has always been next to impossible. In the days before the threat of suicide bombers and the creation of the sophisticated security checkpoint at Erez that put an end to the practice, more than 60,000 Gazans were 'lucky' enough to be part of an army of day labourers.

Every morning this army would board vans, cars and buses, before making its way in the early dawn light to a variety of low paid 'dirty jobs' inside Israel itself. Often the soldiers at Erez would delay the workers for hours without reason. While some stayed overnight in Israel they did so against the law and at great risk. For those that made their way back to Gaza at the end of the working day, their degradation would sometimes be rounded off by the Erez guards forcing them to perform humiliating acts, mimicking barking dogs or braying donkeys before allowing them to pass.

Often I watched these workers returning home just before dusk. The scene was reminiscent of black labourers returning to South African townships from menial jobs in the big cities during the time of apartheid.

Hundreds would arrive at Erez as if on cue, tumbling from an assortment of vehicles, before being 'processed' back into Gaza. A few hours sleep would see them rise again before light, ready to start the treadmill journey back to the jobs so crucial for the money needed to eke out an existence and feed their families.

It was around 4 p.m. on Monday, December 8, 1987 as four Gaza workers were returning home from day jobs in Israel that an Israeli army tank transporter ploughed into a line of cars, killing the four men and injuring seven others. Israeli Radio broadcasts said it was an accident, but in the volatile Jabaliya refugee camp – 'Gaza's Soweto' – where three of the four dead men had lived, the rumour mill had already gone into overdrive.

The Israeli driver of the truck was said to be the cousin of one Shlomo Sakle, a 45-year-old Jewish salesman from the Northern Negev town of Beit Yam. Two days earlier Sakle had gone to the Gaza Souk looking for cheap merchandise when an unidentified Palestinian came up behind him and plunged a knife into his neck. Sakle managed to stagger just a few yards before collapsing in the backstreets where he bled to death.

In the super-charged atmosphere that is Jabaliya, for many Palestinians it naturally followed that the truck crash had been a deliberate and premeditated act of Israeli revenge. Whatever the explanation, in effect the fuse of rebellion had been lit and was burning down fast.

By the time angry mourners returning from the funerals of the four crash victims clashed with Israeli troops the following day, detonation was imminent. Within hours the barricades went up. Oil drums and tyres, sewage pipes, rocks and old furniture blocked the roads across Gaza. Israeli army patrols found themselves increasingly ambushed by hundreds of stone-throwers, but their top brass remained unperturbed.

'It's nothing. You don't know them. They'll go to bed and tomorrow report for work,' one regional army commander told a journalist. How wrong he was.

Just after 8 a.m. on December 9, an Israeli army unit entered Jabaliya camp. It was meant to be a routine mission, but very quickly the patrol found itself cut off and surrounded by dozens of incensed Palestinians. Out of nowhere, two flaming petrol bombs crashed to the ground near the soldiers' jeep, causing panic. Their officer gave the order to fire back using live ammunition, and seconds later an Israeli bullet ripped into the heart of 15-year-old Hatem Abu Sisi, killing him almost instantly.

The 'war of the stones' had claimed the first of its many martyrs. One of the great popular mass uprisings of our time had erupted. The first Palestinian intifada had begun.

Jerusalem, September 2004

Since that day in December 1987, the word *intifada* has taken on an iconic resonance worldwide. From TV news bulletins to T-shirts, it has become a byword for resistance to Israeli occupation, and the weapon with which many Palestinians hope to create a future state. Yet, despite its familiar usage these days on CNN or the BBC, many people remain unclear as to what the word really means. Indeed, many Middle East watchers have often commented on the significance of the Palestinians' choice of the word *intifada* as a name for their uprising.

In his marvellous book *From Beirut to Jerusalem*, the then *New York Times* Jerusalem bureau chief, Thomas Friedman, was struck by the fact that the Palestinians did not call it *thawra*, the standard Arabic word for revolt.

'This was odd,' pointed out Friedman, 'because for years one of the most popular Palestinian chants among PLO guerrillas in Beirut was "Thawra, thawra, hat al-nasr" – "Revolution, revolution, until victory".' Friedman and many others contend that the choice of intifada was borne out of the extent to which Palestinians were integrated or at least living cheek-by-jowl alongside Israelis.

Intifada derives from the Arabic word *nefada*. As a verb it means 'to be shaken, to wake up.' As a noun it means, 'shudder, awakening, uprising,' suggesting 'a shaking off,' as a dog would shake off water, or a person would shake off sleep. In this respect, says Friedman, it expressed the Palestinian desire at that time to purge themselves of all things

Israeli or any sense of 'Israeliness' that had swallowed up their lives.

Back in those turbulent early days, as thousands took to the streets with their slingshots, rocks and Molotovs, rekindling the embers of Palestinian opposition, the intifada seemed indeed at long last to offer a way of 'shaking off' the chains of a 35-year Israeli military occupation.

'We used to have strikes, but that word is too small,' said Hussein Jamal, a young journalist who lived in Jabaliya. 'We used to have demonstrations, but that word is too small as well. What we have today is something completely different. It is intifada.'

But just why did the Palestinian uprising start there and then in the Gaza Strip? Who were the main players behind it, and what was the reaction of both the Israeli government and the Palestinian Liberation Organisation (PLO)? Indeed, what if anything did this new-found faith in collective resistance ultimately achieve?

Travelling often as I did in those days between Gaza and Israel, I had always been struck by the 'two worlds' experience of going from one to the other. Over steak or spaghetti dinners in Jerusalem's fashionable Ben Yehuda Street cafés, Israeli friends would look at me incredulously when I told them of what Palestinians had to endure in Gaza. Only those who had done active service with the Israeli Defence Forces (IDF) in the occupied territories seemed to grasp what I was trying to describe.

Just before the start of the intifada, the Israeli novelist David Grossman wrote in his book *The Yellow Wind* about how Israelis:

Have lived for twenty years in a false and artificial situation based on illusions, on a teetering centre of gravity between hate and fear, in a desert void of emotion and consciousness.

Someday, Grossman warned, 'it will exact a deadly price.' Many Israelis I spoke with in those days seemed to live in this emotionless 'desert' that Grossman had described. It was as if Gaza and the occupied West Bank were home to millions of invisible people. Only rarely did a few more enlightened and curious Israelis venture to ask, 'What's it like there?'

For most Israelis, the humiliation, grinding poverty, curfews, movement controls and extrajudicial killings, which were the everyday life of most Palestinians, might as well have been taking place in the Congo or on the moon for all they cared. As the Israeli writer Amos Elon put it,

'Self deception became a prerequisite for survival.'

For example, how many Israelis would have heard of a Palestinian schoolgirl called Intidssar al-Atwar, who barely a few weeks before the outbreak of the intifada was shot and killed by a Jewish settler as she played in her schoolyard not far from the settlement of Gush Katif. The settler, Shimon Yifrah, was arrested some weeks later but released on bail because the Israeli Supreme Court deemed that the offence was 'not severe enough' to warrant detention. A little less than two years later in September 1989, Yifrah was acquitted of all charges except causing death by negligence. According to the judge he had only intended to frighten the girl by firing his gun at her in the schoolyard, not to kill her.

'This is not a case of a criminal person who has to be punished, deterred and taught a lesson by imprisoning him,' declared the judge, before giving Yifrah a seven-month suspended sentence. At news of the verdict Yifrah's settler supporters in the courtroom instantly broke into celebratory chanting and applause.

That September, almost at the same time as Shimon Yifrah was acquitted, the Israeli press also reported that an army patrol had fired into another schoolyard, this time wounding five Palestinian boys between the ages of six and twelve. Again it was only to 'frighten them.' Again, no charges. Again, next to no attention paid by ordinary Israelis. It was, however, yet more evidence of an emerging pattern, and part of an increasingly common occurrence called 'collective punishment.' As the Israeli media put it at the time, the schoolyard shooting was just another episode in the strategy of 'illiteracy as punishment,' whereby soldiers would close schools, fire tear gas grenades into classrooms, or beat and intimidate pupils.

On one occasion soldiers threatened that if they found children outside they would kick their asses 'and fuck them one by one.' It was all a far cry from the message of 'enlightened occupation' put across in a colourful booklet issued just before the start of the intifada by the Israeli Civil Administration in the territories. Marking 27 years since the 1967 war, it featured on its cover a golden wheatfield. Inside were pictures of playgrounds and clinics.

It was this collective mental block towards what was really happening in the territories by many Israelis, combined with a massive neglect of the conditions under which most Palestinians were forced to live, that largely lay behind the outbreak of the first intifada. It was, in effect, time to pay the 'deadly price' that David Grossman had warned about. As for the Palestinians themselves, their situation was desperate. Since June 1967 they had hoped that their Arab brothers would come to their rescue. They saw the defeat of Arab nationalism, the loss of Egypt into the Camp David peace treaty with Israel, and the successive blows dealt to the PLO in Jordan, Lebanon and within the occupied territories themselves.

On the inside, they watched helplessly as their land slipped out of their hands. Everywhere, their olive, fig, orange groves and vineyards were turned into Jewish settlements to accommodate foreigners who had arrived from the USA, USSR and other far off places to claim what many Palestinians saw as a mythical inheritance.

Once during a lull in a stone-throwing street battle between Palestinian youths and M16-toting Israeli soldiers in the centre of Bethlehem, I asked one Israeli soldier, 'Where do you come from?' Expecting him perhaps to say Jerusalem, Tel Aviv, Haifa or Ashkelon, I was taken aback when he replied 'Uruguay.' Things had not gone well for him in the South American country of his birth, he insisted, so as a Jew he had decided to take up citizenship and settle in Israel.

'My Hebrew's not so good and I'm not especially religious, but this is Israel after all,' he said, with a shrug by way of explanation, before returning to the street to fire rubber bullets at the Palestinian *shebab* who had once again started throwing stones.

To younger Palestinians, the arrival of such outsiders and the spread of Jewish settlements in the West Bank and Gaza looked exactly like the creeping encroachment that cost their grandfathers the other four fifths of Palestine between 1920 and 1948.

The Israeli government was able to use vague laws concerning the ownership of public land to confiscate much of the territory of the West Bank and Gaza to build 'strategic settlements.' While the exact figures are disputed, human rights groups indicate that this covered more than 80 per cent of the West Bank and 40 per cent of Gaza. Likewise the Israelis allocated themselves a huge share – 60 to 75 percent of all the spring water of the West Bank and channelled it to pre-1967 Israel. Even had they been residents in the West Bank, on a per capita basis the Israelis gave themselves twelve times what they allocated to the Palestinians.

For many of that older generation of Palestinians, after more than 40 years of exile, the last hopes of challenging this Israeli occupation and exploitation were fading fast. But just when their rage looked like it had been contained and was cooling off, along came their sons and daughters to resurrect a sense of opposition and fight. The anger of this new generation had long since been simmering and festering.

Brigadier General Ya'acov Orr, the Israeli division commander in the Gaza Strip, once explained to Thomas Friedman how he first realised the depth of this anger during a patrol through Jabaliya camp in the Gaza Strip in the early days of the intifada.

> I was walking down a street when I saw this little boy – I think he was a boy – he wasn't much more than one year old . . . he had just learned to walk. He had a stone in his hand. He could barely hold on to it, but he was walking around with a stone to throw at some- one. I looked at him and he looked at me, and I smiled and he dropped the stone. I think it was probably too heavy for him. I'm telling you he had just learned to walk. . . . I thought about it later, and I thought, for that little kid, anger is a part of his life, a part of growing up – as much as talking or eating. He still didn't know exactly against whom he was angry; he was too young for that. He will know after a while. But for now, he knew he was supposed to throw a stone at someone.

Far from being toddlers, those now taking up the stone of the intifa- da were mainly young adults, many of whom made up the army of labourers who worked daily in Israel. They understood Hebrew and Israeli ways, and witnessed a standard of living that put into perspective their own dire quality of life and the limitations imposed by such a predicament.

Working in Israel from dawn to dusk was to be at the sharp end of such injustice, and many who later became active in the intifada held deep grievances because of their exploitation by Israeli employers. Most of this labour force were hired at what Israeli journalist Yigal Sarna called the 'slave markets' of Ashkelon, Jerusalem, Ramat Gan and other places. Some would pay social security that they knew would never be repaid to them, or they were banned from joining trade unions and in their workplace lived under a callous hire-and-fire regime. Others were compromised to the extent that they themselves became corrupt or even collaborators with the Israeli military authorities.

A few months before the intifada, Yigal Sarna, in an article entitled 'Uncle Ahmed's Cabin,' exposed the conditions faced by those

Palestinians who against the law stayed overnight in Israel rather than run the gauntlet of harassment at checkpoints like Erez in Gaza.

> They are slaves, sub-citizens suspected of everything, who dwell under the floor tiles of Tel Aviv, locked up overnight in a hut in the citrus grove of a farm, near sewage dumps, in shelters that . . . serve rats only.

In one notorious incident in a Tel Aviv hotel, Israeli Border Guards badly beat up Arab workers: they forced them to masturbate, lick the floor of their room and eat coffee mixed with sugar and toothpaste. The guards' parting gesture was to steal from the workers the little money they had earned. Despite the incident being reported to the Israeli Parliament by Knesset member Ran Cohen and complaints to the police and military authorities, no investigation was undertaken.

A regular source of cheap labour when needed, Palestinian workers were instantly expendable when employers turned against them or simply no longer had any use for their services. After the intifada began, just to be in the wrong place at the wrong time could lose a Palestinian more than a job.

I remember once a chain of events that typified those early months and years of the first intifada. It began after the horrific stabbing to death of an 18-year-old off-duty Israeli girl soldier in the fashionable West Jerusalem neighbourhood of Baka.

'Iris the Rainbow' was the name *The Jerusalem Post* gave the girl, alongside its gory front-page description of how the Palestinian murderer had been 'highly trained,' leaving the girl's lungs on her chest. Within hours, a young Palestinian worker had been caught and the more militant of Baka's Jewish community were out for revenge.

At the Baka building site, where the accused Palestinian had been employed, a large angry mob surrounded the perimeter fence. Inside, about 20 terrified Palestinian workers peered nervously from an unfinished building; outside, the Israeli riot police turned the other way as the Arabs' cars were smashed and their tyres slashed with knives. Two Israelis carrying jerry cans of petrol made an attempt to torch the cars and only then did the police move in. Halfheartedly holding back the mob, the police persuaded the Arab workers to come out. They mistakenly thought that they would be escorted to safety, but instead, the Chief Police Officer suggested they 'run for it.' As the workers scattered in panic I watched the younger and fitter of them flee across some waste ground. The older of the men, though, were caught by the mob, punched and kicked to the ground. When eventually the police brought the mob under control, a number of the Palestinians lay badly beaten.

In the next few days the murderer of the girl soldier was convicted and his elderly parents' house blown up by the Israeli authorities under the 'collective punishment' ruling in response to such acts.

Meanwhile, the other Palestinian workers from the Baka site who had nothing to do with the girl's slaying lost their jobs after Yitzak Shamir imposed a ban on Arab workers from the occupied territories entering Israel to work.

And 'Iris the Rainbow' was buried.

The pattern of these events which caused untold suffering on both sides and way beyond those people directly involved in the girl's murder, was to become all too familiar as the *intifada* began to bite and many Palestinians hurried to join its cause. But if many disgruntled Palestinian workers were emerging as the vanguard of the intifada, their ranks were quickly swollen by the 15,000 bitter and bored college and university graduates who had found themselves largely making up the ranks of the unemployed, doomed to choose between indignity and exile.

In Gaza's eight refugee camps, including Jabaliya where the uprising had first exploded, unemployment was running at between 50 and 60 percent. A lot of pent-up frustration, fear, hatred, revenge and sheer hopelessness was coming to a head and finding a release.

'The worker only used to think about how to get to Israel and bring back money. He only thought about his family. Today he no longer goes to Israel to serve the Jews. He stays here with us to demonstrate,' was how a 17-year-old girl called Aya from Shatti refugee camp in Gaza put it when asked how the intifada had changed people.

In Gaza, and across the West Bank towns of Nablus, Hebron, Bethlehem, Jenin and now in Jerusalem itself, the war of the stones had taken hold, and there was no turning back for Palestinians and Israelis alike. As the Israeli journalists Zeev Schiff and Ehud Ya'ari observed:

> In the course of a single month Israel lost its control over the Palestinian population. The reins were snatched from the hands of the military administration . . . the habits of surrender, the obedient deference to the whims of the ruling power, melted away in the

atmosphere of revolt. This was a sharp psychological turnabout for a public that had discovered what it could do – and how to exploit the enemy's weaknesses.

During those volatile and unpredictable days I was almost constantly on the move, touring the hotspots in the company of other reporters, photographers and cameramen, who became witnesses to the extraordinary events that were unfolding.

West Jerusalem, 1988

'Sometimes only 50 shekels a picture. Can you believe it?' asked a colleague, Zeev Ackerman, one morning, throwing a copy of that day's *Jerusalem Post* onto the café table in front of us in disgust. Zeev, himself a Canadian Jew now living in Israel, was another of the many freelance photographers on the intifada beat. Only when things were 'really happening' did he get what he always called 'serious intifada rates' as a stringer with the worldwide news agency Reuters.

That particular morning there were a number of ongoing incidents, but nothing exciting enough to draw Zeev from what he saw as the day's real story. Another stabbing of an Israeli by a Palestinian man had taken place, this time near the Neve Yaakov settlement, and was sure to bring a militant Jewish backlash. For the moment at least, the war of the stones had been knocked off the headlines by this spate of stabbings labelled 'the war of the knives.'

Like most journalists covering those early intifada-related incidents, Zeev used a scanner to monitor police and army radio through a set of Walkman earphones that slipped inside his shirt. 'Not exactly legal, but certainly indispensable. There's some stone-throwing down on Salah e Din Street in East Jerusalem, and a Molotov's just been lobbed at a bus near the American Colony Hotel,' Zeev relayed to me before ordering another coffee.

'Neve Yaakov's what we really want though,' he reminded me. It was a peculiar daily routine that had no real routine at all. Like most intifada chasers, Zeev had quickly become all too familiar with the tactics and moods of both sides. He had been beaten up by Israeli soldiers in Gaza, and cornered by rioting Palestinians in the Nablus Casbah. Like most of us he prided himself on being intifada streetwise. To be oblivious of the vital rules that governed the day-to-day character of the uprising made getting around difficult, and could even cost you your life. For example, drive a car with Israeli-registered yellow plates and you were at the mercy of stone-throwing *shebab*. Territories-registered blue plates on the other hand meant constant Israeli army checks. Any Palestinian driving a car inside Israel with white-coloured Gaza regis-tration plates, however, might as well have had the word terrorist embla-zoned across the sides if the reaction of the Israeli police and army at checkpoints was anything to go by.

While driving inside Israel you had the option of windows down to cool off and seatbelts on as the law required. In the territories, it was windows up to help ward off stones, and seatbelts off in the event of needing to make a rapid exit should the car be petrol bombed.

One afternoon, driving with another colleague down the main Jerusalem to Jericho road, a Palestinian boy appeared from nowhere by the roadside near the village of Abu Dis. He could not have been more than eight years old, but with great accuracy – or luck – put a stone straight through the passenger door window next to me, showering my face with glass. In the few seconds that I saw him, I'll always remember how innocent-looking and nonchalant he was, pausing to give the vic-tory sign with his fingers before launching the stone.

This use of stones as the main weapon of the intifada was of course largely because of their ready availability. But some observers have sug-gested an additional, altogether more symbolic reason. Known as Rajm, throwing stones against evil spirits is what Muslim pilgrims to Mecca do from the top of a mountain. According to some Middle East experts, in that sense, the throwing of stones during the intifada could also be seen as the reflection of an Islamic stance. Certainly for most Palestinians embroiled in the war of the stones, there was little differ-ence between chasing away evil spirits and chasing away Israelis. Not that many Israelis chose to travel to the occupied territories. More than ever since the start of the intifada, these areas had become akin to the dark side of the moon.

To those who dared venture into the West Bank – like the settlers – M16 and Uzi machine-guns, Motorola radios, car phones and crash-proof Plexiglas were all at first offered at discount prices, but increas-ingly became a way to make a fast buck. 'I'm definitely in the wrong business,' Zeev Ackerman once jokingly pointed out. 'The glaziers in Jerusalem are charging 1,500 US dollars to install shatter-resistant car windows. And you know what, people are paying.'

Using a photographic analogy, Zeev once told me he saw both sides in the conflict as 'a kind of moral and political double exposure.' But being Jewish, as the intifada became more bloody and entrenched, his viewpoint had slowly changed. 'I used to be sympathetic to the Arabs,' he confessed. 'Now I see it more as a case of them or us. Especially with the rise of Hamas and other Islamic fundamentalist groups.'

Along with the disgruntled workers and graduates that were making up the spearhead of the intifada in these early days, Islamic militants not unlike those involved in the Iranian revolts a decade earlier, were also beginning to make their presence felt.

Almost from the moment the first stones were thrown in anger in Gaza's Jabaliya camp in December 1987, a group calling itself 'Islamic Jihad' had increasingly become involved. First established in 1981, Islamic Jihad became more widely known when some of its fighters tossed not stones but a grenade at a group of Israeli soldiers and Jewish settlers in February 1986. This no-quarter type of attack was to become something of an Islamic Jihad trademark. Later that same year, some of its fighters threw a cluster of grenades at an Israeli military graduation ceremony taking place at the Western, or 'Wailing Wall,' in Jerusalem.

It was only later, however, once the intifada was well underway, that Islamic Jihad would be joined by another and even larger fundamentalist group – 'Hamas.' In Gaza especially, the emergence of both groups would mark a radical departure from the resistance movements of the past. They would also add a violent new dimension to the future direction of the Palestinian armed struggle and give the Israeli authorities dangerous new security problems to contend with. For the time being though, as the war of the stones spread like wildfire across the West Bank, Israeli commanders continued to insist that they could crush the intifada quickly.

'The disturbances in the territories will not occur again,' Defence Minister Yitzak Rabin said three weeks after it started. 'Even if we are forced to use massive force, under no circumstances will we allow last week's events to repeat themselves.'

Army Chief of Staff Dan Shamron confidently told journalists that Israel had deployed more troops in Gaza alone than it took to conquer armed enemy soldiers in both the West Bank and Gaza Strip in the 1967 Six Day War.

Not everyone shared Rabin and Shamron's confidence. Many ordinary Israeli soldiers who were coming face to face with Palestinian rage for the first time had a different take on events.

'You can't imagine what's happening there. And there are places the journalists don't see,' said one soldier serving in Gaza. 'I'm sitting in front of a riot. Thousands of people are on the rampage, there's smoke everywhere you look, and on the radio I hear some Mickey Mouse announcing the Strip is quiet. Are they having a joke at our expense? Or are they trying to calm things down or something like that? On the radio they say the disturbances are local. Local? I saw how well organised they were . . .'

Though a serious offence, many demonstrators waved Palestinian flags, shouting 'Falastin, Falastin.' Everywhere political graffiti sprayed on the walls was often in one of the four colours of the Palestinian standard. Red in the flag signified the blood of the martyrs: green, the fertility of the Palestinian plains; white, peace: and black, the oppression of occupation to be removed when Palestine was liberated.

The Israeli army considered even the depiction of such flags and symbols as a threat to public order, but Palestinians frequently found novel ways of making sure their colours were displayed despite the prohibition.

'What do you think of our intifada salad?' asked the grinning waiter in a Jerusalem old city café where I regularly ate, as he placed the plate on the table in front of me one afternoon. The salad was made up in the colours of the Palestinian flag: black and green from the olives, red from tomatoes, and white from the cheese.

Back on the streets though, the resistance was a deadly serious business, as the Israeli army was quickly finding out to its cost. Most riots were often carefully timed to break out in one locality and then another. While these street battles often looked chaotic, the *shebab* who took on the Israelis were said to obey strict orders from quickly organised committees set up by the local Palestinian leadership.

To give clear direction and develop the intifada, it needed leaders, and fast. Since the PLO leadership was based in Tunis and were caught out just as much as the Israelis by the speed and scale of the uprising, those ready and able to orchestrate the intifada had to come from within the occupied territories. This local leadership arose from the popular movements. Representatives of the PLO (Fatah) under Yasser Arafat, the Democratic Front led by Naif Hawatmeh, and the Popular Front of George Habash, joined with the Palestine Communist Party to create at times an unlikely alliance against the common foe – Israel. From this alliance, one month after the uprising started, emerged the 'United National Leadership' (UNL), which effectively became the coordinating body of the intifada on the West Bank.

Many of these leaders were also part of student groups, trade unions and women's groups, but by and large considerable efforts were made to keep their backgrounds, names and identities as anonymous as possible. Conscious of their status as local leaders first and foremost, there was some concern among their ranks that the PLO, fearing the marginalisation of its own influence, might apply unwanted pressure. By not revealing their names and accepting the need to act clandestinely, the leaders of the UNL effectively served notice that they posed no threat to the PLO and were not trying to supplant Yasser Arafat and its other leaders based in Tunis. Keeping their identities secret was also a necessity against the more immediate and likely threat of being arrested or killed by the Israeli security services.

Of course, the Israeli authorities already knew many members of the UNL, most having been previously imprisoned for their political activities. It is estimated that perhaps as many as 90 percent of the intifada's local leaders went through the brutal regime of Israeli prisons during the 1980s. Prison was their university. It steeled them in self-sacrifice and taught them about revolutionary attempts in other areas. These lessons learned in prison became crucial for the future leadership of the intifada, and great weight was given to the prisoners' movement and supporting their families.

Alongside the underground leadership, there were also leaders in the field, organised in 'people's committees.' They in turn were responsible for mobilising the villages and refugee camps into 'action committees.' Next to these were the 'shock committees' whose task was to challenge the Israeli armed forces. It is estimated that during the years of the first intifada there were as many as 45,000 local committees of various kinds operating throughout the territories.

I first met Salah (not his real name) during the early months of the intifada, but was to see him again over a year later. Twenty-eight years old, and a leader of the 'people's committee' in the area around his village of Abu Dis near Jerusalem, he was typical of those shaped by their prison experiences.

'Guess who?' he asked with a smile one afternoon while rewinding a videotape to show me a scene again on television. After pressing play, a youth appears on the screen, his face wrapped in a checked *kaffiyeh* headscarf. It's a street scene. And the youth leaps over a smouldering tyre in the middle of the road, picks up the tear gas grenade that has landed and hurls it back at the Israeli soldiers who move towards him flatfooted in their heavy gear and armed to the teeth. All around, other young Palestinians can be heard taunting the Israeli troops in Hebrew with demands for a state of their own, 'Rotzim Medina, Rotzim Medina.'

'We shot this video at the beginning of the intifada. From the roof of the building here,' Salah smiled again, nodding towards the ceiling. Salah smiled a lot for someone who had spent the last few months in one of the notorious Ansar detention camps run by the Israelis.

As well as opening the Dhahariya prison near Hebron, and expanding al-Fara'a detention centre in the West Bank, Israel had constructed three Ansar camps. The first was in south Lebanon, where Palestinians and Lebanese prisoners from the war there were incarcerated. The second was in the Gaza Strip, and had also been enlarged to absorb the latest influx of intifada detainees.

Then there was Ansar III, where Salah had been held. The largest and most notorious of the camps, it was known as the 'camp of slow death,' and stood in the Negev desert where temperatures regularly soared to over 110 degrees. With human rights delegations forbidden to visit Ansar III, the best description of the razor wire enclosed camp was based on messages spirited out by inmates and written up in the Hebrew-language magazine *Koteret Rashft*.

> In the middle of the compound there is a hut with a pit: the central latrine, swarming with flies and giving off a vile smell. There are no newspapers, no books and it's forbidden to walk around, save in the compounds during designated periods. Every disturbance reaps a punishment, usually collective. With their hands tied behind their backs and heads lowered, the prisoners are forced to sit in the sun for hours at a stretch. There is no canteen, and there is no laundry. And there also isn't enough water. The prisoners shower once every 10–14 days. They receive almost no vegetables or fruit. Two prisoners share a single plate.

Inside Ansar III, the physical and psychological abuse of Palestinian prisoners during interrogation was routine.

'Yes, I was afraid at times,' Salah admitted, when asked about his time there. 'Especially the isolation rooms, standing up for such long periods, handcuffed, with a sack over my head. Often all I could hear was screaming coming from somewhere. I learned many things though, about myself, my abilities to organise and maintain security within our prison group. I also learned how to prise out collaborators or informers and deal with them.'

Like the many other people's committees formed throughout the West Bank and Gaza during this time, Salah's group assumed much of the authority not only for the shooting, beating or hacking to death of traitors, but for distributing *communiqués* and leaflets, and the running of riots on the streets.

Outside in the village streets he pointed out the many Palestinian flags hanging from overhead cables and telephone lines, and the walls spray-painted with slogans: VICTORY IS NEAR, PLO, THE INTIFADA MUST CONTINUE.

'The *shebab* last night,' he announced proudly. 'Soon the soldiers will arrive. Our men, women, even the children will be stopped in the street and forced at gunpoint to take down the flags and paint over the slogans.' No sooner would this be done than Salah's *shebab* would go out again that night and replace them.

'I'd like you to have these,' he said, handing me a string of beads fashioned from dried olive seeds. 'I made them last time in prison.'

The following week I tried to arrange another meeting, hoping through Salah to talk to other members of the people's committee in the area. 'Salah's been arrested, prison again,' one of his boys told me. 'But don't worry, we've already got another leader to replace him for now.' Some months later, after his release, I heard that Salah had been killed, shot in the head during yet another street fight with Israeli soldiers. The memory of the perpetual smiler had been transformed into yet another of the grave-looking poster portraits of the martyred, plastered on local street walls and shuttered shop fronts.

By now the protests across the West Bank and Gaza had developed a momentum of their own, and with each new death the scale and ferocity reached a greater pitch. The local leadership or UNL meantime had to work hard to ensure the intifada maintained a sense of direction. Its leaders communicated with those on the street by issuing leaflets or *communiqués*. Sixty thousand copies of the first *communiqué*, NO VOICE WILL SILENCE THE VOICE OF THE INTIFADA, were distributed and pasted to walls on January 10, 1988. It called for a three-day general strike that month and on 'the heroes of the stone and fire bomb war to shake the oppressive regime down to its foundations and create inviolable unity.'

A trade unionist known as Mohammed Labadi, from the DFLP, is credited as being the main author of most *communiqués*. Moving from one location to another in the backstreets of East Jerusalem to avoid the Israeli security services, the UNL representing all the popular movements would sometimes meet to work on strategy and draft its leaflets. The directives of Mohammed Labadi's first *communiqué* were typical of many that would follow:

> All roads must be closed to the occupation forces . . . its cowardly soldiers must be prevented from entering refugee camps and large population centres by barricades and burning tyres. . . . Stones must land on the heads of the occupying soldiers and those who collaborate with them. . . . We must set the ground burning under the feet of the occupiers. Let the whole world know that the volcanic uprising that has ignited the Palestinian people will not cease until the achievement of independence in a Palestinian state whose capital is Jerusalem.

Outside this small circle of the UNL no one knew who wrote the manifestos or *communiqués*. By and large the leaders took decisions by consensus, without favouring any particular organisation. As they saw it, their primary task was that of guiding the people. This anonymity suited the spirit of the intifada. Putting the emphasis on the man on the street, it also marked a waning of influence by notable Palestinian families on any political leadership.

In issuing the *communiqués*, great care was taken by the UNL to keep a finger on the pulse of the mood in the communities. Making sure, for example, not to overburden the people with too many general strikes.

Lots of attention was also paid to new methods of civil resistance. Indeed, today's critics of the current al-Aqsa intifada often point out that the loss of hard-won lessons from these early years have in great part led to the failure of the current uprising in terms of any tangible political gain.

Back during the war of the stones, however, links between the leadership and the Palestinian community at large were necessarily more flexible. *Communiqués* that were unrealistic in terms of their effects on the people were frequently corrected. For example, in the beginning the UNL forbade the buying of Israeli products. However, as it soon became clear that the public was simply unable to abide by the decree, its leaders then limited the boycott to products not found in the territories. Sometimes though, the UNL had to be uncompromising in imposing orders and strike notices.

On one occasion, a local UNL leader in the city of Hebron told how he had received orders to instigate a strike of shopkeepers using whatever means necessary. The night before the strike was due to begin, he and other activists from the local committee went from shop to shop hammering nails with the heads removed into the keyholes of the padlocks that locked the shops. The following morning they then went on to the streets to gauge the reaction of the merchants.

'Okay, if you are men, if you are really patriotic, you have to protect us when the Israeli soldiers come, so wait here with us,' insisted the shopkeepers. Barely minutes later Israeli troops arrived and began telling the shopkeepers to open their doors. When they complained that they were jammed, the troops put hooks through the U-shaped padlocks, connected them by cables to their jeeps and wrenched them open by force.

Nearby, the local Hebron activists who had lain in wait immediately started to lob petrol bombs, setting fire to an Israeli jeep. Others threw stones and were joined by the shopkeepers and other onlookers who hurled rocks and missiles from the windows and roofs of their homes.

'We had wanted to make a spark, and here we were, seeing it catch fire,' said the UNL leader afterwards. Time and again local activists like these would tell me that all they were really doing at this stage was improvising resistance, after consultation with those higher up the command chain. 'The leadership entrusted us with the details. The leaflets said, "Do whatever is necessary: attack Israeli vehicles, burn Israeli property, and boycott Israeli products." This is our chance to kick out the occupation.' Above all, through these actions the local leadership was able to create the impression that the intifada was spreading faster and wider, thus ensuring others would join in.

'We began to move around in cars, carrying petrol, old tyres and all the necessary equipment to begin a demonstration,' explained the same Hebron local leader. 'We burned tyres everywhere in the city – this intersection, that intersection – with five or six cars, in one or two hours we had all the city on fire.'

No one was necessarily manning all these barricades. Driving or walking into such areas, where bonfires or overturned vehicles burned and makeshift barriers were strewn across the street without a soul in sight, was in itself intimidating enough. The sense of impending menace was almost physical, and any Israeli soldier on patrol must have felt that rocks and petrol bombs could begin raining down anytime without warning. These no-go area tactics also got the message through to the local Palestinian community that the intifada was not restricted to the large, volatile refugee camps and casbahs of the Gaza Strip and Nablus. It was right here in their own neighbourhood – wherever they might be.

As these actions and the *communiqués* that triggered them became increasingly effective, the influence of this new breed of internal underground leadership rapidly grew. Not surprisingly, in Tunis, the PLO hierarchy looked on anxiously, fearing it might lose the initiative of its own direct involvement in the intifada.

On January 18, 1988, another *communiqué* – number 3 – was issued. This time its signatories were different. All the leaflets were signed not only by the UNL but by the PLO, and read 'Palestine Liberation Organisation – Unified National Leadership of the Palestinian Uprising in the Occupied Territories.' The message from the 'Tunisians' – as the PLO leadership is often now referred to – was clear. The UNL was no more than an arm of the PLO acting on its behalf in the occupied territories.

In one sense the acceptance of the PLO's primacy despite the misgivings of many Palestinians about its leadership abilities was almost inevitable. Shortcomings the PLO most certainly had, but it was still the one organisation perceived by most Palestinians to have kept their collective sense of national identity alive through long and difficult times.

It was the astute and politically talented Abu Jihad, the *nom de guerre* of Khalid al Wazier, who took the initiative in ensuring the PLO's efforts to support the local leaders and stone-throwers of the intifada. Abu Jihad had been Arafat's deputy commander after the formation of Fatah, and as the intifada gained momentum he activated every cell he had created since the 1970s in support of the intifada leaders in the occupied territories. He was also ensuring that the intifada would not be sacrificed – for the time being at least – to Yasser Arafat's diplomatic initiatives, and saw it as an opportunity to potentially reform the PLO's style of leadership and dubious handling of its finances.

In Gaza things were different. While a similar body to the UNL operated there, the influence of Islamic Jihad and Hamas made for a more insular, self-contained core of activists, less prone to direct pressure from the PLO in Tunis. The fortunes of both Islamic Jihad and Hamas had grown proportionally as people reverted to religion in these crisis-wracked times.

Just like their nationalist counterparts, the Islamist groups had nurtured their own strongholds, turning mosques into centres of propaganda and platforms from which fiery sermons could galvanise resistance. They supported needy families, controlled refugee camps and neighbourhoods, and called their own strikes. Like the locally bred leaders of the UNL they presented another kind of challenge to the PLO, and an uncompromising one to the Israelis.

But while leadership tussles were one thing, the violence on the streets was something else, having assumed a scale that even the Israelis admitted was unprecedented. Just like their archenemies the PLO, they too had been caught out from the start. Barely three months after the start of the intifada, the Israeli writer Amos Elon pointed out that the status quo, which Likud politicians had long regarded as the best of all possible worlds, 'is shattered forever.'

So complacent had the Israelis been, that as far back as December 10, 1987, just a few days after the intifada flared into life in Jabaliya, Defence Minister Yitzhak Rabin refused to cancel a trip to the United States, on the grounds that the disorder was insufficiently serious. While in the US, amongst other duties, Rabin was to settle a price with the Americans for the buying of 70 of the world's most sophisticated weapons – F-16 fighter planes. These awesome weapons might have their role to play against the intifada in the years to come, but for now they were useless against the kind of popular uprising the Israelis were facing. Nevertheless, Rabin was confident of Israel's ability to crush the uprising in its tracks.

'Don't worry, the army will assert control very quickly,' Rabin reassured Shimon Peres, speaking over the phone from the US with the Israeli Foreign Minister who was in Brazil at the time. Not long after Rabin was back in Israel and the West Bank some ten days later, he was telling Israeli troops in Ramallah to use 'force, power, beatings' to suppress the Palestinians. The then more liberal *Jerusalem Post*, decried the minister's 'jarringly brutal language.'

But Israeli soldiers took Rabin's 'break their bones' advice literally.

In the territories it was not uncommon to meet Palestinians disabled for life by the blows they received during these beatings. Ironically many of the firms that manufactured the truncheons and clubs used in these beatings employed mostly Palestinian workers from the Gaza Strip.

'Our task now is to recreate the barrier of fear between Palestinians and the Israeli military, and once again put the fear of death into the Arabs of the territories so as to deter them from attacking us anymore,' demanded Rabin.

Having apparently come to its military senses, and shaken off any initial tactical inertia, Israel struck back in characteristically dramatic fashion. But the payback came not in the occupied territories, as most people expected, but in the North African base of the PLO itself.

On a clear night on April 16, 1988, barely four months after the start of the intifada, an elite Israeli 'Sayaret Matkal' special forces unit – the equivalent of the British SAS – slipped ashore from small boats on the Tunisian coast. Led by pathfinders who had entered Tunisia under false passports and set up a surveillance operation, the unit, supported by agents from Israel's Mossad secret service, lay in wait outside the home of Khalil al-Wazir, the PLO's key intifada coordinator and godfather, otherwise known as Abu Jihad.

As chance would have it, Wazir was working on a memo to the underground leadership of the intifada when the Israelis stormed his home shortly after 1.30 a.m. Fighting back with only a pistol as the Israelis rushed upstairs to his bedroom, the Palestinian leader only managed to fire one round before he was riddled with more than 70 bullets, as his wife Intissar looked on in horror. So intense was the gunfire that his pistol hand is said to have been virtually severed from the wrist. As a final warning, one of the Israeli assassins fired a burst of automatic fire into the wall above the bed of Wazir's baby son, Nidal.

Only a week earlier, the Israeli cabinet, led by Prime Minister Yitzak Shamir and Defence Minister Rabin, had met and decided to assassinate Wazir. The decision was based on the urgent need to eliminate the PLO's key man behind orchestrating attacks in the territories and building the momentum of the intifada. Yet, far from having the desired effect of undermining the uprising, the legend of Abu Jihad, the martyr, became yet another symbol of resistance for countless Palestinians. Even before his bullet-riddled body was laid to rest at a mass funeral in the Syrian capital Damascus at which hundred of thousands marched, many were swearing revenge for Abu Jihad's 'sacrifice.'

In the riots across the territories that followed Wazir's killing, at least a dozen Palestinians fell to Israeli bullets in the worst single day of violence the intifada had yet seen. By this time, the Israeli government seemed to have taken to heart former US Secretary of State Henry Kissinger's comments to a private group of Jewish American leaders in New York on February 1988. According to the *New York Times*, Kissinger had suggested that Israel should put down the intifada as quickly as possible, overwhelmingly, brutally and rapidly.

'The insurrection must be quelled immediately, and the first step should be to throw out television, *à la* South Africa. To be sure, there will be international criticism of the step, but it will dissipate in short order,' insisted Kissinger. But despite Kissinger's calls for a media ban, atrocities were not going unnoticed by the outside world. Early in February 1988, Israeli soldiers attempted to bury alive four Palestinian youths in the village of Salem near the West Bank town of Nablus.

A few weeks later, American CBS television crews filmed four Israeli soldiers systematically breaking the limbs of two Arab men they had arrested inside Nablus. It was a sickening prolonged beating that many TV viewers found almost unbearable to watch.

Inevitably, as the arrests, clubbings, tear gas, rubber bullets and house demolitions failed to stop the uprising, Israeli troops resorted again and again to live ammunition, and the casualty toll soared. In Gaza and elsewhere I came across hospitals full of youngsters suffering from gunshot wounds, broken arms, legs, or both. However, the *shebab* were undaunted and reckless as ever in facing off the Israelis.

On one occasion, at the intensive care unit of the Israeli Hashomer Medical Centre near Tel Aviv, a badly wounded 17-year-old Palestinian youth was wheeled in. Asked his name by the surgeon in charge, Dr. Raphael Wolden (Shimon Peres's son-in-law) the only reply the teenager groaned was '*Jihad, jihad*' (holy war, holy war).

It was estimated at the time that, on average, two out of every five Palestinian males over the age of 15 in the occupied territories would have been imprisoned for political reasons during the previous ten years. According to Al Haq, a Palestinian human rights monitoring group based in Ramallah (and affiliate of the International Commission of Jurists in Geneva), 410 Palestinians were killed during the first year of the uprising and more than 20,000 wounded. During the same period, two Israeli soldiers, two Israeli women and three children were killed by the rioters. Day in, day out there were reports of Israeli military excesses; of pregnant Palestinian women who aborted, and babies who died of suffocation after being exposed to tear gas fired into closed rooms; of young boys tied to army jeeps as human shields against stone-throwers, others not so lucky thrown off speeding vehicles to their deaths. As ever, many Israelis seemed able to live with the atrocities they heard and read about daily. For some – sheltering just beyond the shadow of such bloodshed – the self-deception required to do so was made easier by the fact that the carnage was largely confined to the territories and rarely trickled onto their own streets.

Not everyone turned the other way though. In the autumn of 1988 the Israeli novelist A.B. Yehoshua was so disgusted by the complacency of his fellow citizens that he said he now understood how so many Germans after World War II could say they had never seen or heard of the Holocaust concentration camps. Yehoshua's comments went straight to the heart of the Israeli psyche and generated a bitter backlash. But whether Israelis liked it or not, the irrefutable evidence of widespread human rights abuses against ordinary Palestinians was there to see for anyone who took the time to go and look for themselves.

Mount of Olives, Jerusalem, June 1989

It was a sweltering summer's day with yet another wave of violence sweeping across the territories, as I drove up through the Mount of Olives to visit the Makassed hospital in East Jerusalem. As the largest Arab hospital in the West Bank and Gaza, more than 700 of the severest cases resulting from the intifada had been treated here. Just outside, as I paused to buy some boiled corn on the cob and falafel from a street vendor, I watched a group of Palestinians sitting patiently in the shade waiting on word of relatives and loved ones who were being treated in the emergency rooms inside.

In the company of Dr. Wahib Dajani, head of Anaesthesia and Intensive Care at the 200-bed hospital, I was taken to meet 14-year-old Ali Mohammed Fannoun and his family.

But for the occasional tilt of his head on the hospital pillow, it was difficult at first to tell if Ali was alive. On one side of the bed his father sat silently watching as Ali's mother stood gently forcing spoonfuls of gruel between the youngster's lips. Inside the intensive care cubicle the air was heavy with the odour of faecal waste from the tubes connected to Ali's lower abdomen. But his mother was oblivious; working with a single-mindedness she slipped spoonfuls of the soup between his shriv-elled lips, as though feeding her son with some kind of elixir, which might, just might, claw him back from death.

Seven weeks and three operations ago, an Israeli bullet had ripped through Ali's body, causing severe damage to the kidney, liver and spinal cord, paralysing him immediately. Since then Ali had made little progress and Dr. Dajani was pessimistic.

'We doubt that he is going to make it,' he said quietly as we left the room and I looked back at Ali. The portents were etched into the young-ster's face. His eyes bulged from emaciated features yellowed by jaun-dice that had resulted from the annihilation of his digestive system.

According to the Israeli authorities, Ali, from Nahalin near Bethlehem, was shot when soldiers opened fire to disperse stone-throw-ing Palestinians resisting a search and arrest raid in the West Bank vil-lage. There is, however, an alternative account of what happened.

It was just before the beginning of the all-day fast for the Muslim festival of Ramadan as villagers were finishing a meal, that a single jeep-load of Israeli soldiers arrived in Nahalin. Among them were some set-tlers who began harassing people on their way to the mosque and forc-ing other villagers out of their homes. At some point shooting began, and Ali was hit as he left the mosque with some of his eleven brothers and sisters. An ambulance ferried him to Makassed, where half a kid-ney and part of his colon were removed in emergency surgery.

Whatever really happened that day, an official Israeli army inquiry into the raid concluded that seven of the men had lost control and used excessive violence, firing live ammunition without first using tear gas, or rubber or plastic bullets.

The story of the circumstances surrounding Ali's wounding was a familiar one at Makassed. In another room at the hospital, Bassem Hamdam and his wife Samira waited anxiously outside an intensive care unit where their eight-month-old son Mohammed lay motionless, his tiny skull connected to a tube following an operation to retrieve a 'rubber' bullet.

Mohammed had been in his mother's arms when soldiers fired on demonstrators with rubber-coated metal bullets. As she was about to step inside her door, Samira looked down at her son and found him cov-ered in blood.

'We have had many fatalities from this type of bullet,' said Dr. Dajani, holding up another example of a 'non-lethal' round he had dug out of a patient. Dajani kept his collection of bullets and fragments in small plastic bags. All had the date, the types of wounds they inflicted, and the names of the victims written on labels on the outside.

It was difficult to see how a 15g metal ball coated with rubber and fired from a high velocity rifle can be anything other than an instrument of death, especially when the victim is a baby.

Dr. Dajani then looked over the medical notes, which revealed that the tissue that had oozed out of tiny Mohammed's skull during the operation had left a cavity of 5 x 5 x 6 centimetres.

'Imagine, there's nothing left,' he sighed.

Palestine Square, Gaza, September 1989

One afternoon, in Omar Muktar Street in Gaza, I lay huddled against the wall of a petrol station. From on top of a nearby building, Israeli soldiers had opened fire on some Palestinians next to me in the street below after they had thrown rocks at a passing patrol. Very quickly, everywhere around us, all hell was breaking loose. It was such a precarious position, with not much cover from the gunfire, that I decided to make a run for it across the street to the comparative sanctuary of the main al-Ahli Arab hospital, where many victims of Gaza's street clashes ended up.

A fairly impoverished freelance reporter in those days, I couldn't then afford the body armour that later became such a necessity for working in these street battles. That moment of fear waiting to make the dash across the street, it was always as if all my senses rushed to the back of my neck. Like when I was a boy, going off the high board at the swimming baths for the first time. 'Will I, or won't I?' Then suddenly you are out there, committed, exposed. Later, I would often imagine the sniper squinting through the cross-hairs. What if he didn't see the cameras around my neck, and in the chaos mistook me for a rioter not a reporter? What might be going through his mind at the moment he took aim? Bullets travel faster than sound, so I'll never hear the one that gets me, I reassured myself.

'I'm going to run to the hospital,' I announced to a teenage Palestinian boy cowering beside me behind the wall, almost as if I needed his permission or reassurance.

'Me too,' he replied nervously, as we both got to our feet and bolted across the street. From the corner of my eye I saw some bullets kick up the dust barely feet from me, before collapsing at the hospital entranceway on the other side of the road. Almost instantly, the boy who had been running in my wake fell against me. For a moment I was sure he had been shot, then he turned and gave me an enormous grin.

'You okay, *sahafi*?' (journalist) he inquired, before picking himself up and walking casually into the hospital grounds as if he was simply going to visit a relative on a quiet afternoon. But even here, inside the hospital, it was far from quiet and there was little respite from the furious clashes now well underway outside.

All around, I watched as young Palestinians, many with blood dripping onto the dust from their wounds, were carried or dragged by their comrades into the hospital grounds. After about thirty minutes the Israelis had clearly decided to quell the rioting once and for all that day. On hearing warning shouts from some Palestinians who were peering through gaps in the hospital walls, I turned to see men, women and children scatter in panic.

Almost instantly, there was an enormous bang as an Israeli armoured jeep rammed the hospital gates, bursting its way into the tree-shaded compound followed by three or four other vehicles. Soldiers streamed from the jeeps and quickly fanned out, searching the hospital grounds. Some shoved their way past angry medical staff to enter the wards in the hunt for recently admitted wounded and those that had ferried them there. Anyone, patients, relatives, or staff, who tried to intervene was beaten or arrested.

I lifted my camera to photograph one man lying semi-conscious against a wall after being struck by a soldier's truncheon. Even before he shouted, the look on the face of an Israeli officer who caught sight of me said it all. 'Who are you? Show me your identification. There will be no pictures, this is a closed military zone,' he bellowed, pushing my cameras against my chest and me against a wall. It wasn't the first or last time I would encounter the 'closed military zone' rule. Issued almost arbitrarily by soldiers on the spot, rather than as a considered order from higher up the chain of command, it provided an instant way of preventing journalists recording or gaining access to events on the ground. Even with an officially issued Israeli government press card, I had long since learned how impossible it was to negotiate or reason with soldiers in these situations. If the sanctuary and well-being of patients in a hospital – many of whom were uninvolved in the street riots – were to be ignored, it was hardly likely the army would take any notice of a complaining reporter.

'Such behaviour is against all conventions and regulations,' pointed out Jorgen Rosendahl, the Danish Director of Administration at al-Ahli hospital, as he stood back helplessly and watched the soldiers go from ward to ward in search of the newly admitted wounded. An otherwise unassuming man, Rosendahl was a courageous critic of the methods used by the IDF. 'I have already sent three complaints about the army to the Israeli Knesset, with copies to UN Secretary General Perez de Cuellar, the Danish and American embassies, the Director of the United Nations Relief and Works Agency and the Red Cross,' Rosendahl told me. Rosendahl had arrived in Gaza barely days after the intifada had broken out and had been witness to the escalating heavy-handedness of the Israeli army.

'I am shocked by what I have seen here. Twenty-seven percent of all intifada casualties are under 15,' he told me, as we walked through the wards in the wake of the Israeli soldiers. 'The youngest, so far, is a baby of seven months; among the oldest is a woman of about 70 with a bullet through her jaw,' Rosendahl continued.

Small clusters of women and children were sitting by the bedsides of their injured menfolk. Some, whose husbands or brothers had been hauled from their beds by the soldiers, were weeping hysterically; others sat impassively, as if resigned to yet another brutal incursion into their lives.

Rosendahl had kept scrupulous records of the type of casualties treated at the hospital since his arrival. This information allowed him to argue that there had been a conscious shift in IDF policy from beatings to shootings, with shooting injuries now outnumbering beating injuries. 'If you look at gunshot wounds between January and May 1989, the total for the period is 37 percent higher than the 12-month total of 1988,' he said.

As we entered the casualty ward, in the first six beds only one patient was older than 25. All the others were aged between 14 and 17 and had suffered gunshot wounds, mainly from the now familiar rubber-coated steel bullets the Israelis always insisted were less harmful. They had been shot in the legs, the buttocks, the testicles, the stomach and the abdomen. Some of the young wounded lay below a large brass plaque on which was inscribed a quote from Psalm 103, Verse 17: 'The merciful goodness of the Lord endureth forever . . . and his righteousness upon children's children.' The plaque, I was told, was put there by a British Army Captain, G.A. Schofield, who had dedicated the casualty ward to the memory of his mother and father back in November 1917. It was that very same month that Lord Balfour, then a member of the British government, made his famous declaration that 'His Majesty's Government views with favour the establishment in Palestine of a national home for the Jewish people.'

How things had changed. The Jewish people had indeed found a home. But at what cost to themselves and the countless Palestinians deprived of the right to live in their own home without fear and repression?

'I came here at the same time as the intifada started and everybody told me then, in January 1988, that it would be over in a few weeks. They have been saying that since and now it is September 1989,' said Jorgen Rosendahl, as we headed back to his office.

Over a cup of Turkish coffee, I wrote up my own reflections of the day's events. In the streets outside, the cries and crackle of gunfire reverberated from more erupting riots, and Rosendahl sat down to type up yet another complaint about the IDF to a seemingly oblivious international community.

Beach Refugee Camp, Gaza, September 1989

A strong warm breeze blew off the Mediterranean, carrying the stench from Gaza's open sewers and rotting garbage into our nostrils, as we drove through a labyrinth of tumbledown streets heading for Beach Refugee Camp. In one deserted alleyway hemmed in by low stone buildings and almost too narrow for our car to pass, a few lumps of concrete and twisted metal beams had been laid across the street as a makeshift roadblock.

The gunman seemed to come out of nowhere. His head was covered in a black ski mask with only the eyes and mouth visible, and he carried a pistol at the ready. Two other men, dressed almost identically but cradling Kalashnikovs, lurked nearby in the shadows, watching for passing Israeli patrols.

'Hamas,' announced my driver and fixer. 'Let me talk to them, it should be okay,' he said, his voice still betraying a certain nervousness. It was my first encounter with the Islamic Resistance Movement, or Hamas, which as well as meaning 'courage' or 'zeal,' is also an Arabic acronym for Harakat al-Muqawama al-Islamiya.

Growing out of the Muslim Brotherhood, a religious and political organisation founded in Egypt and with branches throughout the Arab world, Hamas was set up by Sheikh Ahmad Yassin and six other leaders of the Brotherhood in the occupied territories. Among them were Abd al-Fattah Dukhan, Muhammed Shama, Ibrahim al-Yazuri, Issa al-Najjar, Salah Shehadeh and Abd al-Aziz Rantisi. In its founding charter, Hamas pledges the group to carry out armed struggle, try to destroy Israel and raise 'the banner of Allah over every inch of Palestine.'

The rise of Hamas in the mid-1980s had coincided with a return to a more traditional Moslem way of life. Where once at the end of the 1967 war there were 77 mosques in Gaza, by the outbreak of the intifada the number had risen to 160. Underpinning this growing influence of the Muslim Brotherhood and Hamas was an impressive social, religious, educational and cultural infrastructure, called Da'wah, that worked to ease the hardship of large numbers of Palestinian refugees living on the very edge of existence. This social influence quickly evolved into a political one in Gaza, before then spreading to the West Bank.

Unlike the PLO, which was secular, leftist, and promoted Palestinian nationalism, Hamas wanted to set up a transnational state under the rule of Islam, much like that of Ayatollah Khomeini's Iran. Financed in part by contributions from an Islamic tax called a *zakat* levied on its supporters, Hamas was well organised by the time it entered the intifada in February 1988. In response to its new role, it quickly divided itself into three separate wings. The political wing, staffed by Sheikh Yassin's closest allies, produced leaflets, recruited members, co-opted mosques, and raised funds from the *zakat*. Its intelligence apparatus, known as al-Majd (glory) was established mainly for internal policing, especially in Gaza. It later merged with the military wing called the Izz al-Din al-Qassam Brigades, after the leader of the Arab uprising against the British from 1936 to 1939.

Salah Shehadeh, whose codename was '101,' led the brigades and by the third month of the intifada they were playing a leading role in the resistance. Yet, strange as it might seem, the rapid growth of Hamas, like that of its fundamentalist counterpart Islamic Jihad, was not simply a result of an Islamic resurgence. It also had to do with a strategic miscalculation on Israel's behalf in the years before the intifada.

According to documents from the Israel-based Institute for Counter Terrorism, Islamic movements in Israel and Palestine were 'weak and dormant' until Sheikh Yassin legally registered Hamas in Israel in 1978 as an Islamic association by the name of Al-Mujamma al Islami. It was around this time that the Israeli intelligence and military leadership made a tactical decision to provide the Islamists with direct and indirect financial aid over a period of years. The plan was simple, if somewhat controversial and ultimately flawed. In one instance, Israel decided to encourage the growth of an organisation known as the 'Islamic Centre' that was based in the Gaza Strip. Those running the Islamic Centre were the self-same leaders with connections to the Muslim Brotherhood and the founding fathers of Hamas in the Gaza Strip.

'The Israeli government gave me a budget, and the military government gives to the mosques,' said the then Israeli military governor of Gaza, Brigadier-General Yitzhak Segev. The mosques to which Segev channelled government cash were the ones run by the Islamic Centre.

In 1980, when Muslim fundamentalists burnt down the Red Crescent Society building in Gaza City – a body funded indirectly by the PLO – the Israeli army looked the other way. Some years later in 1983–84, Moshe Arens, Israel's Defence Minister, would confirm that the army and intelligence services had been complicit in the incident. 'There was no doubt that during a certain period the Israeli governments perceived [Islamic fundamentalism] as a healthy phenomenon that could counter the PLO,' he wrote in his memoirs.

Arens' admission was also backed up by one former senior CIA official who described the Israeli plan as 'a direct attempt to divide and dilute support for a strong, secular PLO by using a competing religious alternative.' But turning Hamas into a potential counterweight to the PLO was not the only reason for Israel's duplicitous support. Financial aid was also a way of infiltrating Hamas and helping Israeli agents to identify and channel towards them those members who were dangerous hard-liners. While aid to Hamas may have looked clever at the time, in the long term for the Israelis it only helped create a Frankenstein monster within the intifada, which it would later have to tame at great political and human cost.

Not surprisingly, many key players within the US intelligence community were less than impressed by Israel's efforts to manoeuvre Hamas for its own ends. 'The thing wrong with so many Israeli operations is that they try to be too sexy,' said former CIA official Vincent Cannestraro.

It was only by the second year of the intifada that the Israelis realised that reining in Hamas was not as simple as they first thought.

The group had fast become a resistance power to be reckoned with, and unlike other Palestinian groups, which held back from the use of arms, was readily preparing caches of guns and explosives. In the end, as Hamas set up a very comprehensive counter-intelligence system, many collaborators with Israel were weeded out and shot. Armed resistance and violent acts of terrorism became a central operational strategy as the Islamist groups, unlike the PLO, became increasingly unwilling to compromise in any way with Israel. That the situation was in part of Israel's own making might have been ironic, but it was also annoying to its allies.

'The Israelis are like a guy who sets fire to his hair and then tries to put it out by hitting it with a hammer. They are their own worst enemies when it comes to fighting terrorism,' said Larry Johnson, a former US State Department counter-terrorism official, when later asked about Israel's attempt to manipulate Hamas. But even despite Israel's now apparent tactical blunder, there were still those in the country who saw some benefits to be gained in trying to support Hamas. 'The thinking on the part of some of the right-wing Israeli establishment was that Hamas and the others, if they gained control, would refuse to have any part of the peace process and would torpedo any agreements put in place,' claimed one US government official on condition of anonymity.

By the middle of 1988, the Israeli military had begun to see the error of their ways and decided to strike back hard at the fledgling Islamist movement. In July and September of that year, around 120 Hamas activists were arrested as the Israelis attempted to liquidate its command. But within only a few weeks Hamas was back in business and stronger than ever in the frontline of the intifada.

By the time I encountered the Hamas men in Gaza that September afternoon in 1989, the movement was already well embedded within Gaza's refugee community. Though still only a few hundred volunteers strong, they had nevertheless been able to divide the entire Gaza Strip into five operational districts. Each was headed by a commander and a liaison officer, whose job was to maintain regular contact with Islamic activists on the West Bank. At the checkpoint that day, the gunmen were brusque but polite. Ever careful not to hand over my Israeli government press card as proof of my journalistic credentials, I instead offered my international press ID.

'You are welcome here, but remember that any pictures you take, the Israelis can take from you, and could be dangerous for us,' the gunman warned, before waving us through in the direction of the camp. Just as we pulled away, he suddenly rushed forward again to the passenger side window. Braking hard, my driver cast me an anxious look as the gunman leaned inwards.

'You are Scottish, yes?' asked the Hamas man in clear but halting English.

'Yes,' I replied, never for a moment expecting what was coming next.

'So are you a fan of Glasgow Rangers or Glasgow Celtic?' he inquired, a smile clearly filling the hole in the mask around his mouth. For a second I thought it was some kind of trick question, designed to trip me up and prove that I wasn't who I claimed to be.

'In my city, it can be dangerous to say one or the other,' I pointed out, smiling in the hope he would get the joke, and understand the nature of the Protestant and Catholic sectarian rivalry between the two football clubs.

'Here in Gaza, sometimes it is also best not to say too much,' the gunman replied, waving us ahead again, his grin still clearly visible in the wing mirror as we drove off, kicking up the sand that had blown into small heaps in the road.

Within minutes, we pulled up again in another rutted dirt street inside Beach Camp itself. Home to more than 50,000 people, half of them under the age of 15, all across the camp these kids moved in wandering bands, scavenging, cursing and falling into stone-throwing battles with the Israeli patrols. The place was a warren of flimsy huts with asbestos sheeting on the roofs. Here and there, rivulets of raw sewage ran through the camp, which overflowed when the rains came, flooding the place with waste. Rough open latrines lay outside shacks. From time to time these pits also overflowed, the filthy water sloshing into the cramped rooms where people ate and slept. What, I wondered, had forced families to come and settle in such squalor, and how were they coping with the latest pressures the intifada had brought into their lives?

Khadeja Ayoup Gharab was nine when her family was driven out of Ashkelon by the fighting, mass expulsions and massacres of the war against the Israelis in 1948. She remembered the '*Nakba*,' or 'catastrophe' as Palestinians have since called those days, as the time when seven of her family were killed in a bombing attack that destroyed their home. Rescued from the rubble, alive but injured, Khadeja, her parents, two brothers and a sister, walked all the way from Ashkelon to Gaza, arriving with only the clothes they were wearing.

As is so often the case with people who have next to nothing, the moment I arrived at her door in Beach Camp that day, Khadeja invited me to take a seat, before disappearing inside her tiny house to make tea and collect some documents she insisted I should see. Nearby, two bearded men wearing long white *galabias* – Egyptian cotton robes – had turned up, and perched themselves on some rocks in a patch of sand to watch us from a discreet distance. Further out on the white-capped waves of the Mediterranean, the Israelis were also keeping tabs on what was going on in Gaza. Clearly visible just on the edge of the horizon, was the menacing grey silhouette of a naval gunboat.

'Hamas,' my driver announced again, his voice barely audible as he nodded imperceptibly in the direction of our two bearded watchmen.

Khadeja reappeared with a tray carrying glasses of black tea laced with fresh mint, that she had sent her 14-year-old son Khalid to buy as a special treat for the guests who had turned up unannounced on the doorstep.

'Mohammed, one of my other sons, was shot by the Israelis four months ago. He died in the dunes, where he had been throwing stones,' she said quietly, placing the tray on a tiny table in front of us on the sand outside the house. 'He was 17 years old.'

It was too soon to press her on such a recent and painful experience. Instead, I asked Khadeja what she remembered about first coming to Gaza.

'We had nothing, but picked up some cardboard and wood on the seashore and built a shelter. We lived in this for almost two years before UNRWA (United Nations Relief and Works Agency) gave us a tent,' Khadeja recalled. On the foundations of this same site, the Gharab family had built their present concrete shack with its five rooms shared by 20 people from Khadeja's extended family.

As we sipped our tea she reached into a worn leather pouch and delicately unfolded some wafer-thin, sepia-coloured papers. The documents, from the government of Palestine in the days when it was a British mandate, were title deeds. They had been issued under the land settlement ordinance of 1928, and were proof of the registration and ownership of Khadeja's family house in Ashkelon.

'This shows that the house and land is ours, and that it was taken away from us by force,' she told me, before delicately folding the faded paper away again in its pouch.

'Yes,' she shrugged, 'we still call Ashkelon our real home, but I doubt we can ever go back. Can you imagine the Israelis allowing that?' she asked, rubbing the palms of her hands together in that familiar Arab gesture that suggests the subject is *khalas*, finished or closed.

It was also near impossible for the Gharab family to move anywhere else outside Beach Camp, Khadeja told me. Like most families living here, they had little money, and to do so would mean losing their refugee status, and the few kilos of lentils, rice and flour from UNWRA they received.

As we talked more, Khadeja began to relax, and I noticed some barefoot boys on the filthy beach beyond. They were flying kites made out of polythene and laughing hysterically.

'Can you tell me about Mohammed?' I ventured, unsure as to whether the wounds of grief were still too raw for her to talk openly about her dead son.

'He was with Hamas. He volunteered as soon as they would let him, even though he was so young,' Khadeja began slowly. 'He shouldn't have been throwing stones with the other boys that day. Hamas told him that he would be trained as a *mujahed* (holy warrior) and should keep his anger for the right moment,' she continued. Khadeja described how Mohammed's rage against the occupation had long since consumed him. That afternoon in the dunes the soldiers' taunts over the loud-speakers mounted on their jeeps had brought his blood to the boil.

'Your mothers are whores. What's wrong? Are you afraid of us, you sons of whores?' the soldier's voices boomed, recalled Khadeja, shaking her head at the memory.

When the clashes began, Mohammed at first had heeded the orders of his Hamas commander, and held back. 'Then an Israeli tear gas cannister cracked the skull of his best friend, and Mohammed ran to the dunes. The bullets were flying everywhere and he was shot right here,' said Khadeja, gently touching the side of her face as the tears welled in her eyes.

I sensed it was time to take our leave, and as we said our *shukrans* and *ma'as Salaams* – thank-yous and good-byes – I noticed the Hamas men also getting to their feet, ready no doubt to speak with Khadeja after we had gone. As we paused by our car, Khadeja spoke one last time. 'If I caught a Jew now, to be honest, I would kill him or eat him alive. I have lost my home. They have killed my brothers and sisters, my son. We don't want them here. We simply want them to leave us alone.'

By now, the intifada had become what writer Amos Elon astutely described as an 'irresistible force colliding with an immovable body.' As the resistance reached a full head of steam, covering its twists and turns became a part of my life. It was also becoming clear that what I was often witnessing among ordinary Palestinians was the social discipline of a genuinely revolutionary movement. As the hardships became greater, so too did the sense of solidarity. Food and other necessities were often shared; the families of victims given whatever support could be mustered. Rural Palestinian communities organised the collection and transport of food donations to the besieged Gaza refugee camps and later to West Bank towns and cities under curfew. Farmers in the Jordan Valley, the most fertile region of the West Bank and a centre of agricultural production, sent truckloads of local vegetables to the Gaza Strip. Some of the better-off merchants and factory owners contributed merchandise from their stores and warehouses. People went from door to door collecting money from those who could afford to give, and then bought food supplies to be stockpiled and later distributed in times of curfew and siege.

In February 1988, the Nablus popular committees were ready when the IDF imposed a 13-day curfew. Hoarded foodstuffs were distributed from house to house across the flat rooftops or by foot during intermittent one-hour liftings.

One senior Israeli army officer at the time described the intifada as a 'deeply entrenched state of mind. Anyone who believed that the old status quo could be restored,' he added, 'just doesn't know what he is talking about.'

With their rocks, this first crop of activists had not only caught the Israelis and their own PLO leadership on the back foot, but were showing other Palestinians that the rest of the world was watching. For millions of television viewers in the outside world the intifada came across as the *cri de coeur* of a downtrodden minority.

'What we have lost in lives is tragic. But what we have gained in publicity, in exposure to our cause, is worth far, far more,' an old man once told me in Gaza. Heaped around him was what was left of his home after the Israelis had dynamited it as an act of collective punishment. This demolition of homes was done under a then still valid British emergency regulation issued in 1946 to put down Jewish terrorists. It was also conducted under a law that prevented the Palestinian householders from rebuilding their homes.

Before the outbreak of the intifada, demolishing a house had needed the special approval of the Defence Minister; now it was left to the discretion of individual local military commanders. Cutting off electricity and telephone lines, uprooting trees or orchards – ostensibly to deny cover for ambushes – and extending the duration of curfews were all stepped up. While localised curfews were imposed in the West Bank, in Gaza they were often blanket shutdowns of days at a time when almost nothing moved.

During 1988, no fewer than 1,600 curfew orders were issued in the territories, and overall more than 60 percent of the Palestinian population were living under this regime. It was estimated by human rights groups that on a number of occasions, more than one million Palestinians were confined to their homes in mass curfews imposed on the whole of the Gaza Strip, major West Bank towns and cities, and on many rural villages. Even when not under curfew there were new restrictions on movement imposed with the introduction of special 'green' identity cards. First issued to recently released detainees in the Gaza Strip, and later to former prisoners in the West Bank, these cards were only valid for a period of three to six months and renewable at the discretion of the Israeli authorities. The card carriers were not allowed to cross the 'Green Line' border that separates Israel from the occupied territories for any purpose, including employment. Stopping travel to Israel thus not only served as a movement restriction, but an economic sanction as well. In effect it was a bit like being under town arrest.

In the months and years ahead, the situation would only get worse. There seemed no end to Israel's ingenuity in devising novel and ever more draconian measures to repress the intifada. As early as January 1988, Palestinians charged with 'incitement' were being served with expulsion orders.

Despite international condemnation of the measures, including a UN Security Council resolution calling on Israel not to carry through the deportations, on January 13, 1988 the first four deportees of the intifada were on their way to Lebanon. In carrying out many further 'transfers' Israeli claimed it was simply removing the uprising's ringleaders. But even this was not enough for Defence Minister Yitzak Rabin. 'Ten months is too long a time to wait between issuing a deportation order and actual deportation. And it's not just the punishment that counts – it's the timing, too,' complained Rabin to Israel's Foreign Affairs and Defence Committee. Not only was the right of the deportee to appeal the expulsion order suspended by the Ministry of Justice, but it became possible for deportations to take place from 72 hours to one week after arrest. But the intifada's ringleaders were not Rabin's only targets. Another measure employed by the authorities was called 'invisible transfers.' In effect this meant that hundreds of Palestinians, mainly women and children, were denied the right to remain in the West Bank and Gaza on the grounds that they did not have the necessary residency or visitors' permits.

First introduced shortly after the Israelis' victory in the 1967 war, 'invisible transfers' were designed to deal with the 'demographic problem,' or to be more precise, the problem of too many Arabs in the Jewish state. Over 90 percent of the victims of 'invisible transfer' were women and children. In many villages the Israeli army would arrive and separate the men from women. Those women targeted would have minutes to pack and leave with their children, often having to take an Arab taxi to the bridge over the River Jordan, and pay a fee to cross after being fined for their 'illegal residence.'

One of the few ways to avoid transfer or expulsion was to agree to become an informer for the Israeli authorities. Shin Bet, the Israeli internal security service, had long cultivated a network of informers as part of its system of controlling the Palestinian population and their participation in the intifada. Coerced through a combination of threats and bribes, individuals and sometimes entire families would become part of the Israeli intelligence network. Many of these people were known as 'wastanaries.' In the local Palestinian dialect, the word 'wasta' meant a broker or middleman. Most wastanaries began as collaborators with the Israeli security forces. As their involvement with the Israeli administration became institutionalised, they let it be known within their communities that they had connections and influence with the Israeli authorities. In this way the wastanaries became part of a system of patronage, whereby Palestinians in need of, say, an official document from the Civil Administration – a licence for trade or construction – were often forced to go through these informers. They acted as middlemen, wielding influence with the Israeli department concerned in return for a fee. This system would mean that Palestinians were often forced to pay twice for the privilege of obtaining a travel permit: once to the middleman, a second time to the Civil Administration itself.

In the early stages of the intifada collaborators were called upon to 'repent' or sever their links with the Israeli authorities. Many who had been equipped with Israeli automatic weapons turned them in, but the amnesty and dissolving of the network was short-lived. As the military occupation tightened its grip, increasing numbers of informers took up the Israeli shekel or relented to intimidation and blackmail. Not surprisingly, as the intifada progressed, Palestinian hostility towards informers and collaborators became veracious and frequently bloody.

On more than one occasion I covered what were alleged collaborator killings. Once, near Nablus, we arrived shortly after the body of a young Palestinian man had been discovered in an old olive grove. His hands still bound behind his back, he had been shot at point blank range in the head, the blood soaking into the parched earth, staining it black. Rumour had it that he had informed on the whereabouts of local popular committee activists who were wanted by the Israelis, but as with so many of these deaths the real motive or those responsible was never really clear.

Many Israeli media reports simply presented the killings as signs that the intifada had 'turned in on itself,' the result they said of internecine Arab violence and political power struggles. Some of the killings were no doubt a result of this, but many were almost certainly extrajudicial executions carried out by the Israelis themselves.

Tel Aviv, September 1988

I would never have taken him for an assassin. I'd never have believed that the hand I was shaking had held a Beretta .22 calibre pistol and fired a bullet into someone's skull at point blank range, or tugged on a steel wire to silently garrotte a victim's throat. Nobody, except Rafael 'Rafi' Eitan himself, knows how many times he has done such things. But by his own admission he had often been an executioner, killing sometimes up close enough 'to see the whites of their eyes.'

It was towards the end of summer in 1988 when I met Rafi Eitan in his office at the then largest state-owned business enterprise in Israel, the Israel Chemicals Company in Tel Aviv. Our meeting was a mistake, a chance encounter; the result of some crossed wires and misunderstanding at the Israeli Embassy in London.

I had come to Tel Aviv to interview another man called Raphael Eitan, a former chief of staff of the Israeli Army, who was about to become a candidate in the country's forthcoming general election. It was only after 'Rafi' responded to a question from a colleague accompanying me, who enquired about his most memorable moment in the service of the state of Israel, that the penny dropped and we both realised the real identity of the man talking to us.

'Probably the Eichmann operation is what I'm most proud of,' Eitan replied, before launching into the story of how he and his Mossad secret service team had been sent to Argentina in 1960 to kidnap the Nazi war criminal Adolf Eichmann and bring him back to Israel for trial. 'I had him here, this close to me, with a gun at his head,' recalled Eitan, holding up his hand a few inches from his face. 'I could have killed him but I was under orders to bring him back alive,' he shrugged, clearly disappointed at being deprived of the opportunity to deliver the *coup de grâce* to Eichmann there and then.

Born in Kibbutz Ein Harod, Eitan in his youth served as a fighter in the underground army, the Palmah, against the British. After his discharge he joined the General Security Services (GSS) or Shin Bet, and later Mossad, where he became head of the operations department. By the time of our meeting Eitan was an elderly man, small and stocky, bespectacled and partially deaf from an old wound received during the days of Israel's 1948 war. It was difficult to associate the figure sitting before me with his near legendary reputation as the ice-cold hit man *par excellence* of Israel's famed Mossad intelligence service – a man whose operational maxim was said to be: 'If you are not part of the answer, then you are part of the problem.'

At the time of our encounter, Eitan had officially retired from his deadly undercover trade; his only continuing involvement, he insisted, was occasional lecturing on counter-terrorism in places like Belfast or at the home of the British Special Air Service (SAS) in Hereford, England. But early in 1988 the intifada is said to have troubled Eitan so much that he sent a letter to Israeli Prime Minister Yizhak Shamir, outlining a solution for dealing with the uprising's leaders. Eitan suggested killing those behind the riots in the dead of night, in their homes, quietly, in the assassination style that had epitomised the Mossad operations of the past.

'One bullet and that's it,' he wrote to Shamir and suggested that the Prime Minister summon him for a secret meeting to discuss the plan further. As operations chief at the Mossad, Rafi Eitan had, for decades, been the master in this murky, violent and dangerous trade. Their's is a shadowy world of which little is really known, but one that film director Steven Spielberg set out to explore in his controversial film *Munich*.

It tells the powerful story of an Israeli Mossad assassination squad dispatched to revenge the kidnap and murder of 11 Israeli athletes at the 1972 Munich Olympics by Palestinian 'Black September' terrorists. Not surprisingly, *Munich* bitterly divided opinion over both its historical accuracy and the political and moral issues that it wrestled with, namely, Israel's use of assassination and extrajudicial execution in response to Arab attacks at home and overseas. If the Mossad of which Rafi Eitan was once part was Israel's retaliatory response arm around the world, then the Shin Bet and other special forces groups were its domestic weapon in the ceaseless undercover war it waged against Palestinians in the occupied territories.

In October 1989, less than a year after I met Eitan, Reuters filed a story detailing the existence of Israeli 'death squads' set up to target intifada activists. Codenamed Duvdevan (Cherry) and Shimshon (Samson), these undercover units, sometimes disguised as Arab women, were deployed almost from the beginning of the uprising. While Duvdevan operated in the West Bank, Shimshon covered Gaza, and between them they were believed to have been responsible for the murder of as many as 160 Palestinians. Undercover squads also used Palestinian vehicles to gain entry to remote villages. Though this was initially denied, Yitzak Rabin eventually conceded that the 'security apparatus' was permitted under military law to commandeer Palestinian cars for security missions.

Yasser Abu Ghosh, a young Palestinian activist in Ramallah, was walking along the street in July 1989 when one of these commandeered vehicles rolled up behind him. Two men in civilian clothes got out of the van and shot him in the back as he tried to flee. Abu Ghosh died several hours later while in Israeli custody.

In another incident on August 19, 1989, an undercover unit disguised as tourists in Bethlehem shot five Palestinian youths at point blank range, killing 21-year-old Radi Salah and wounding the four others. Sharif Zawahara, one of the wounded, told an Israeli lawyer that during the incident he had been shot in the leg from a distance of about six feet by one of the four 'tourists' who had stepped out of a shop after an Israeli patrol had been stoned. As Radi Salah lay dead, Zawahara was shot again in the other leg before uniformed soldiers dragged him by the hair along the pavement to a nearby army base. According to eyewitnesses, as the terrified crowd dispersed, the civilian-clad assassins laughed and joked with the Israeli soldiers who arrived at the scene.

Just as these Israeli counter-insurgency tactics became more wide-spread and sometimes indiscriminate, so too did the use of the hi-tech weaponry at the military's disposal. Newly developed types of tear gas and other kinds of smoke or vapour grenades were used daily.

'Look here *sahafi*, look how new these are,' a boy in Hebron called out to me one April afternoon in 1988 after picking up one of the used cannisters in the wake of some street clashes. As the manufacturer's date on the can confirmed, it had taken a little over a month for the tear gas to make its way from the factory to the streets of the West Bank. Often the words MADE IN THE USA or FOR OUTSIDE USE ONLY were stencilled on the casing of the grenade. Not that this prevented the Israelis from firing them into homes, schools, mosques and even hospitals.

So widespread were reports of gas being fired deliberately into these places, that in May 1988 one of the US-based manufacturers, Transtechnology, suspended shipments to Israel 'until such a time as Israel demonstrates that it is prepared to use the product in a proper and non-lethal manner.' But even when the gas was used outdoors, if fired into the close confines of refugee camps or the narrow alleyways of many West Bank streets, the high concentration of toxic gas created in the air could easily kill.

Some Palestinians also spoke of grenades that released what they called *ghaz aasad* ('nerve gas') that gave off orange- or red-coloured smoke when thrown. If inhaled, this gas, it was said, made people 'hysterical.' 'Nothing would stop it . . . the effect was incredible. You would suddenly find yourself starting to panic for no apparent reason. Everyone around would start to panic and experience extreme confusion,' recounted one activist.

On a number of occasions during large-scale clashes, I was to witness saturation gassing of large built-up areas by Israeli helicopters. Often the bombs were of a strange 'bouncing' variety. To neutralise them, demonstrators would wait and watch them being dropped from the helicopters before tearing off towards where they estimated the bombs would land. Immediately they would try to grab them and bury them in the sand or plunge them into buckets of water.

'One time as I arrived, I suddenly realised they were dropping stones. It took us a moment to work out what was happening. We stupidly relaxed for a few seconds and then the actual bombs came down. The stones had been a decoy,' remembers one Palestinian activist called Abdo. 'Four or five of us got really screwed. It became necessary for others to come and carry us away from the place before we were able to breathe again.'

Israeli tactics were not always so crude. At 5 p.m. on July 7, 1988, Israeli tax collectors along with IDF troops raided the homes of 50 Palestinian merchants in the sleepy town of Beit Sahour about two miles south of Bethlehem. By Palestinian standards this was a fairly affluent middle-class community, far removed from the teeming refugee camps of Gaza. Home to many Palestinian Christians, Beit Sahour had also produced a number of writers, artists and intellectuals. Like most educated Palestinians, many of these people were supporters of the PFLP, DFLP and the local Communist Party.

Here though, just like other parts of the West Bank, citizens had refused to pay taxes levied by the Israeli authorities as a protest against military actions. Occupation taxes imposed on Palestinian businesses and the commercial sector had been widely resented. Not least, because it did not entitle Palestinians to the same social benefits that Israeli citizens received in return for the tax. By early spring 1988 what had begun as an act of protest was fast turning into a widespread tax revolt. The refusal to pay taxes, said intifada leaders, was part of the disengagement process. As the raids got underway in Beit Sahour, the local merchants' precious ID cards were confiscated, only to be returned, said the Israelis, once payment of outstanding taxes had been made. Earlier that same day, military checkpoints had been erected at all the entrances to Beit Sahour, and passing vehicles were pulled over for inspection. Some were confiscated and impounded in the playground of a local secondary school. In protest, hundreds of Palestinians marched on the local police station and turned in their ID cards in an act of solidarity against the tax raid. As ever in this eye-for-an-eye struggle, the Israeli response was to impose a two-week curfew and cut all the local telephone lines. Beit Sahour's first tax 'revolt' was over, but not for long.

Almost a year later, in mid-September 1989, the Israelis launched another more intensive tax collection operation on the community. This time, the raids on homes and businesses were unrelenting. After houses were emptied of $1.5 million worth of furniture, televisions, fridges and stereos, the seized goods were then auctioned off to the Israeli public. Even a YMCA rehabilitation centre set up to treat children traumatised by the intifada was raided. But the people of Beit Sahour remained defiant.

'We will not finance the bullets to kill our children, the growing number of prisons, the expenses of the occupying army, the luxuries and weapons provided to collaborators,' read a statement issued by the town's residents during their bitter six-week strike. Despite international outrage, the Beit Sahour tax boycott proved a difficult story to cover from inside the community.

With the town almost entirely cut off, and local reports beginning to leak out of Israeli troops ransacking or looting shops, I set out one morning with a few colleagues to try and see for ourselves what was going on. It wasn't long before we were stopped in our tracks. 'Closed military zone,' I mimicked to the reporters with me, as our car was pulled over by some tough-looking Israeli paratroopers on Beit Sahour's perimeter. 'This is a closed military zone,' began an officer almost the moment we had rolled down the window, much to the amusement of my snickering colleagues in the car. 'I don't care if you are Press, if you come here again you will be arrested,' added the soldier, with a look that left us in no doubt he meant what he said. Still determined, we backed off, only to make a two-hour detour in an attempt to gain access to the town from the other side on a more remote road. As we drew closer to Beit Sahour, passing the familiar clusters of whitish cheese-like stone houses surrounded by cypress trees, it was quiet and things looked promising. Then suddenly, on a blind bend, we ran slap into another Israeli checkpoint. It was too late to back off as the paratroopers raised their weapons, gesturing and shouting at us frantically to pull over. My heart sank as I saw an officer approaching and realised instantly it was the same one that had stopped us on our previous attempt to enter two hours earlier. We were sure to be arrested this time.

'Out! out! Get out of the car!' he screamed, before ushering my two colleagues and myself over to a nearby wall which we were told to face with our hands on our heads. One by one our press cards were confiscated, while the officer radioed his headquarters and relayed our details. Should the authorities decide to keep the cards or withdraw them, working in the territories would become next to impossible for us. There followed a few anxious minutes while we waited on the reply from the IDF press officials. Finally, a call came through establishing that our accreditation was official, along with confirmation that we had no previous black marks against us. As our cards were handed to us, three mightily relieved journalists were herded back into the car, the lieutenant still nipping at our heels like some overzealous sheepdog. 'Listen to me, all the roads are blocked and if you try again your press cards vanish,' he warned again while we nodded in reply like chastised schoolboys. I could not believe we had escaped so lightly.

For the best part of two months in complete isolation, the people of Beit Sahour stuck to their tax revolt. Like the press, delegations of foreign consuls, church dignitaries and Israeli peace groups were all turned back when they tried to visit the town. In the end the Israelis even blocked food supplies from getting in. Tax resisters were arrested and held in detention pending trial for refusing to pay. Of the first 40 to be tried, all opted for imprisonment with sentences in some cases of more than a year.

Meanwhile, in distant Oslo, at a conference held on Beit Sahour, the town was mentioned as a potential nominee for the Nobel Peace Prize. Beit Sahour was a landmark in the *intifada*. Here was a way of confronting the occupation with more than violent street resistance. It had been an innovative and highly organised campaign of civil disobedience. It was the most serious challenge to Israeli authority since the uprising began, and had the added benefit of throwing the intifada into the international spotlight. By now there were even times when it seemed the revolt was spreading to Israel itself. In July 1989, a Palestinian refugee from Gaza grabbed the steering-wheel of a passenger bus from its driver and sent it over a cliff, killing fifteen people.

On 20 May of the following year, a former Israeli soldier opened fire on about 50 Palestinian casual construction workers as they waited to be picked up at an intersection in Rishon Le-Zion, a southern suburb of Tel Aviv. After ordering the men to sit in rows on the ground he shot into the group indiscriminately, pausing only to reload. Seven Palestinians were killed and 11 wounded. The man might have been 'deranged' as the Israeli authorities described him, but the resultant violent backlash was one of the worst the *intifada* had yet seen.

Against this backdrop of bloodletting, wider diplomatic moves were being initiated that somehow seemed dislocated from what was happening on the ground. For example, Yasser Arafat was courting the United States in an effort to begin peace talks. Not that his call for a 'peace of the brave' did much to impress the Israeli leadership. Arafat starting a dialogue with the Americans was a victory in one way. At least it had peeled away the excuses Israel had always hidden behind in deciding not to deal directly with the Palestinians and face the harsh realities of the intifada. But the US refusal to accept the idea of a Palestinian state, or to bring real pressure to bear on its ally Israel over the occupation and response to the intifada, belittled Arafat's claims of success.

The Beit Sahour tax revolt might have resulted in the Arab states tabling a UN resolution calling for the condemnation of Israeli measures and a lifting of the siege, but the Americans vetoed it. Beit Sahour was also a reminder to Arafat of how tenuous his grip on the intifada could at times be. Just as at the beginning of the uprising he had feared the potential of the local leadership to undermine his own control, the tax revolt had shown that the PLO was still not always able to call the shots. If the determination of ordinary Palestinians had ensured that the intifada gained international recognition as it entered the 1990s, then a terrible political miscalculation by Arafat was about to deal it a near fatal blow.

3

APOCALYPSE TOMORROW

'This is Israel; there are no guarantees.'

—An Israeli shopkeeper to Thomas Friedman, in
From Beirut to Jerusalem

Jerusalem, January 15, 1991

At Café Gizmo, my favourite watering hole in West Jerusalem, a poster plastered to the window billed it as the APOCALYPSE TOMORROW PARTY.

'Are you coming?' asked Ilan Yigal, the café owner and a good friend. The son of an Israeli diplomat and himself a former officer in the IDF, he had always been wonderfully hospitable during my stays in Israel. In a comparatively short time we had become good drinking buddies at his café on Helene Hamalka Street in the Russian Compound district.

'Listen, David, war is nothing new for us Israelis, let's have some fun,' he said with a familiar grin, thrusting into my hands one of the fly-ers he'd had printed to advertise the Apocalypse party planned for that evening. Walking on a few hundred yards towards Ben Yehuda Street, I came across a crowd surrounding two other young Israelis who were running a street stall. In the best barrow boy tradition, they called out the indispensable qualities of the items they had on offer. 'Heavy duty, three shekel per metre. Lightweight, one shekel!' One of the men held up the plastic sheet, while the other dished out rolls of sticky tape from a stack piled up on a table in front of him. 'The complete do-it-yourself home protection kit against a gas attack,' he assured me, pausing for a moment before adding with a telling shrug, 'along with your personal gas mask of course.' Waiting for the start of the Gulf War in 1991 in Jerusalem was a serious business in every sense.

At Café Gizmo, Ilan had crossed off the days on what he'd dubbed the 'Saddam calendar' that hung above the bar, confirming that the countdown to war with Iraq was all but over. The current crisis had of course started back in the summer of the year before – 1990 – when at 2 a.m. on August 2, Iraqi troops and armour trundled over the border into neighbouring Kuwait. So taken aback was Yasser Arafat at news of the invasion that he is said to have thrown up his hands and said: 'Nothing can be done: only by God the powerful.'

Saddam Hussein's regime had insisted that Kuwait was illegally tap-ping into Iraqi oilfields that straddled the two countries' ill-defined bor-der, but everyone knew this was merely a pretext for the assault on Iraq's wealthy neighbour. Iraq had long considered Kuwait to be part of its territory, and relations between Baghdad and Kuwait had been badly strained following the Iran–Iraq war. Almost immediately following

Iraq's invasion, the United Nations responded with sanctions, but as time dragged on and these failed to persuade the Iraqi leader to withdraw, a coalition of forces from some 30 nations led by the United States and Britain stood poised to take military action against Saddam's Ba'athist dictatorship.

Strolling around among Jerusalem's shoppers on January 15, it seemed odd to think that in less than 24 hours the coalition onslaught would be unleashed. Few would have imagined that those Israelis I saw pretty much behaving as normal were in effect part of a nation bracing itself for the potential backlash of Iraqi Scud missile strikes, their warheads perhaps loaded with chemical or biological weapons. All kinds of horrors had been spoken about: anthrax, botulism, mustard or nerve gas. Like everyone else who lived or worked in the Middle East, I knew about Iraq's use of such weapons during the Iran–Iraq war, and against Kurdish civilians. I had seen the pictures and spoken to colleagues about the chemical attack using mustard gas and the nerve agent sarin on the Kurdish town of Halabja in 1988, in which many thousands of innocent Kurdish men, women and children had died.

In Café Gizmo, like everywhere else in Jerusalem and across Israel, the talk was of 'defensive capability and retaliatory strikes,' and 'what if Iraq's missiles and gas get through?' In the supermarkets and stores off Ben Yehuda Street and elsewhere throughout the entire country, tinned foods were bought up and the prerequisite rolls of sticky tape and plastic sheets had all but run out. Gone now were Jerusalem's tourists and almost all those foreigners who had been willing to brave the violence of the *intifada* in a city tense at the best of times.

At Tel Aviv's Ben Gurion airport an hour or so away, the last flights taking foreigners out of Israel had already left. Even some Jews – notably Americans – had gone, their tearful farewells in sharp contrast to the bewilderment and apprehension of arriving Soviet Jews, still coming in daily by the hundreds. At the taxi rank outside the airport I watched some who – apart from their newly issued gas masks – could have stepped from the pages of a 19th-century Russian novel. In their heavy overcoats and fur hats they struggled to stack a pile of tied-up bundles and torn cardboard boxes filled with belongings onto a taxi roof-rack. The term 'out of the frying pan...' was never more apposite.

Heading back to Jerusalem after doing some interviews for a story I was writing on those who had decided to get out fast, I shared a taxi with Elsa Siegel. Elsa was a 20-year-old Jewish American girl who had just spent an emotional three hours at the airport with her father. He had flown in from Boston in an attempt to persuade her to return with him on the next flight home. He had left alone. 'I can't explain it,' she told me. 'I'm a Jew and I suppose it's that sense of collective responsibility that so many of us here in Israel feel when faced with difficult times.'

It had always struck me that if there is one thing Israelis and Palestinians do have in common it is that both peoples are no strangers to difficult times. Since its birth and throughout its turbulent evolution, Israel has lived in an almost perpetual sense of uncertainty. The collective mindset resulting from this constant living on the edge was sharply observed by the *New York Times* Jerusalem bureau chief Thomas Friedman in his book *From Beirut to Jerusalem*. At one point, Friedman recalls the response of an electrical shop salesman after the writer had returned a broken cassette player to the store where he had bought it just a few days earlier. 'It's still under guarantee,' Friedman assured the salesman, to which he received the instant reply: 'This is Israel, there are no guarantees.'

On the eve of war that day in 1991, guarantees were once again in short supply. Arriving back in Jerusalem from the airport, the streets were quieter than usual. The khaki-clad young soldiers with their kit bags and M16 rifles were still thumbing lifts, but there were fewer now. Most had already joined their units on a high state of alert.

Hotels were empty except for foreign journalists. At the Jerusalem Hilton, CNN World News service broadcast 24 hours a day as clusters of people gathered around each screen waiting for the latest bulletins. At the tiny Cliff Hotel beyond the Arab east of the city, near the village of Abu Dis, I was the only guest, save for Joan Turner, a woman in her forties. Joan from Cheltenham had until recently worked as a matron in St. John Hospital in Jerusalem. Committed to her work there, she too felt the need to stay on. As the UN deadline for Iraq's withdrawal from Kuwait drew closer, we both prepared our rooms in line with the Israeli Civil Defence instructions. Windows and vents were sealed off with plastic sheeting. Supplies of bottled water and boxes of tinned foodstuffs were installed, along with bags of bicarbonate of soda and bottles of bleach in an effort to neutralise the effects of gas, should the need arise.

'If the worst comes to the worst, I'll just have to sit it out. I've got plenty of taped music,' Joan told me, the epitome of stiff upper lip.

Though few of us in Jerusalem fully realised it then, the dramatic events about to unfold in the coming days and weeks would have a profound effect on the future course of the intifada. It would also dramatically shape the nature of resistance to Israeli occupation and the way in which many around the world would perceive the Palestinian cause. After all, this would be a conflict unlike any other Palestinians or Israelis had known. For the moment at least, the intifada was overshadowed by an imminent Gulf War that threatened to suck in the entire region.

'Iraq and Palestine represent a common will. We will be together side by side and after the great battle, god willing, we will pray together in Jerusalem,' Arafat proclaimed to a rally in Baghdad on January 7, 1991.

Back in my hotel in Abu Dis it was looking increasingly as though sitting it out in a well-sealed room with a gas mask was as good as it was going to get.

Just a few days before the expiry of the deadline for Iraq to withdraw and the outbreak of war, *The Jerusalem Post* ran a question and answer series entitled 'What To Do If An Alert Is Sounded,' in an attempt to cover every kind of eventuality.

> *Question*: What happens if we haven't received our gas masks and there are signs of an attack – rising and falling air raid sirens; birds, cats and other animals showing signs of poisoning; sounds of muffled explosions; or the air smelling of garlic, rotten fish, or mustard? *Answer*: Prepare, for every family cloths soaked in a baking soda solution. Use one 25-mg package to a litre of water. Breathe through the cloth, covering the nose and mouth and moving the cloth periodically to unused areas. *Note*: Do not use this method if you have gas mask equipment, it is much less efficient and the decision could be deadly.

Another decision that was likely to prove deadly at the time was one made by the Israeli Defence Ministry, that Palestinians were not considered likely targets of a gas attack. Even the Israeli Citizens Rights Movement had charged that the selective distribution of gas masks as the Israeli authorities intended amounted to 'discrimination on grounds of race.' The argument of the Rights Movement was that chemical weapons or gas would be unlikely to distinguish between those that

lived inside Jerusalem and those Palestinians that lived a few miles outside further over the 'green line.'

Khaled Ayad lived barely three miles east of Jerusalem. In his village
of Abu Dis, gas masks had not been distributed. A few days before the
start of the Gulf War his wife gave birth to a baby boy. Without a
Protective Infant Carrier (PIC), or 'gas cot,' like those given to families
the Israel authorities deemed to be living in the immediate Jerusalem
area, his son, like the rest of his family, was at risk. 'I will seal off the
room the best I can,' he told me. 'If an attack happens, I will lie on the
bed with my son. We will die together if we must.'

As the countdown to war entered its last few hours, Jerusalem also
braced itself for what many were sure would be a dramatic escalation in
street rioting by Palestinian activists. On January 15, the same day that
I walked around West Jerusalem and visited Ben Gurion airport, the
intifada's leadership declared a general strike and clashes broke out in
and around the Old City's Damascus Gate area.

'Do you think that if war comes we will sit on our hands?' enquired
my Palestinian taxi driver as I headed back to my West Bank hotel that
night after a few drinks at Gizmo's Apocalypse party.

A little over 48 hours later, the wail of air raid sirens echoed over
Jerusalem, Tel Aviv, Haifa and other cities. The first of Saddam
Hussein's Scud missiles had plummeted into Israel.

Abu Dis, January 18, 1991

There can never be a right time for such an experience. But standing half naked and half asleep at three o'clock in the morning, bleary-
eyed and struggling to understand the instructions on my gas mask kit,
seemed to me such a prosaic way to die. Seconds earlier I had woken to
the sound of my hotelier banging on the door, accompanied by the rise
and fall of Jerusalem's air raid sirens. Overhead, I could just make out
the sound of jet engines – Iraqi, Israeli, plane or missile? It was impossible to tell.

With Israeli state radio confirming a Scud missile attack and the
need for immediate civil defence procedures to be taken, I sealed the
main door with tape. I then placed bleach-soaked towels along its base
and put on my gas mask. Only then did I realise that I was only half
dressed; a ridiculous sight no doubt, standing there in my underpants
and mask, with a blur of questions racing through my brain. Can this

really be happening? What bloody difference could some bleached towels under the door, or cling film sealing off the toilet bowl make against sarin? Why had I not left Israel myself when I had the chance? Rummaging through the contents of my civil defence kit, stored in a little cardboard box that I had been issued a few days earlier at the Jerusalem press centre, did little to reassure me. Among the items were a plastic bottle full of chemical decontamination powder and an auto-injector syringe full of atropine to relieve the effects of nerve gas.

For the next two hours I stayed in my 'sealed' room wearing the claustrophobic gas mask with its strange rubbery odour, listening to the continual sound of what I now knew to be Israeli aircraft overhead. The radio announcer confirmed that both Tel Aviv and Haifa had been hit, and that up to eight missiles had streaked in, exploding in balls of flame as sleepy residents scrambled like myself for their gas masks. Initial reports that one of the missiles had a chemical warhead proved wrong. While no one was killed, there had been casualties, and the strike would come as a huge psychological blow to Israelis. It was, after all, the first time in the history of the Arab–Israeli conflict that Tel Aviv had been hit.

In the streets of West Jerusalem later that morning the mood was a mixture of anxiety, defiance and black humour. At a newsstand on King George V Street, Israelis queued for the early morning newspapers. Many were carrying their gas masks out of the carton, hanging from neck straps for immediate use.

I asked Arie Kimelmen, an advertising manager, how he had coped with the previous night. 'It was terrifying, the noise of the planes all the time. I have a five-year-old boy and my hands were shaking as I tried to fit his protective hood,' Arie admitted. In many cases the strain of those few hours proved too much. Israeli medical sources said that there had been a dramatic rise in the numbers of those admitted with suspected cardiac arrest – close to 200 people across the country. Many people felt that Iraq's attack had been inevitable, and that it was now time for Israel to retaliate effectively but wisely.

'The mood of the people reminds me of the run-up to the Six Day War. I was only 17 then, but I remember the determination to come through,' one army commander told me. 'I think Israel should launch a strategic bombing attack, but keep ground forces out unless absolutely necessary. Not that I have much confidence in the Americans in that capacity. As for the French, well, look at history. Look at Marshal Petain,' the officer added disparagingly.

As US President George H.W. Bush issued an appeal to Israel to hold back from any retaliation, Israeli Prime Minister Yitzhak Shamir called an emergency meeting of his defence committee to decide on his country's response. After many hours, Foreign Minister David Levy emerged to tell journalists that no decision had yet been taken. He added, however, that 'Israel reserves the right to retaliate in the manner and with the scale and method of its own choosing.'

Few doubted that US pressure had been brought to bear on the Israelis. Any military response by Jerusalem would almost certainly have broken apart the multinational coalition against Iraq by provoking the Arab members to withdraw their support. This was precisely what Saddam wanted, and had tried to provoke by launching the Scud strikes in the first place.

Israeli fortitude under pressure was well known and was once again going to be put to the severest test. The country's reputation as a nation forged on solidarity and its people's ability to stand shoulder to shoulder against outside aggressors had in the past taken on near-mythical proportions. But in this crisis there were much wider tactical and political considerations. There was also the question of those Jews I had witnessed at Ben Gurion airport queuing to leave before the going got tough. Could it be that things had changed in Israel? That perhaps the kaleidoscopic make-up of its people had eroded their solidarity irrevocably?

I had always been struck by how much more fragile and disparate Israel's true identity was than many of its politicians and religious leaders would have the outside world believe. Within its cosmopolitan community lay a multitude of social tensions and a range of potentially lethal maladies. The effect of its illegal occupation of Palestinian land and the resistance of the intifada was the most obvious thorn in its side. Internally, tension between its secular and religious communities was another problem. Then there was what many Israelis saw as the overbearing US influence on its political decision making and culture, not to mention the latest influx of immigrants adding to an often fractious melting pot. But, despite these concerns, on the morning after that terrible night of the first Scud attacks, and in the immediate days after, it was that familiar resilience and Jewish sense of black humour that instantly kicked in as coping mechanisms.

Tel Aviv, January 22, 1991

By now there had been almost a week of nighttime missile attacks. Every morning Tel Aviv's citizens would emerge onto the streets, eyes heavy-lidded and smudged with dark shadows. While some set out to buy fresh food and restock their supplies in case things got worse, others would walk their dogs along the city's promenade in the chill damp January air.

'Don't you think it's ironic, the name of this place, at a time like this?' asked Abraham Ravina, an elderly local man, as we sat drinking breakfast coffee in the Baghdad Café on Ben Yehuda Street. Abraham told me how he had left the Soviet Union, then Germany in 1936, and served in the British Royal Engineers during World War Two. 'Fifty-five years I've been here in the Middle East, and still war, war,' he sighed. 'First it's the Palestinians and their intifada, now the Iraqis and their Scuds.'

'Did you hear the missiles last night?' I asked him,

'Yes, it's a little bit worrying,' he told me quietly as he got up to go.

'You have a gas mask though,' I inquired, noticing that he wasn't carrying one.

'Yes, at home,' Abraham replied, 'but not with me. That would be something of an over-reaction, don't you think?' Abraham Ravina's nonchalance was typical of the attitude shown by many older Israelis for whom hard times were nothing new.

Now, across the country, it was time for a new generation to prove their mettle and show that same unflappable resilience. Sometimes it would take on an almost surreal air. One columnist in *The Jerusalem Post* observed that songs like 'The Air That I Breathe' by The Hollies, 'I Have No Other Country' by Corinne Alal, and 'Big Hero' with the lyric 'wars don't happen in the winter' by Si Hi-Man, seemed to have become regulars on Israeli radio shows. Even Tel Aviv's Mayor, Shlomo Lahat, whose city bore the brunt of Israeli casualties from the falling Scuds was able to crack a joke about the situation on Israeli TV. 'Sure, it takes Iraqi missiles five minutes to get to Tel Aviv. But it will take them an hour and a half to find parking,' quipped Lahat. But while Israelis busied themselves with playful morale boosting and defending themselves against the brutally indiscriminate bombardment raining down on their cities, in the West Bank and Gaza it was an altogether different story.

Abu Dis, January, 1991

In the potholed village streets around the Cliff Hotel, loudspeaker warnings from passing Israeli army patrols rang out with monotonous regularity. It wasn't necessary to speak Arabic to get the message: 'Stay indoors'; 'Do not break curfew'; 'You do so at your own risk.' 'At your own risk' effectively meant the possibility of being shot. A few hundred yards away, like others in the occupied territories, the main road from the Jordanian border to Jerusalem was manned with young soldiers. Spiked grids had been laid across the street at their checkpoints forcing the handful of cars on the road to stop for ID checks.

Since the start of the war and the enforcement of a blanket curfew, few vehicles had been able to pass through Abu Dis, and I was lucky to hitch a lift into Jerusalem. The driver, Mohammed Halad, a Palestinian Jerusalemite, was on his way home from Jericho, having been stuck there for the past three days because of the curfew. Like many Palestinians at that time, his take on the Gulf War was pro-Iraq and Saddam Hussein. But his views also hinted at a certain caution and astuteness that came of his people having been a political football for far too long. 'Saddam and the war are good for Palestinians,' Mohammed told me. 'But we must be careful, it could backfire on us.'

What if Israel entered the war against Iraq, I asked him, would it help the intifada?

'Of course, it's what Saddam wants, and we Palestinians, too. Then perhaps Arabs might stand together against the Israelis. Who knows, maybe even Hosni Mubarak,' he laughed. Like many Palestinians, Mohammed clearly had little time for the Egyptian president, who was seen as too eager to please the United States.

Rarely since the start of the intifada had I sensed such a rekindling of Palestinian spirit as I did at this time. Just as the Israelis had closed ranks to outside aggression, so had the Palestinians. All of a sudden, it was as if the fate of the Palestinian people was inextricably tied to events in Iraq and the rest of the Arab world. An article during those weeks in *The Jordan Times* referred to it as 'Linkage by Scud.' But despite this renewed sense of solidarity across the West Bank since the start of the war, the anticipated escalation of the intifada had failed to materialise beyond the usual run of clashes.

Throughout the day and evening near my hotel, was the persistent sound of gunfire and tear gas rounds, but the large-scale unrest we had anticipated never materialised. The Israelis sent massive reinforcements into the territories, with orders to impose one of the strictest curfews ever. Dan Shomron, Defence Force Chief of Staff, had made it clear that violent street demonstrations would be seen as an act of war. Israel had so far complied with a US request to keep a most uncharacteristic 'low profile.' But there was always the sense that if it came to the crunch, Israel would also handle things in its own inimitable way.

At one press conference in the Tel Aviv Hilton Hotel following another night of Scud attacks on the city, a reporter next to me asked the IDF spokesman what Israel's response might be if one of Saddam's missiles contained, say, sarin or some other chemical or biological agent?

'We would turn Baghdad into a sheet of glass,' came the immediate reply. It was a chilling moment. No conferring, no hesitation – just an implied nuclear strike. While the spokesman was doubtless shooting from the hip, it was an indication of the mood that had gripped the nation since the attacks had begun. Whether many Palestinians realised the extent of this anger, or how unforgiving the Israelis would be after hearing that many of them had stood on their West Bank and Gaza rooftops cheering and banging pots as the Scuds fell on Tel Aviv and Haifa, was doubtful at the time.

That day, barely a week into the war, when I stepped from Mohammed Halad's car, I still recall the remark he made after I offered to pay for the lift. 'Don't worry, Saddam is paying,' he insisted, not for a moment realising how much time would prove him wrong.

A few weeks later, I was sitting in an East Jerusalem coffeehouse – the sort of place in which only Arab men gather, the room alive with the hubbub of card play and talk, amid the smell of pipe smoke and black Turkish coffee. Only a single television silently showing CNN news, an obvious concession to the war, imposed itself on this otherwise traditional male reprieve from the outside world. Onscreen, a news report cut to some early footage of a beaming Yasser Arafat greeting Saddam Hussein with a hearty embrace. 'You can expect to see that film a few times,' said the Palestinian man next to me, glancing up from his hand of cards. 'Believe me, the Israelis will not let the world forget it now, intifada or not.'

Certainly, Palestinians publicly supported Saddam Hussein almost to a man and woman during the war. They did so largely from a collective sense of frustration at the failure of the intifada thus far to bring them justice or something politically tangible and positive. But private-ly, lurking beneath that gut support for Saddam, lay a veracity in the belief that they, more than most, would be called to account in the wake of Saddam Hussein's defeat. As one Middle East commentator irrever-ently put it: 'In that sense Saddam Hussein was the biggest Zionist henchman who'd ever lived. If Israel did get a blank cheque after the war it was because of him.' Of course Israel did benefit from outside financial promises as a result of the war. Predictably the Palestinians lost most of theirs.

Remittances from the oil-rich Gulf States, a handsome $200 million a year, virtually dried up. At Jerusalem's Makassed hospital, which I had often visited and where most of the *intifada*'s casualties were taken, the 70 percent of its funding that had come from Kuwait not surprisingly had almost gone – the Kuwaiti government was less than forgiving for what it saw as Palestinian support for the Iraqi dictator whose army had invaded their country. Faced with such demoralising economic and political setbacks, the gains of the intifada had been squandered. Once again for a people whose fate seemed constantly to vacillate between catastrophe and neglect, there now seemed even fewer options for the future.

Jerusalem, 1993

The Oslo peace process began while the official, public negotiations that followed the 1991 Madrid conference were still going on. But after ten sessions those talks had stalled again in the spring of 1993, this time over the status of Jerusalem, and it was becoming clear they weren't going anywhere. Madrid's failure quickly increased interest among the highest-level officials on both the Israeli and Palestinian sides in the still secret talks underway in Oslo. Those talks, initially involving Israeli academics and mid-level Palestinian officials brought together by Norway's Foreign Minister, had gone much further than the Madrid talks. They culminated in September 1993, with an announcement that letters of mutual recognition and a Declaration of Principles (DOP) had been agreed. Wasting no time, Washington quickly moved to take over the sponsorship of the process. The finale to the Oslo agreement took place at the now famous White House signing ceremony where, as Yitzak Rabin and Yasser Arafat exchanged handshakes, President Clinton looked on like a proud father.

Oslo's Declaration of Principles separated the various issues that divided Israelis and Palestinians into two types: easy and hard. The theory was that the 'easy' issues – such things as release of prisoners, economic cooperation, construction of Palestinian seaports and airports, and security considerations – would all be dealt with first, during a five-year interim period. Discussion of the hard 'final status' issues – including borders of a Palestinian state, settlements, Jerusalem and refugees – would not even begin until the third year, and their resolution would be delayed till the end of the interim period, which was eventually extended from five to seven years. However, the reality was that the United States was a terrible sponsor of the peace process. It succumbed to Israeli pressure on just about everything, leaving the beleaguered Palestinian leadership – especially after the Gulf War – pushed deeper and deeper into a corner.

'The fact is that Palestinians are dramatically worse off than they were before the Oslo process began. Their annual income is less than half of what it was in 1992; they are unable to travel from place to place; more of their land has been taken than ever before; more settlements exist; and Jerusalem is practically lost,' declared the great Palestinian writer and thinker Edward Said. His assessment should have registered as a warning of things to come. But like other alarm calls it went unheeded, and the resulting cost to Palestinians and Israelis alike in the years ahead would be high indeed.

Hebron, October 1995

His accent was knife-like 'New York,' his delivery pure Woody Allen. 'The name's Arnold Foyerstein, lived here 27 years. These are my friends; Nidal, Qassem, Mustapha and Khalil,' he said, pointing to each of the four Palestinians sitting alongside him on the wall. 'Khalil, here, is my oldest buddy, done business together a long time. He's a terrific carpenter.'

'For an Arab, you mean,' jibed Khalil, butting in good-naturedly and slapping Arnold on the back. It was an unlikely scene. Arab and Jew sharing pointed jokes in the middle of what locals of the West Bank town of Hebron called 'the corridor' – the most fiercely contested city centre street, in a town that itself was at the heart of the intifada.

Even as we spoke, an Israeli patrol, kitted out in flak jackets and carrying M16 rifles, came thundering down an alleyway in response to renewed stone-throwing in the old part of the city.

'Been like this for days, since some Palestinian schoolgirls put a PLO flag on Kortuba School opposite Beit Hadassah,' said Arnold. 'Army tore it down, said it provoked the settlers.' Himself a settler in Kiryat Arba, home then to 4,000 Jews north of Hebron, Arnold's conciliatory views had made him something of an outcast among Hebron's hardline settler community.

Drawn from the West Bank's Gush Emunim and Kach settler movements, Hebron's settlers were better known for their mix of religious fundamentalism and ethnocentric nationalism. Beit Haddasah, which lies adjacent to the infamous 'corridor,' was one of four Jewish enclaves in the heart of Hebron's old commercial district. Surrounded by 100,000 Palestinians, over 400 settlers lived there at that time.

'The settlers believe Hebron is every bit as important as Jerusalem,' Arnold Foyerstein explained. 'Hell will freeze over before they share with the Arabs what to them is Judea and Samaria.' Few as they were, Gush Emunim's supporters consistently tried to put their beliefs into effect. Seizure of Palestinian property, harassment attacks, at times even murder were used to re-Judaise Hebron. According to Foyerstein, every day militant settlers came to pray at Baruch Goldstein's memorial in Kiryat Arba.

It was in February of the year before that Baruch Goldstein, a well known Kach leader and doctor from the Kiryat Arba settlement, had entered the Ibrahimi mosque, or the Tomb of the Patriarchs as Jews call it. At around 5 a.m. Goldstein emptied two clips of a machine-gun into Moslem worshippers during the dawn prayers.

'He was dressed in military clothes and carrying a machine-gun and had passed the Israeli soldiers standing guard near the door of the mosque,' said Ashraf Mitzab, a taxi driver and eyewitness. 'He began shooting from the back of the mosque and had time to run to change the clip on his gun and continue shooting. People tried to run away but soldiers came into the mosque and used tear gas at the entrance and also opened fire on people. It was impossible to tell who was shot by the settler and who by the soldiers.'

Twenty-nine Palestinians were killed and scores more wounded by the high velocity ammunition from Goldstein's weapon. Ashraf Mitzab ferried four injured people in his taxi. One was shot in the head. The Israeli army had forbidden anyone to come or go into Hebron after the shooting and Ashraf's car was fired on as he left the area with the casualties. 'When I left there were helicopters spraying gas over the whole city,' he recalled.

A Palestinian response was inevitable, and by 2 p.m. that afternoon more than 30 Palestinians had been wounded across the West Bank and Gaza in clashes. Israeli Prime Minister Yitzak Rabin called the massacre at the Ibrahimi mosque 'a murderous act by a psychopath against innocent civilians.'

Goldstein's many settler supporters disagreed, subsequently holding celebrations at a shrine dedicated to him in Kiryat Arba on which the inscription read:

> Here lies the saint, Dr Baruch Kappel Goldstein, blessed be the memory of the righteous and holy man, may the Lord avenge his blood, who devoted his soul to the Jews, Jewish religion and Jewish land. His hands are innocent and his heart is pure. He was killed as a martyr of God on the 14th of Adar, Purim, in the year 5754.

Inadvisable as it was to be seen accompanying Jewish settlers in any West Bank town, I took up Arnold Foyerstein's invitation of a tour of Hebron's old city. He was clearly a little apprehensive, discreetly making sure his *yarmulke* (skullcap) was well and truly stuffed out of sight inside his pocket, before stepping from his battered Ford pick-up into Hebron's bustling central market. 'That's the only place I wouldn't go alone. Might just get a knife between the shoulders,' he warned in his nasal drawl, as though talking about some unsavoury Bronx neighbourhood. He was, in fact, referring to Hebron's casbah; a labyrinth of slit-like alleyways at the entrance to which hung the heads of two young camels dripping blood from a butcher's hook on to the greasy cobbles below.

Despite Arnold's fluent Arabic and cordiality, there was no disguising the very muted response in his encounters with Arab acquaintances. Most were market traders, men whose livelihoods had suffered badly under the draconian measures imposed by Prime Minister Rabin's government. Following the Goldstein massacre, Rabin, instead of moving against Hebron's settlers (as many Israelis also hoped) moved against the Palestinians. Curfews were imposed and the central market was closed. This, and the tension of a still very visible occupation – despite Oslo – had continued to sour Hebron's spirit and economy.

Andul Awda, a Palestinian, helped run his friend's grocery store on

Salaam Street to supplement the cost of his language course at Beir Zeit
University. 'There used to be 76 shops along this street where the settlers live, now there are only 27 open because of loss of business, and
the fear of working next to these crazy people,' he told me. At that time,
Andul believed that ultimately the settlers would have no choice but to
leave. He saw them as little more than expendable bargaining chips,
whether as a factor in Rabin's prospects in the forthcoming Israeli elections, or as part of a trade-off involving the removal of settlers from
Hebron in exchange for sovereignty over Palestinian villages around
Jerusalem. 'We give up villages and towns where 40,000 Palestinians
live and Israel kicks out 400 settlers from Hebron. Not much of a deal
is it, though?' he asked.

Often unable to attend university, Andul sat in the shop between
customers with a cheap battery-powered laptop, translating words into
Hebrew, English and French. The combined effects of a meagre 20-
shekel wage (then £5.00), curfews and the pettymindedness of individual soldiers manning checkpoints, conspired to prevent his daily access
to lectures.

Not far away from his stall, outside Beit Hadassah, crack Israeli
'Golani' soldiers stood guard over settler children at play. One soldier,
the warning I KILL FOR FUN stencilled on his flak jacket, removed a
spiked grid from across the road to allow a relay of Ford mini-buses
with reinforced windows to transport settlers and deliver provisions.
One settler, Miriam Weiss, baby son in her arms, watched her husband,
shouldering an Uzi machine pistol, unload boxes of cornflakes and
Goldstar beer.

'Does your son have a future in Hebron?' I asked. 'Of course,' she
told me. 'His presence, like all Jews' here, is living proof that the city's
Jewish history will not be forgotten.'

And what if Mr Rabin insists that she leave, I put to her? 'That's
something the government should bring before the Jewish people. Either
it stands for the right of Jews to live in Hebron, or for those Arabs who
would, if they could, make the whole country *Judenrein*,' Miriam Weiss
replied sharply.

I think it was at that moment, there in Hebron's streets, that it
struck me just how divided Israelis and Palestinians remained, despite
all the talk of peace since the signing of the Oslo agreement on
September 13, 1993. Officially the intifada had been over now for two
years. Yes, the mass mobilisations, the daily commercial strikes and tax

resistance had by and large come to an end, but the intifada had not. It was only catching its breath.

Nothing had been resolved through Oslo. If anything, the sense of frustration, especially among ordinary Palestinians, was greater than ever. The sense of uncertainty among Israelis and settler families like that of Miriam Weiss was all too apparent.

The Palestinian youngsters who had been the intifada's foot soldiers were still on the streets. The rocks, as ever, would continue to fly, even though the handshakes on the White House lawn had signalled that the war of the stones was over. A new, even more vicious intifada, one inhabited by the suicide bomber and characterised by the Qassem rocket, D-9 armoured bulldozer and Apache helicopter gunship, was just around the corner.

4

THE BULLDOZER IN THE CHINA SHOP

'First, you create great expectations. Handshakes on the White House lawn. A rhetoric of peace. ("No more war. No more bloodshed.") Elections, giving them a flag of their own. Then secret meetings, summit meetings, dinners, retreats, peace treaties, interim agreements, promises, tantalising benefits held before hungry eyes. More handshakes, more 'gestures.' Then you create a framework of peace that guarantees you negotiating superiority. Take out international law, human rights covenants, UN resolutions, and for good measure enlist your strategic ally, the strongest power in the world, the one who supplies you with all your arms, as the "mediator." Then, as you talk peace in Oslo, Washington, Paris, Cairo, the Wye Plantation, Stockholm, Amman, Camp David, Sharm, you "create facts" on the ground that ensure your continued control and prejudice the negotiations altogether.'

—How To Start An Uprising, Jeff Halper

Haram al-Sharif, Jerusalem, September 28, 2000

It was Dennis Ross, US Special Envoy to the Middle East at the time, who hit the nail on the head. 'I can think of a lot of bad ideas, but I can't think of a worse one,' he reportedly commented, on hearing of Israeli opposition leader Ariel Sharon's intention to go walkabout on Haram al-Sharif.

While the Haram is the third holiest shrine in Islam, its site is also equally revered by Jews, who call it Temple Mount, the location of the Biblical First and Second Temples, and the most sacred place on earth. Sitting high overlooking East Jerusalem, which has been under Israeli occupation since 1967, this 35-acre esplanade has lain at the heart of the Israeli–Palestinian conflict, and it remains one of the greatest obstacles to securing a meaningful peace. Given the obvious sensitivities such a place invokes, few doubt that on the day 72-year-old Ariel Sharon, the hard man of Israeli politics, set out for the Haram, he knew exactly how his visit would go down with Muslims throughout the Arab world, and Palestinians in particular.

In a play on words using Sharon's nickname, a Palestinian colleague I knew at the time likened the gesture to that of 'the bulldozer in the china shop.' Surrounded by more than a thousand Israeli soldiers, riot police and a handful of Likud politicians, Sharon marched up to the site of the al-Aqsa mosque and the burnished golden Dome of the Rock, a landmark that is to Jerusalem what the Eiffel Tower is to Paris. Almost immediately the barrage began. Chairs, rubbish bins, stones, whatever came to hand, scores of young Palestinians threw at the man they had long since come to revile. As Sharon descended the hillside flanked by a phalanx of police and bodyguards, Palestinian protestors set off in hot pursuit, one group narrowly missing a potentially lethal clash with Orthodox Jews who called on them to 'go back to Mecca.'

'Murderer, murderer,' some Palestinians jeered at Sharon in reply, while others chanted over and over their promise to redeem the Haram 'with blood and fire.' In all, Sharon's visit could not have lasted more than 45 minutes – 45 minutes that would leave in their wake a trail of fury that ignited like a brush-fire across the Palestinian territories, and would lead to one of the bloodiest-ever periods in the Israeli–Palestinian conflict.

Thirteen years earlier, the killing of four Palestinian workers in Gaza lit the fuse of rebellion that led to the war of the stones. Now, it was

Sharon's 'desecration' of a sacred place, as Palestinians saw it, that provided the new spark. But that is all it was – the spark. For once again, just as in 1987, the real causes of the new uprising were much more deeply rooted. If the fuel for the first intifada was the frustration born from the inequities and hopelessness of the occupation, then what lay behind the latest stirrings was the bitterness bred by the protracted Oslo peace process. Its failure to deliver any positive tangible change meant that Palestinians continued to live in what was effectively an apartheid state.

Convened by US President Bill Clinton seven years after the signing of the Oslo Accords, the Camp David summit in July 2000 was meant to tackle the tough 'final status' issues head-on. 'Chairman Arafat, come try your best. If it fails, I will not blame you,' Clinton encouraged the Palestinian leader on the eve of the summit. Just around the same time that Clinton was extending his invitation, Israeli Prime Minister Ehud Barak – who had initiated the summit – was busy reassuring the Knesset that his own participation in the talks would never amount to a sell-out of Israel's position. Determined to 'act with courage and resourcefulness,' Barak insisted that there would be no compromise on separation from the Palestinians. No return to the 1967 lines; a united Jerusalem under Israeli sovereignty; and that Israel would not accept moral or legal responsibility for the refugee problem. Almost from the moment the summit opened on July 11, it quickly became bogged down over two of these crucial issues. The right of return of Palestinian refugees from previous wars – mainly 1948 – to Israel proper, and the fate of Jerusalem, notably control over Haram al-Sharif – the Temple Mount. Clinton clearly had his work cut out, if anything remotely resembling a deal was going to be reached. As so often in the past, the thorny issues of borders, settlements, refugees and, especially, the question of who controlled Jerusalem, were always the most intractable and potentially inflammable.

As the summit got underway I would often sit in Jerusalem's coffeehouses or bars in the company of Palestinian or Israeli friends, watching news updates on the latest political wrangles and manoeuvrings. 'Look, look, they can't even decide who should go through the door first,' laughed an old Palestinian man one evening. Onscreen, caught by television cameras, we watched in disbelief a farcical scene unfold in which Barak and Arafat each insisted in turn that the other lead the way into one of Camp David's secluded cabins to begin the next round of talks. Standing in the doorway alongside the 'peacemakers,' a clearly embarrassed and bemused President Clinton could only look on at the battle of body language and the uneasy stand-off that spoke volumes about the relationship between the two Middle Eastern leaders.

For those Palestinians watching back home in the living rooms of Ramallah, Hebron or Gaza, such signs were hardly reassuring. What's more, that same audience – unlike some of the Palestinian leaders themselves – was already wary of Clinton and his negotiating team's motives in bringing the two sides together. Time and again over endless cups of Turkish coffee or mint tea, Palestinians would recall that when Egyptian leader Anwar Sadat went to Camp David in 1978, the American negotiating team included only one Zionist Jewish official. Now, they warned me, with the exception of Clinton himself, all the American team were Zionist Jews. The Palestinians had long questioned America's credibility as a mediator. How they asked, was it possible for the country that supplied the warplanes, tear gas grenades and attack helicopters used against them, to act as an 'honest broker' in such negotiations? Like them, I only had to cast my mind back to those first few weeks of the Gulf War in 1991 to remember how quickly Washington responded to its ally's needs in moments of crisis. During those dangerous early days of the conflict, we would watch the giant US Air Force Galaxy transport aircraft land at Tel Aviv's Ben Gurion airport.

On board were batteries of the Patriot ground-to-air missile system that would provide protection for Israeli cities by intercepting the Iraqi Scud rockets that had been falling almost nightly on Tel Aviv or Haifa. Conscious that Israel might be provoked into retaliating against Iraq, Washington pulled out all the stops to encourage its ally to hold back. A deal between the two nations was struck. Not only were the Patriot batteries delivered at breakneck speed, but cash incentives, and a green light from Washington for Israel to continue with its controversial settlement expansion in the West Bank was also given the nod of approval. Once again for most Palestinians the message was clear. Whenever Israel needs help to consolidate its military or political role in the region, Uncle Sam was ready and willing to answer the call.

But as those Palestinians I met in cafés during the Camp David summit had been quick to point out, this was a partnership based on more than Israel simply being a regional ally, or America a ready supplier of military hardware. It was also a pact shaped and influenced by the political brokering of America's Jewish lobby in Washington's corridors of power. So influential was this lobby on US policy that at times it was difficult to tell just who was cracking the whip. The extent of the lobby's power always seemed to me best summed up by the slogan emblazoned across T-shirts for sale in Arab shops in Jerusalem's Old City bazaar. DON'T WORRY AMERICA, ISRAEL IS BEHIND YOU, the message ironically reassured Washington doubters, beneath the diving silhouette of an Israeli F-16 fighter-bomber.

One Israeli government source explained the measure of the lobby's leverage another way. 'The Palestinians always complain that we know the details of every proposal from the Americans before they do,' he remarked. 'There's good reason for that: we write them.' It was against just such a backdrop of Arab suspicion over US–Israeli complicity that the Camp David summit played out in July 2000.

Keen for a diplomatic 'victory' in the Middle East before it left office, the absence of any international or legal parameters for the negotiations mattered little to the Clinton administration. While this suited Barak's agenda, Arafat on the other hand only had America's 'goodwill' to rely on. The refugee issue was the first of the 'final status' questions to hit the Camp David buffers. For years the United Nations had reaffirmed its ruling that the Right of Return was an 'inalienable right.' But as Barak had previously made clear to the Knesset before arriving at Camp David, it remained simply the fault of the Arabs, and an issue for which Israel refused to accept any moral or legal responsibility. After a heated but superficial discussion, the Israeli negotiators made the concession that a few thousand refugees could return over a ten-year period, but only based on humanitarian criteria. Israel also agreed to support an international fund that would compensate some of the refugees. For Arafat and his team, it was an untenable position. As members of the PLO – which itself has its roots in the Palestinian refugee diaspora – how could they without conscience sign away the rights of return for some 3.7 million fellow Palestinians who remained outcasts after being driven from their homes by Israeli tanks and guns? But if the refugee issue was the first serious nail in the Camp David coffin, then it was the wrangling over the fate of Jerusalem that would effectively bury it.

At the heart of the debate lay the super-sensitive issue of sovereignty over the city. Early in the summit, at least two formulae were initially proposed but almost immediately fell apart, revealing the extent of Washington's tilt towards its Israeli ally. Clinton's team repeatedly used what they called 'bridging proposals' to repackage terms the Israelis had come up with in the first place. As Arafat himself pointed out to Clinton, far from being new offers, they were little more than reiteration of proposals the Palestinians had already received through secret channels from the Barak government. As if the dressed-up bridging proposals were not bad enough, anyone giving more than a cursory glance at their terms would have realised that they had little international legitimacy, specifically relating to UN Resolution 242, which called for Israeli withdrawal from territories they had occupied in 1967. Despite this, on the fourteenth day of the summit, in an attempt to break the deadlock on the Jerusalem issue, Clinton came up with yet another bridging proposal. In it he suggested that Israel would take the Jewish neighbourhoods, the Palestinians would take most – but not all – of the Arab neighbourhoods, while the Haram Al-Sharif and Temple Mount would come under Palestinian custodianship. Overall sovereignty would remain in Israel's hands. Not surprisingly Arafat rejected it. For not only would it deny Palestinian sovereignty over the heart of Jerusalem, but as the Holy City's self-appointed guardian, Arafat knew that any compromise on Jerusalem would brand him a traitor in the Arab world for all history.

'Do you want to attend my funeral? I will not relinquish Jerusalem and the holy places. . . . I have led my people's revolution, and the siege of Beirut was easier on me than the siege of Camp David,' Arafat complained to Clinton as the summit effectively collapsed.

As ever, each side blamed the other. While Clinton publicly sided with Barak, lavishing praise on the Prime Minister for his 'courage and vision,' as well as his 'understanding of the historical importance of this moment,' he chided Arafat for his lack of flexibility. For many Palestinians all the wrangling represented nothing more than a wasted seven years, and their resentment grew not only against the Israeli occupation, but also against Arafat himself.

Life for most ordinary Palestinians during six of those seven years had been spent under the authoritarian and incompetent governance of Arafat's Palestinian Authority (PA). Now they were faced with the harsh reality that Oslo had been much more about 'process' than it had been about peace. On the strategic level it had done little more than change the form of the occupation instead of removing it. In terms of day-to-day living it benefited only those Arafat loyalists who had come with him from Tunis, plus a *coterie* of wealthy cronies from within the PA.

More and more Palestinians expressed their anger to me at what they saw as flagrant opportunism among their leaders. 'They think only of their own private interests,' complained one young unemployed man called Nidal that I met in Gaza, voicing the feelings of many. 'They prefer to put up with what Israel is willing to give, and cooperate with them economically and on security issues while we carry the burden,' he continued. He was 'finished' with being a member of Fatah, he insisted, and had decided instead to offer his allegiance to the Islamist group Hamas, whose influence throughout the territories was rapidly growing.

As this disgruntlement with the PA simmered and steadily grew, Israel's military occupation had become increasingly harsh. Closures preventing Palestinians from entering Israel were expanded to prevent travel within and between the West Bank and Gaza. Military checkpoints proliferated throughout the maze of Israeli and partial PA-controlled areas. House demolitions continued and settlement construction had nearly doubled throughout the occupied territories since Oslo. Hardly surprising then that the combined effects of this multiple oppression were pushing many Palestinians to the limits of their endurance and stirring them to action. Add to this volatile mix Ariel Sharon's provocative march across Haram al-Sharif and the potential power keg was complete.

It was not the first time he had tried to upset Muslim sensitivities in Jerusalem. In December 1987, the same month that the first intifada broke out, Sharon had bought and moved into an apartment in the heart of the Muslim quarter of the Old City. In the months and years that followed, some of Sharon's supporters, mainly groups of right-wing students, did likewise. Strolling down from Damascus Gate through the *mêlée* of Arab stallholders, it would always catch me by surprise to come across the entranceway leading to Sharon's apartment tucked under a little archway. Beneath a Star of David flag hanging limply from the building, three or four heavily armed Israeli soldiers would stand guard in the narrow passageway, voices crackling over their radios as they eyed those who went past. Sharon liked such gestures. It was his way of saying to the Palestinians, 'See, we can go where we want, whenever we want, and what can you do about it? Nothing.'

As Housing Minister in 1991, Sharon also took it upon himself to help Jewish extremists take over a house in Silwan, an Arab village within the Jerusalem municipality. 'We have set a goal for ourselves of not leaving one neighbourhood in East Jerusalem without Jews, not one,' he declared defiantly. It was around this time that I covered a tense

and sometimes violent stand-off, after a group of extremist Jewish settlers forcibly took over a building belonging to the Greek Orthodox
Church in the Christian quarter of the old city. The move, not surprisingly, had Sharon's blessing. From time to time, surrounded by bodyguards, he would squeeze his way past protestors and waiting journalists to visit the settlers, who would peer out nervously from doorways
and windows, protected by police sentries carrying tear gas launchers
and machine pistols. Even Jerusalem's Mayor, Teddy Kollek, was forced
to denounce what he called Sharon's 'messianism' at the time.

Back then, and now again in September 2000 after his march
around the Haram al-Sharif, the 'bulldozer' was in a characteristically
unrepentant mood. 'What provocation is there when Jews come to visit
the place with a message of peace? The Temple Mount is in our hands
and will remain in our hands,' Sharon announced after his descent.
Some political observers have also suggested that provoking the
Palestinians was not Sharon's only aim. Knowing the controversy his
Haram visit would cause, it might also conveniently serve to divert
attention away from his Likud rival, Benjamin Netanyahu, who was
making something of a political comeback at that time. Just prior to
Sharon's visit, Palestinian and American officials fearing violence had
urged Prime Minister Ehud Barak to prohibit the move. But Barak also
saw Sharon's attempt to visit the Haram as the act of an internal political opponent and he decided not to stand in his way. Whatever Sharon's
intention, the consequences were catastrophic.

In Salah e Din Street, the main commercial district in Arab East
Jerusalem, I watched as clashes between troops and Palestinians continued intermittently for hours after his visit. The tension ratcheted up further as news began filtering through to the streets that in the West Bank
town of Qalqilya a Palestinian policeman working with Israeli police on
a joint patrol had turned on them and gunned down his Israeli counterpart. It was clear that the blaze of violence was catching fast. But it was
nothing compared to the inferno that would come in the days, weeks
and months ahead.

US Special Envoy Dennis Ross had been right when he described
Sharon's walkabout as a bad idea, but what made the gesture so much
worse and certain to raise Palestinian hackles was its timing. In a part
of the world where anniversaries all too often have a particular resonance and potency, the 'bulldozer's' trundling across Haram al-Sharif
also just happened to coincide with one of the blackest events in mod-

ern Palestinian history. The cry of 'murderer' at Sharon from protestors on the Haram was a reminder to him of an infamous incident 18 years earlier.

As Israeli Defence Minister at the time, Sharon gave his full approval to an operation that resulted in the massacre of perhaps as many as 2,000 Palestinians in the Sabra and Shatila refugee camps on the outskirts of Beirut in Lebanon. Robert Fisk, one of the Middle East's greatest-ever correspondents, was among the first eyewitnesses to arrive in the camps during mid-September in 1982. He recalled how the millions of flies and the stench of the dead filtering through the thickest of handkerchiefs held over his mouth first brought home the horror of what had gone on there. 'When we had seen a hundred bodies, we stopped counting. Down every alleyway, there were corpses – women, young men, babies and grandparents – lying together in lazy and terrible profusion where they had been knifed or machine-gunned to death.' As Fisk and a few colleagues waded through the evidence of the slaughter at Sabra and Shatila, he clearly remembered Israeli soldiers watching them though binoculars from the top of a tower block on the Avenue Camille Chamoun.

'That fucker Sharon!' cursed a *Washington Post* reporter as they moved through the bloated corpses, the realisation slowly dawning that the Israeli Defence Minister bore some of the responsibility for the massacre they were encountering. As Defence Minister in Menachem Begin's government, Sharon had led the Israeli invasion of Lebanon. Ironically dubbed 'Operation Peace for Galilee,' it was aimed at destroying PLO bases in the country and bringing about the establishment of a Lebanese government led by Maronite Christians.

In September of that same year, Sharon, having helped to fund and arm Israel's Christian militia allies – the Phalangists – gave the green light for their gunmen to enter Sabra and Shatila to root out Palestinian 'terrorists.' Meanwhile, the Israeli army, under orders not to interfere but clearly within sight of the killing and raping underway, did nothing as thousands of innocent people were butchered. During a subsequent commission of inquiry into the massacre, one Israeli officer, Lieutenant Avi Grabowski, testified that he had been witness to the murder of women and children. In his evidence Grabowski told how on Friday, September 17, the second day of the massacre, he had asked a Phalangist why they were killing civilians. 'Pregnant women will give birth to terrorists; the children when they grow up will be terrorists,' the militiaman replied.

In December 1982, the United Nations declared the Sabra and Shatila massacre an act of genocide, while Israel's own Kahan Commission found that Ariel Sharon bore 'personal responsibility' for what happened. Now, 18 years after the bulldozers had tried to bury some of the evidence of the massacre under the bloody earth of Sabra and Shatila, 'the bulldozer' was still goading and gunning for his Palestinian enemies on the sacred ground of the Haram al-Sharif. For most Palestinians this latest outrage renewed their anger, but came as little surprise. To them, even long before Sabra and Shatila, Ariel Sharon had always been an Israeli leader with 'form.'

Born in 1928 in Kfar Malal, ten miles from Tel Aviv, Sharon's original family name was Scheinermann before it was later changed. His was an early start to a military career when he became involved with the Israeli Haganah, the largest of the Jewish underground organisations during the 1948 war. But it was five years later in 1953 that Ariel Sharon first leapt into history's spotlight, with a military modus operandi that was to become all too familiar in the years ahead.

It was a bitterly cold night on October 14 when Sharon and his newly formed 'elite' commando squad known as Unit 101 crept into the sleepy village of Qibya in the West Bank. The Israelis' orders were simple, and called for the 'blowing up of houses' and 'hitting the inhabitants,' ostensibly in retaliation for a grenade attack two days earlier which had killed an Israeli woman and two children. Whoever the Arabs were that had carried out that attack, there was no known or suspected connection between them and Qibya, which at that time was under Jordanian administration. Such details mattered little to men like Moshe Dayan, head of the Israeli Army's operations department, and David Ben-Gurion, leader of Israel's first government. Like many Israeli chiefs at the time, they shared the belief that Arabs only understood force, and felt that Israel needed to exercise that force as often and assertively as possible.

As the brainchild of Dayan and Ben-Gurion, Sharon's Unit 101, nicknamed 'the Avengers,' was a semi-clandestine force raised to deliver that message in devastating 'reprisal' attacks against Palestinians and neighbouring Arab populations. In time, Unit 101 would later evolve into the Duvdevan (Cherry) and Shimshon (Samson), the undercover units that today still carry out retaliatory and other planned hits against Palestinians involved in the intifada.

Back in 1953, as Sharon's men swept into Qibya that chill October night, the silent desert air was quickly filled with the thump of grenade explosions, the rattle of automatic weapons and screams of wounded and dying villagers. Barely two hours after Sharon and his men had finished their work, UN observers arrived in the village. What they found shocked them. Jordanian pathologists later confirmed that the bullet-ridden bodies near the doorways of the demolished houses indicated that the villagers had been forced to stay inside until their homes were blown up over them. Eyewitness survivors time and again told UN officials the same account: how the Israelis moved about the village dynamiting houses, lobbing grenades and firing into doorways and windows. Despite it being the middle of the night when the raid took place, Sharon claimed that his men were unaware that people were inside the houses as they carried out their mission. By the morning of October 15, 1953, though still not quite a household name, Ariel Sharon had nevertheless managed to elicit the strongest possible condemnation of the United Nations, the United States State Department and most of enlightened world opinion after his Avengers' attack on Qibya.

Though estimates vary, as many as 69 men, women and children were slaughtered in the raid, and there seems little doubt that if a similar operation were carried out today it would be condemned as an act of terrorism. It was a notorious start for the man his followers liked to call 'Arik,' but would do little to halt Sharon's dogged climb to the highest levels of power in Israel. The massacre at Qibya was only an ominous portent of things to come as Sharon in the years ahead resorted time and again to crushing military action against the Palestinians.

Jerusalem, September 29, 2000

We all sensed it would be no ordinary Friday. For years throughout the first intifada, the arrival of the Muslim holy day and the start of Jewish Shabbat had always been viewed as potentially the most volatile day in any week. 'The Friday matinee,' a journalist friend called it. Once a week we would roll up at mosques in Gaza or Jerusalem, knowing full well that a heavily armed Israeli presence on the streets outside and a politically charged sermon inside the mosque made for an explosive brew.

But that Friday the sense of foreboding was almost palpable. I'd had the same feeling a few times in the Middle East just before momentous events. Call it a buzz, a vibe; whatever the explanation, sometimes it's almost as if the air crackles in anticipation.

The airwaves of the Arab radio stations were buzzing that day. All morning following Sharon's walkabout of the afternoon before, the same passionate mantra had filled Arab radio broadcasts. In call after call, the message went out to 'Come protect Haram al-Sharif.'

As Muslim worshippers made their way through the cobbled streets towards the mosque, Jerusalem's old city stood fortified as if awaiting a rerun of some bygone assault on its ramparts. From its walls and inside its alleyways, Israeli soldiers and police had taken up key positions, their guns trained on the massive stream of worshippers that crept past like slow-moving lava. One Hebronite women is said to have later described the events that were about to unfold as being 'like the Day of Judgement.' She was not far wrong.

Watching the Muslim faithful shuffle into the Haram, I could only guess at the fervour with which the *imam* would deliver his *khutba*. As expected, he did not hold back.

> They have no right to the Haram. . . . They claim the presence of a skeleton only to destroy the Aqsa. . . . They're enslaving us, they're stripping us of our dignity. . . . May Allah grant peace to all of His martyrs, may Allah permit the release of all our brothers in prison, may Allah make us stronger by uniting the Arab world.

The atmosphere was electric. The holy place was under threat. As the imam's words echoed around the esplanade, adrenaline and anger were already coursing through the veins of the Muslim worshippers. Outside, Israeli security men checked their weapons for the umpteenth time. Visors were dropped on their protective helmets, and tear gas rounds were slotted into the barrels of their launchers.

The first shots came from the direction of the Western Wall. From along its top edges, Palestinians had begun stoning Jewish worshippers at the face of the famous site beneath them. As Jews scattered for cover, the soldiers opened up on the rock throwers. *Cra–crack*. The bullets began to whack against the sun-drenched limestone walls of the Haram compound. Others quickly found their mark, and the bodies began to fall. There were no half-measures now. The lid was off, and it would be a long time before the cauldron cooled sufficiently for it to be replaced. Bullets criss-crossed the Haram. The Israelis were shooting to kill.

Taking aim above the waist, necks, shoulders, chests and wrists were ripped open by the live rounds. Palestinian women and children trying desperately to escape the prayer area tripped and fell. Others stood frozen to the spot, shrieking in fear and panic. 'Let's get the fuck out of here, to the other side of the gate,' a TV cameraman next to me screamed, as we tried to shove our way through the crush and panic of people at Lion's Gate.

On the other side of the narrow archway the Israeli police and soldiers were swinging batons at the skulls of those who made it through. Behind us, the sound of yet more gunfire and tear gas grenades being launched brought another wave of worshippers fleeing the battle. I watched two Palestinians half carry, half drag the body of a wounded friend, their shirts spattered in his blood. There was a gaping hole in the man's chest and a steady thick trickle of red from the side of his mouth. Though he seemed to me almost certainly dead, his left hand still clenched a set of faded plastic prayer beads.

On the steep hillside street outside Lion's Gate that leads down towards the Jericho Road and the Church of Gethsemane, there was chaos as worshippers tried to distance themselves from the clashes taking place in and around the Haram. Ambulance sirens and those of Israeli army jeeps rose and fell around East Jerusalem, and gunshots could increasingly be heard in all directions.

At nearby Makassed Hospital, where during the first intifada I met the family of 14-year-old Ali Mohammed Fannoun keeping their bedside vigil as life drained from their wounded son, the wards were awash with the fresh blood of the young pitched into this new uprising.

Arab radio broadcasts kept up a commentary of those who had already fallen for good: 'Haythem al-Skafi, Hebron; Osama Geda, Jerusalem; Bilal Anafani, Abu Dis.' The numbers of dead rose interminably: five, seven, twelve. Those counted wounded were already in the hundreds. As reporters, we struggled to keep up with the pace of events on the ground.

Over the next 24 hours there were outbreaks of fighting in Jerusalem, Abu Dis, Ramallah, Bethlehem, Jenin, Tulkarm, Nablus, Hebron, and hell on earth in Gaza. In no time, all of the occupied territories were on fire, and the Palestinian Authority had declared a general strike.

As we tried to make sense of what was going on around us, it was clear from the start that this was different from the first intifada.

Everywhere it seemed, the *shebab* were rushing headlong to sacrifice themselves. Such wanton forfeiture was an uncomfortable thing to witness. Something had snapped in so many of these young men, for whom the value of life versus death had become blurred. Anxiety, frustration, tragedy, confusion and manipulation ruled the day.

For this generation of Palestinians, it was clear the handshakes on the White House lawn, Oslo, the summit meetings, dinners, retreats, peace treaties, interim agreements and promises of their leaders had meant only one thing – betrayal. To my eyes, many appeared at one with their rage. It was almost as if they had become resigned to a long slow-burning fuse that they knew sooner or later would finally detonate and lead to God only knows where.

I thought back to what Khadeja Ayoup Gharab had told me that day in September1989 as we sat and drank tea at her home in Beach Refugee Camp in Gaza. How for such a long time prior to her 17-year-old son Mohammed being gunned down in the sand dunes of Gaza, his rage against the Israeli occupation had eaten away and ultimately consumed him. Now, it was a collective rage that was exploding, unleashing this al-Aqsa intifada. One senior Israeli intelligence officer at the time is said to have joked about how this was the start of a 'Six Year War.' He might have been indulging in some word-play by comparing the intifada, which he saw as a long-term sore, with the quickie Six Day War, which pitched Arabs and Israeli against each other in 1967, but he wasn't far off the mark. For not only would it take a long time for this latest uprising to burn itself out, but with it would come events, tactics, strategies and a no-quarter struggle that would eat like never before into the psyche and lives of both Palestinian and Israeli alike.

Netzarim Junction, Gaza Strip, September 30, 2000

The Friday afternoon riots in Jerusalem were showing on television later that evening, as 12-year-old Mohammed al-Durra sat down to watch at his home in Bourij refugee camp in Gaza. Like most youngsters his age, Mohammed always wanted to be where the action was. When not attending to his pet love birds in their pink cage that had been given to him as a gift by his teacher, he would often disappear for hours to watch the older boys throw rocks. As the drama of Friday's events unfolded on news bulletin after news bulletin, Mohammed turned and asked his mother if he could join the protests that were expected throughout the next day, Saturday, at one of Gaza's most notorious flashpoints – Netzarim Junction. Amal, his mother, said nothing in reply. Like many Palestinian parents, she and Mohammed's father, Jamal, didn't want him to go. There was sure to be the violence that so many youngsters saw as a rite of passage, and at barely 12 years old, martyrdom was the last thing they wanted for their son. But little did the al-Durra family know that within hours across the Arab and Islamic world Mohammed would be just that – a martyr; a boy whose final few seconds of life would be beamed around the globe in TV images that turned this youngster with a sense of wanderlust into a tragic icon of the intifada. In Baghdad, they would name a street after him. In Morocco, a public park. In Jordan, the Tai Kwon Do Association gave his name to their annual championship. In other Arab countries, postage stamps were issued carrying his picture.

From somewhere in hiding after the September 11 attacks and the US invasion of Afghanistan, Osama bin Laden told President George W. Bush in one of his messages that he 'must not forget the image of Mohammed al-Durra . . . if he has forgotten, then we will not forget,' the al-Qaeda leader warned ominously. A few years later in 2002, when Islamist kidnappers in Pakistan beheaded *Wall Street Journal* reporter Daniel Pearl, visible in the background during a videoclip of the horrific killing was a poster depicting the last moment of Mohammed al-Durra's life. Around the globe, those final eight frames of Mohammed crouched in terror, before bullets ripped through his torso and the dying boy's grip loosened on his father, became the first searing image of the al-Aqsa intifada.

This was the end game that Mohammed's father had deliberately tried so hard to avoid, by offering to take his excited son to a used car auction in Gaza City that Saturday morning to prevent him sneaking off and joining the Netzarim protests. They had left home by taxi, and like most Palestinians from Bourij or the other refugee camps to the south who want to visit Gaza City, had no choice but to travel the coastal road and pass the Israeli military post at Netzarim. For years this fortress of reinforced steel and concrete with its watchtowers on the northwest corner of the junction has been the frontline defence for the 60 or so Jewish families who lived to the west in the Netzarim settlement. Like City Inn Junction on the outskirts of Ramallah, the volatile Netzarim crossroads has long since been the target of Palestinian fury. At full pitch the riots here were terrifying to witness.

'When the people of Palestine are crying out against Israel, they find this place to throw stones. It is a target for all the anger against the people sitting in their belly and in their bedroom,' was how a Palestinian soldier, Brigadier General Osama al-Ali, once described the turbulent flashpoint.

By the time Mohammed and his father were on their way home from the auction, the air around Netzarim was full of stones and Molotovs, and their taxi driver declared he would go no further. Leaving their taxi behind, the al-Durras headed quickly hand-in-hand across the rock-strewn junction hoping to catch a taxi on the other side. Just as they were about to pass a small Palestinian security post that sat diagonally opposite the larger Israeli one a few hundred yards away, the stones hurtling through the air were joined by a salvo of bullets as Palestinians and Israelis exchanged gunfire. Jamal and Mohammed rushed for cover against a concrete water barrel. The images that followed caught live on television made for heartbreaking viewing, and to this day remain the subject of anger, controversy and debate. In the footage, Jamal is seen waving frantically as if pleading with the Israelis to stop firing, as Mohammed cowers terrified in the crook of his father's arm. But the shooting went on and Mohammed was hit first in the leg. 'Don't shoot, don't shoot,' Jamal shouted, his voice drowned out by the rattle of gunfire. For about five minutes after Mohammed was wounded, his father continued yelling: 'My son is dying, my son is dying.'

Bassam Al-Balbisi, a 45-year-old Palestinian Red Crescent ambulance driver, bravely made his way through the hail of bullets towards the pair to try and get them out, but he was instantly shot dead. Another of his colleagues, who tried to do the same was wounded. It was now around 2.30 p.m. In all, the shooting lasted over 40 minutes, during which time Mohammed was seen to become quiet and the desperate clutch on his father slackened as a fourth and final bullet entered his stomach and he slumped over dead. Even then the firing continued, and still trying to protect his son, Jamal was shot again and again, his body jerking convulsively as the bullets struck his legs and torso. Like so many viewers around the world, Amal al-Durra watched her dying son's last moments on television pictures caught by Talal Abu Rahma, a Palestinian freelance cameraman working for the network France 2. 'I went crazy. I was screaming and crying,' she recalled a few days later as mourners filled the al-Durras' spartan concrete house where 'Rami,' as Mohammed had been nicknamed, had been born 12 years earlier. Even amidst the commotion in the house, Mohammed's five pet birds could still be heard chirping noisily in their cage.

The day after Mohammed al-Durra's killing, newspapers in the occupied territories and around the world ran a sequence of still pictures from the television report in which the fear and pain of those last seconds was eerily frozen. Like countless other people in Gaza, Jerusalem and elsewhere, who woke up to the images over breakfast that day, I wondered just for a moment whether maybe, just maybe, something good might come from such a tragedy. Perhaps at long last, from the haunted look on the face of this little boy, the realisation might dawn that the eye-for-an-eye score settling between Israelis and Palestinians could not continue forever. But I knew the reality was something quite different; knew that the face staring out at me was simply yet another icon in this dance of death.

On shuttered shop fronts and cinderblock walls like the one where a circle of fifteen bullet holes and a fading smear of darkening blood were all that marked the place of Mohammed al-Durra's death, Rami's face was already on the posters that lined the martyrs' street galleries. Like countless Palestinian parents, Amal al-Durra and her husband Jamal, who miraculously survived that day, would try not to make too much of how Mohammed had died in front of their other children. To do so could mean that they too might fall under the *shahid*'s spell. As Amal went to visit her recovering husband in hospital, his first words to her were: 'Be patient.' Elsewhere others were far from patient, seeing instead a quick opportunity of making political capital from Mohammed's death.

When the Israeli army opened an investigation into the killing, its soldiers insisted that Mohammed and his father were among the protesters who had assaulted their outpost at Netzarim. 'First of all I am very, very sorry about this kid,' said Major General Yom Tov Samia, chief of the Israeli Army's southern command, 'but we are sure they were not there by accident. People were throwing stones and Molotovs. If a person finds himself under those conditions he must know his life is in danger.' But much of the real bitterness and subsequent controversy surrounding the killing centred on the footage shot by Talal Abu Rahma, the freelance cameraman.

On October 30, 2000, Abu Rahma gave a sworn affidavit to the Palestine Centre for Human Rights about what he had witnessed that day. In part of his statement he confirmed that 'the child was intention-

ally and in cold blood shot dead and his father injured by the Israeli
Army.' Others insisted Abu Rahma's footage had been staged. One of
the first and most vocal was Richard Landes, a Boston University professor, who despite his unlikely specialisation in medieval cultures took
it upon himself to study the footage in detail before concluding that it
had probably been faked. 'I came to the realisation that Palestinian cameramen, especially when there are no Westerners around, engage in the
systematic staging of action scenes,' he said, calling Abu Rahma's
footage nothing more than 'Pallywood cinema.'

Major General Yom Tov Samia of the Israeli Army re-entered the
debate when he commissioned two men to open a second investigation
into the case. Nahum Shahaf was an Israeli physicist, and Yosef Duriel
an engineer; both had worked together previously during an enquiry
into the assassination of Yitzak Rabin in 1996. In short, their investigation and its findings, which they managed to persuade America's CBS 60
Minutes to air, was an attempt by the IDF to prove that Palestinian gunmen, not Israeli soldiers, had been responsible for Mohammed al-
Durra's death. In an interview at the time, Duriel took the controversy
a stage further by stating that Mohammed had not only been killed by
Palestinian gunmen, but that they were collaborating with the France 2
TV crew and the boy's father with the intention of fabricating an anti-
Israeli propaganda symbol. Even in death it seemed, Mohammed con-
tinued to be a target in this, a conflict where there must always be two
stories.

Ironically, it took an Israeli Knesset member, Ophir Pines-Paz, who
then sat on the parliament's Foreign Affairs and Defence Committee, to
point out what many people suspected about the real motives behind
the Israeli army investigation. 'One gets the impression that instead of
genuinely confronting this incident, the IDF has chosen to stage a fic-
titious re-enactment and cover up the incident by means of an enquiry
. . . the sole purpose of which is to clear the IDF of responsibility for al-
Durra's death,' Ophir Pines-Baz stated bravely. His views were endorsed
by an Amnesty International report entitled Broken Lives: A Year of
Intifada, published on November 13, 2001. In its pages, cameraman
Talal Abu Rahma's sworn affidavit to the Palestine Centre for Human
Rights again cast eyewitness light on that day's events. This time it
pointed out that the gunfire from the Palestinian outpost at Netzarim
had stopped 45 minutes before Mohammed al-Durra was shot. The
report also says that photographs taken by journalists at the scene

showed a pattern of bullets indicating that the Israeli post opposite them targeted father and son.

Before that fateful Saturday afternoon, Jamal al-Durra had been employed as a house painter for Israeli contractors in the suburbs of Tel Aviv. As one of the lucky Gazans still to have a job inside Israel at the height of the first intifada, he had once worked at the home of Helen Schary Motro, a Jewish American writer and columnist for *The Jerusalem Post*. Like so many Palestinian workers in those days, Jamal would rise at 3.30 a.m. to take a bus at 4 a.m. to the Erez border crossing, before boarding another bus to ensure he would be in Israel to start work at 6 a.m. 'Was it this backbreaking cycle of physical labour that made the 35-year-old man look like he was 50?' Motro asked, remembering Jamal in her *Jerusalem Post* column a little over a week after the al-Durra story had swept across the world. The mother of a daughter almost the same age as Mohammed, Motro called Jamal barely a week after his son had been killed.

Despite all the wrangling and controversy still surrounding Mohammed's death, Jamal showed few signs of any lingering bitterness. Towards the end of their conversation, Motro asked him what he wished for his remaining children. 'My children? To grow as all children in the world,' he told the writer on the telephone line from Amman, his voice shaking with emotion. 'That they will be surrounded by all good things and nothing bad, nothing bad.'

Khalil Sakakini Centre, Ramallah, March 2001

A catapult, a paramedic's uniform, crayon drawings of a boy flying a kite. As I passed the objects one by one, they seemed to emanate a quiet eloquence. Each was serenely at odds with the screams, pain and anger that had accompanied the deaths of their owners. Mohammed al-Durra had been buried six months ago. Since then, more than 400 other victims, 80 percent of them Palestinians, had died in the al-Aqsa intifada.

Hot and weary after a day spent talking to some Palestinian youngsters about where they thought the uprising was now going, I had sought sanctuary from the hectic bustle of Ramallah's streets in the cool and calm of the Khalil Sakakini Cultural Centre art gallery. Inside, I was instantly enveloped by the mausoleum-like silence that so often in the Middle East inhabits buildings that sit just yards away from the frenzy of the world outside. Here, only the tapping of shoe heels and gentle sputtering of the candles that lined the dimly lit gallery floor intruded on the quiet. Already I had witnessed so much killing in the years that I'd spent covering this battle of wills. But little did I know then, as I made my way through this exhibition of photographs and objects entitled 'The Hundred Martyrs,' that over the next few months, death would become an even more commonplace experience.

Indeed, at times, it would often seem as if the ranks of these first 100 people killed by the Israelis since the start of the al-Aqsa intifada grew so quickly, that the names of the victims and the circumstances surrounding their deaths blurred one into another. Over the coming year, barely a few miles from the silence of the gallery space where I then stood, I would come across the pale, bloodless, bullet-ridden corpse of a dead colleague, and see countless men blindfolded and bound being herded off for interrogation and torture. On more than one occasion I would also find myself walking among the body parts of Palestinians and Israelis alike, torn apart and strewn across the streets by the impact of missiles or detonation of the suicide bombers' deadly cargo.

As I strolled around the gallery looking in turn at the black and white photographs of the deceased, it occurred to me that death has two faces. One is non-being; the other is the material being that is the corpse. After years as a war reporter I had long since learned which one I feared most. Anyone who has ever lost a loved one understands this.

The relatives of those whose memories were represented here in this quiet place certainly understood.

During my visit, the exhibition's curators told me how they had been inundated with requests by the relatives of other intifada victims who wanted their loved ones' belongings and memories to be part of this temporary monument. Each of the objects that I saw displayed underneath the photographs in transparent plastic cases represented individual shrines. Their value was not material, but purely symbolic in that they belonged to a 'martyr.' In each case curators' assistants had journeyed out through the Israeli checkpoints and cordons that surrounded Palestinian communities to collect these personal artifacts.

Mohammed al-Durra's shoes were here. As were a Gameboy, a football and the blue bicycle of 14-year-old Yazan Halayqa with its heart-shaped cushion on the handlebars that read: I LOVE YOU THIS MUCH. The objects stood alone as testament to an individual life. Lives not just remembered, but preserved, along with stories equally powerful and emotive. I remember stopping before the empty birdcage belonging to 15-year-old Nizar Eideh of Ramallah, who on the morning of his death released a bird he had bought a few days earlier, worried that the bird's mother might miss him.

But it was the photograph of another 15-year-old, Fares Odeh, from the Zaitoun quarter of Gaza, that held my gaze longest. Everything about the image suggested an anxious, guilty look. From the intensity of his coal black eyes, to the way he seemed to be biting his bottom lip, it was as if the camera shutter had closed at precisely the moment he had been caught misbehaving. He was just the kind of boy you would expect to own the rough handcarved catapult that lay in the case beneath his picture. I remember thinking that I too had whittled a catapult just like it, which I would use to fire stones at the watchmen on a building site near where I lived. Tanks though, not unsuspecting watchmen, were Fares Odeh's targets. Up until the day he was shot, he had become renowned for stoning tanks on his way to and from school in Gaza. By now, the famous news photograph of him face to face with a giant Israeli Merkava tank barely yards away, arm flung back about to launch a stone, had long since become one of the intifada's icons.

Fares was always one of the closest to the tanks. This was his badge of honour, his trademark. It was early morning when Fares left his house on November 8, 2000, telling his friends he wanted to stone tanks again before getting to school. On this occasion, however, the soldiers tried to chase him. As Fares ran they opened fire, and one of the bullets hit the boy in the neck, killing him instantly. Like so many young Palestinians who died during the intifada, Fares Odeh came from a poor family. So poor were many of those remembered in The Hundred Martyrs exhibition, that they possessed few belongings, and had never had a photograph taken of themselves in their entire lives. Young men like Bilal Affaneh, who was one of the first to die in the second intifada, was represented in the gallery by nothing more than the single sock his family had donated. His story and others like it recounted with depressing regularity how they had been forced to leave school to help their families survive.

'All my children are disabled and Fares was the only one without a disability,' Fares Odeh's mother explained after his death. 'I dreamed that my son would grow up to help us raise his brothers and sisters.' A dream was all it was. For instead of preparing to throw Fares the birthday party she had promised him, his mother was now simply left to mourn the passing of another Palestinian son and potential male bread-winner.

All those trappings of young manhood that surrounded me at the exhibition – the cassette tapes, T-shirts and training shoes – were all mute witnesses to a generation of young Palestinians in peril. What, I wondered, would my Israeli friends and colleagues make of all this? Would they, indeed could they, really care? After all, they had lost so many of their own young men and women to the intifada and the grow-ing violence that fueled it.

Just four months or so before I visited the The Hundred Martyrs exhibition in Ramallah, two Israeli soldiers, Sergeant Vadim Novesche and First Corporal Yosef Avrahami, had one afternoon somehow found themselves alone inside the city. Though the Israeli army later insisted that the two men had been reservists and simply got lost, there was something strange about their presence in what was effectively enemy territory. What's more, they had been travelling in an unmarked car, and according to some Palestinian eyewitnesses, at least one of them was wearing an Arab headscarf. Few probably know the real answer as to why the two soldiers were there that day. The only subsequent certain-ty was that it cost them their lives.

For many Israelis, the grisly events surrounding the soldiers' deaths also confirmed what they had always suspected as being the real driving force behind the Palestinian intifada – an almost congenital hatred. Tensions in Ramallah were running high that October day when the sol-diers drove into the city. For two weeks there had been intense clashes, and over 100 funerals of Palestinians killed, nearly two dozen of them children. Earlier that same week the pressure gauge had risen even fur-ther after the badly beaten body of another Palestinian, Issam Hamad, had been found dumped on the outskirts of Ramallah. Locals were in no doubt that Israeli settlers were to blame for his killing. To the horror of Sergeant Novesche and Corporal Avrahami, it was bang in the mid-dle of this Ramallah tinderbox that they found themselves stuck that day.

To make matters even worse, their fateful entrance to the town also coincided with the funeral of another 17-year-old Palestinian boy shot dead the day before by other Israeli troops. Within minutes of their car pulling up in the city centre, the two Israelis were hauled from their car by Palestinian policemen and taken to a nearby station. There the police hoped they would be able to protect the soldiers from the large crowd of angry Palestinians that had started to gather. But rumours quickly spread that the two men belonged to one of the feared and hated under-cover assassination squads that regularly struck in the heart of Palestin-ian towns.

Colonel Kamal al-Sheikh, Ramallah's Chief of Police, was in a meet-ing when he received a call on his mobile phone telling him that the police headquarters in Ramallah where the Israelis had been taken was surrounded, and that he should make his way there urgently. 'I some-how got into the building and found that the two Israelis were indeed inside. One of them was in his undershirt. I asked the officers why, and they told me that people in the street had torn off his shirt,' al-Sheikh recalled. The police chief had a mere 12 officers at his disposal, and only six of them were armed. The rest of the staff inside the station were either clerks or kitchen workers.

Across the road from the police station, the *muezzin*'s call to prayer reverberated across the rooftops. But later as thousands of funeral mourners left the mosque, it was chants of 'Kill the Jews!' and 'Allah o Akbar!' that echoed ominously around the streets as the crowd began baying for blood.

Colonel Kamal al-Sheikh frantically called for backup, but the police crowd control unit could not make it into the area. Most of al-Sheikh's men were already engaged in duties at flashpoints like Psagot, Beitunia and the Ayosh junction, where Palestinians were mustering after funerals to engage Israeli troops in street battles. Not that the 40 or so men under the police chief's command would have made much dif-ference against the small army of close to 5,000 Palestinians who were now beginning to move on the station. 'I took the two Israelis to the safest room in the building, on the second floor. I offered one of them a cigarette. His cheeks were bleeding. They were both hurt, but fully con-scious. I reassured them, saying that I would do whatever I could to save them. They were very frightened,' al-Sheikh remembered.

As the Colonel barricaded himself with four of his officers and the two Israelis in the second-floor room, the crowd outside broke past the main gate and headed upstairs. Others swarmed in through the window. Al-Sheikh threw himself on top of one of the soldiers in a vain attempt to protect him, but the crowd pulled him aside. An Italian TV crew at the scene captured on film what happened next. Their pictures broad-cast later that day emanated the same terrifying power as the last moments in the life of Mohammed al-Durra gunned down only 12 days earlier. Clearly visible in the footage was the frenzied beating and stabbing of the two Israelis, before one of the young Palestinian attackers came to the window and proudly showed his bloodsoaked hands to the jubilant crowds below. Moments later, the body of one of the soldiers plummeted from the window, smashing into the street, where the mob then beat and mutilated the corpse before dragging it behind a car into Ramallah's Manara Square.

Sergeant Vadim Novesche was a father of three small children; First Corporal Yosef Avrahami had been married for only four days before both were ripped to pieces in Ramallah. In the days that followed, Israeli press reports told how the soldiers' wives had tried to call them on their mobile phones after hearing news of the attack. Hani Avrahami said her husband Yosef's phone rang until a strange voice answered, saying 'I just killed your husband.'

By noon prayers the next day, Israel's wrath was unleashed with wave after wave of missiles raining down on Ramallah and elsewhere across the West Bank. The Palestinians called it war, but an Israeli army spokesman described it as nothing more than a limited operation intended as a 'symbolic message' to the Palestinian leadership. But many ordinary Israelis had a very different take on events. To them, this was proof of the futility in making distinctions between Arafat, those directly responsible for the lynching of the two soldiers, and Palestinians as a whole. 'How will we ever be able to negotiate a permanent peace treaty with people like that?' one Israeli man asked me, as we sat in a café near Jerusalem's Beit Agron Press Centre, pondering the horrors of the previous day in the morning newspapers. It was a difficult question to answer. Not least for a non-Jew and someone who was effectively an outsider. To many Israelis – and indeed Palestinians – I was little more than a bystander to a conflict in which their lives were quite literally being torn apart. To such people, I was at best a concerned reporter, at worst a mercenary voyeur who could have got on a plane and left at any time. As far as they were concerned, any thoughts or reflections I had on such things as The Hundred Martyrs exhibition or the killing of the two Israeli soldiers were easily dismissed as irrelevant.

'This is a dangerous neighbourhood,' an Israeli student and former paratrooper sharply reminded me one evening at a dinner party. 'Don't fall for all this eye-for-an-eye crap. On the whole it's better to blind the opposition the first chance you get,' he insisted. To Israelis like him, the exhibition in Ramallah was nothing more than another Arab way of manipulating the memory of the dead; a blatant glorification of martyrdom and a cynical attempt to portray all Israelis as child killers.

But set against voices like these, there were other Israelis who thought differently, people not blinded by the prevailing eye-for-an-eye demands of the mob, who knew that dialogue was ultimately the only way forward. I knew such Israelis existed because I had met them, spoken to them. These Israelis could relate to the lives and memories The Hundred Martyrs exhibition marked, because they too understood what it was like to be bullied, humiliated, occupied. Because they too realised what it was like to lose one's self-esteem and sense of identity, becoming just another anonymous victim and statistic in a long and bitter conflagration. Such people refused to live in that desert void of 'emotion and consciousness' that David Grossman had warned so eloquently and prophetically about in his book *The Yellow Wind*. The way ahead, the way towards some kind of peace, some kind of solution – if there was one – depended on the existence and determination of such thinking people on both sides of the divide. There were no alternatives – only oblivion.

5

THE RESISTANCE ESCALATES

'These days I try not to tell too many people of my
plans in advance.'

—Marwan Barghouti to David Pratt, June 2001

Netanya, March 4, 2001

It was just before nine o'clock on a Sunday morning when Ahmad Ayam turned into Herzl Street near the central market in the Israeli city of Netanya. The few days he'd spent before setting out for the coastal town had been a busy time for the 22-year-old Palestinian, who worked as a *muezzin* at the local mosque in the Tulkarem refugee camp where he lived with his family. First, he'd had to draft a letter ensuring that his monthly salary of 930 shekels would be given over to help build a minaret for his mosque. Then there was the matter of a smaller sum, the five other shekels that Ayam had promised to repay his father after borrowing the money the week before. There were also lots of photographs to be taken. A series of portraits shot at the local photographic studio of him posed in traditional Arab dress, and in front of a tacky backdrop depicting a poppy-filled landscape – a vision of paradise.

The intersection in Herzl Street was busy with shoppers as Ayam adjusted the shoulder strap on his backpack, and crossed the street to avoid an Israeli police car that was parked a few yards away. Thirty-year-old Galit Shahar didn't see Ayam while she was ringing up another sale on the till in the clothes shop where she worked. All she remembered was a bright light and the blast that thudded against the building, throwing glass and a severed human head across the street outside. Another Israeli shop owner, Sarit Bar-Aviv vividly recalled a car being hurled in the air. 'There were body parts, flesh and blood on the rooftops of the cars parked along the sidewalk. People were screaming, there was great confusion,' she remembered.

In a split-second, Ahmad Ayam had detonated explosives in his backpack, blowing himself to pieces in the name of Islam. The young *muezzin* turned human bomb had begun the journey to his poppy-garden paradise, and caused untold suffering among the 50 wounded survivors and relatives of the three Israelis he had killed. Almost before the dust from the bombing had settled, more than 20 Palestinians were rounded up in the area on suspicion of being inside Israel illegally. At the scene itself, enraged crowds of Israelis gathered, shouting 'Death to the Arabs!' whenever they noticed that television cameras were pointed in their direction.

It wasn't long before the reprisals started. Salah Bassam, an Arab worker in the Netanya market, was attacked by a lynch mob of 30 or more Israelis and beaten unconscious. From the tone of the interviews given by Israeli police officers in the district, it was clear that feelings were running high and any sympathy for innocent Palestinians caught up in reprisals was in short supply. 'After the explosion, a number of minorities (Arabs) fled to the market and some of the people of the market tried to attack them,' explained Police Assistant Commander Ahron Franco, adding that at least his men had 'managed to prevent a lynching.'

Ahmad Ayam's suicide mission had not only enraged the people of Netanya, it had set in train a series of events that would have profound implications for both the intifada and long-term territorial concerns of the Israeli government itself. Though few recognised it at the time, the bombing was something of a real tipping point in a conflict that seemed characterised by so many make-or-break moments. Certainly Ahmad Ayam wasn't the first-ever Palestinian suicide bomber in the annals of the al-Aqsa intifada.

Five months earlier that dubious honour had gone to Nabil Arir, a 24-year-old attendant at a school for the disabled in the Gaza Strip. It was on a bright October morning that Arir, a deeply religious man described by his friends as 'gentle,' cycled up to an Israeli army post and detonated his lethal cargo, killing no one but himself. His individual 'sacrifice' might have been the very first of the intifada's 'ticking bombs' as Israeli soldiers came to call these latter-day Kamikazes, but without enemy deaths it failed to resonate in the way some within the resistance had hoped.

Only a stark mural painting on the wall of Arir's family home in Gaza's Shujayah neighbourhood, showing him surrounded by explod-ing Israeli watchtowers, provided lasting testimony to his desperate act. But in the case of Ahmad Ayam's suicide attack in Netanya a few months later, it was an altogether different story. To begin with, the operation marked the first time ever that the ticking bombs had struck outside the occupied territories and inside the borders of the Jewish state itself. What's more, though few knew it then, the attack signalled the start of a prolonged and bloody campaign by a deadly cell of Hamas bombers from Tulkarem. Their run of devastating blasts would ulti-mately provoke an unprecedented Israeli military backlash and severely set back the course of the intifada.

Just a day before the bombing, Israel's Army Chief, Shaul Mofaz had warned that Israel was 'obliged to raise the threshold in our amount of action and our pressure on the terrorists, and those who send them.'

As is so often the case with such pivotal events, everything hinged on its timing. Put another way, it was hardly accidental that this bloody opening shot from the Hamas suicide cell happened to coincide with the swearing in three days later of Ariel Sharon as Israel's new Prime Minister, following his defeat of Ehud Barak in an election the month before. The enormous wave of electoral optimism that had helped propel Ehud Barak, the negotiator and 'doveish' Prime Minister, to power, had long since waned after the collapse of the Camp David summit and the arrival of suicide bombers on the doorsteps of Israeli citizens.

Even the Palestinian Authority seemed caught out by the escalating use of this scarcely believable suicide weapon and the dangerous ratcheting up of the conflict that its use inevitably signified. While reluctant to publicly condemn the blast, privately the PA was said to be furious with the Netanya attack. 'Operations of this kind, which are an honest expression of Palestinian rage over the ongoing Israeli occupation, damage the Palestinian interests. Now we will be blamed for injuring innocent people, and that is not what we want,' commented one PA source angrily. Even so, almost within hours of Ahmad Ayam's mission, Hamas's military wing, the Izz al-Din al-Qassam Brigades not only claimed full responsibility but announced that it had ten suicide bombers poised to strike inside Israel. 'One down, nine to go,' remarked my local newsagent depressingly as he handed me a copy of *The Jerusalem Post* the day after the Netanya outrage. Buying a newspaper, travelling on a bus, shopping in the market or sipping coffee in a café, it was obvious that the fear of random death had begun to infect even the most mundane aspects of Israeli life. As a Netanya storekeeper summed it up: 'There's a feeling of zero security. You don't have to be a combat soldier to die. You just have to be an ordinary citizen. It can't go on like this.'

The al-Aqsa intifada might have started as the spontaneous boiling over of ordinary Palestinians' frustration with the occupation and failed peace process, but increasing numbers of Israelis were becoming convinced that much more sinister and fanatical forces were now orchestrating the violence. Indeed for some Israelis, the theory that this was an 'intifada from the bottom up' had never held any credence. Among them were numerous hawkish commentators and analysts, who through websites, the media and other platforms, quickly played up remarks made by various Palestinian leaders as evidence to support their case for a conspiratorial pre-planned intifada.

Perhaps quoted most often were remarks by Marwan Barghouti, by then an increasingly influential leader of the Tanzim, a grassroots cadre within Fatah. Consisting mainly of Fatah's 'inside' leadership from the first intifada and fighters from the PA's own security forces, the Tanzim had begun to assume the contradictory functions of being on the one hand the PA's main armed wing and on the other its opposition from within.

A hardened graduate of the generation who fought the war of the stones, Marwan Barghouti and his Tanzim had not only become the voice and force of the Palestinian 'street' but had done so by advocating armed struggle as much as negotiation and diplomacy. 'This intifada has laid down a new rule: Let those who want to negotiate do so, but we will no longer be captives of the negotiation table,' declared Barghouti defiantly, shortly after Arafat had returned from the Sharm al-Sheikh Summit in October 2000. Seen as the first international effort to halt the escalating violence of the al-Aqsa intifada, Arafat had returned from the summit and instructed the heads of Palestinian security organisations to enforce the ceasefire negotiated under American auspices. But Marwan Barghouti was not for turning. While initially he had exerted control over the intifada's direction with Arafat's approval, clearly now Barghouti, a hugely popular orator and charismatic street fighter, had no intention of winding down the powerful momentum the uprising had generated. This tension between Arafat and Barghouti was first and foremost indicative of the perennial struggle for power between the exiled PLO leadership, or 'Tunisians,' and the 'insiders' who took charge of the first intifada. But it was also stoking up trouble for a bitter showdown that would reverberate across the Palestinian movement as a whole in the years to come. For the time being, however, Barghouti acted as an ever sharpening political thorn in Arafat's side. Equally, he was fast becoming one of the biggest Palestinian bogeymen that Israeli hardliners were keen to keep in their sights.

These Israeli hawks had always insisted that the intifada was based on a pre-planned blueprint. To backup their assertions they frequently pointed to comments made by the Tanzim leader in a 'revealing' interview Barghouti gave to the London-based Arabic daily *Al-Hayat* in September 2001. 'I knew that the end of September (2000) was the last period (of time) before the explosion, but when Sharon reached the al-Aqsa mosque, this was the most important moment for the outbreak of the intifada. . . . After Sharon left, I remained for two hours in the pres-

ence of other people. We discussed the manner of response and how it
was possible to react in all the cities and not just in Jerusalem.' Later
that same day in the early evening, Barghouti is said to have travelled to
a conference by car during which he finalised the incendiary document
that ignited the al-Aqsa intifada. 'While we were in the car . . . I prepared a leaflet in the name of the Higher Committee of Fatah, coordinated with the brothers (eg Hamas), in which we called for a reaction
to what happened in Jerusalem,' Barghouti is quoted as saying in the
same interview.

It was this leaflet and its distribution throughout an already volatile
and mobilised Palestinian 'street,' not Sharon's provocative walkabout,
that was the real spark for the intifada, insist some Israeli analysts to
this day. Even six months before Barghouti's comments in the *Al-Hayat*
interview these same commentators were busy citing Imad Falouji, the
Palestinian Authority's Communication Minister, as evidence of how
advanced the shadowy plotting behind the intifada really was. In an
article in *The Jerusalem Post*, Falouji is said to have told a rally in
Lebanon in March 2001 that the violence had been planned as far back
as July of 2000. 'Whoever thinks that this started as a result of Sharon's
despicable visit to al-Aqsa is in error. It was planned since Arafat's
return from Camp David,' the newspaper reported Falouji as saying.

Whatever the truth about the extent to which the intifada's outbreak was spontaneous, planned or a combination of both, there seems
little doubt that Yasser Arafat and the PA had been facing challenges on
a number of political fronts for some time. On the one hand, there was
a hardening of the Israeli political and military response to the violence,
and on the other, the emergence of new forces within the ranks of the
Palestinian resistance – even within Arafat's Fatah itself. When the
intifada broke out, the then Israeli Prime Minister Ehud Barak is said to
have told US Secretary of State Madeleine Albright and French President
Jacques Chirac that Arafat could have stopped the intifada with just
two telephone calls. The reality was somewhat different, and Barak's
remark perhaps reveals just how out of touch the Israelis were with
many of the dynamics going on inside the PA, Fatah and the intifada as
a whole.

For many years since the 1980s there had been growing pressure
from outside the PLO for the need to reform. Many people in the occupied territories were fed up with what they saw as the virtual dictatorship of Arafat and Fatah. Inside the PLO, there were also voices urging

change, men like Abu Mazen, who wanted Arafat to shift the PLO from being an organisation that represented the Palestinian cause to a political institution that would effectively govern and provide services in the occupied territories. Reformers of this kind saw the need to put aside many of the PLO's traditional concepts such as struggle and solidarity, in favour of building a hoped for mini-state through elections and democracy. But not all groups or individuals pushing for reform saw it that way. There were those who recognised that any such fundamental shift would not only negate the armed struggle and the PLO's revolutionary credentials, but also leave those fighting for the Palestinian cause with one hand tied behind their back. By contrast, the reforms these groups sought were simply a means to create a new leadership not tainted by corruption, or blinkered and deluded by the elusive promises of the Oslo peace process that Arafat and his cronies had relied on for their legitimacy and political survival.

The PLO hierarchy had been busying themselves with high-flying politics in the global spotlight, while these new Palestinian opposition groups had become popular by working at street level, in the refugee camps and local committees. Though drawn from very different roots and with varying motives, Barghouti's Tanzim and the Islamist Hamas were among them. Of course this new movement wanted transparency, political accountability and progress, but not at the cost of throwing the armed struggle and the intifada out from their range of options.

If indeed Marwan Barghouti or others among this new breed of Palestinian leaders and activists had drawn up a blueprint for the launching of the intifada, as some Israelis claimed, then they were not alone in their scheming. As far back as May 2000 Ehud Barak and his advisors had themselves drafted operational and tactical contingency plans of their own to halt the intifada in its tracks. These included the massive use of IDF snipers, which resulted in the high numbers of Palestinian dead and wounded in the first few days of the uprising. It was these tactics as much as any advanced planning that many believe transformed a series of violent clashes into a full-blown intifada.

By the time Ariel Sharon took over as Prime Minister from Barak on March 7, 2001, what had begun as intense but conventional clashes between Palestinian demonstrators and Israeli security forces had pretty much evolved into all-out low-intensity warfare. Unlike in the previous intifada the use of firearms and bomb attacks by the Palestinians was now widespread. Following Ahmad Ayam's suicide attack in

Netanya and Hamas's promise to send yet more ticking bombs into Israel itself, Sharon was in no mood to take prisoners, and he wasted little time in pointing the finger at his old adversary. As far as Sharon was concerned Arafat was simply up to his old tricks; a leader who, politically speaking, was forever running with the hare and hunting with the hounds. A master of ambiguity, Arafat delivered radical speeches to his followers one minute and talked of reining them in the next. 'We know very well that the most loyal forces of Arafat are involved in the attacks,' Sharon warned, vowing that no negotiations would be held with the Palestinians until the attacks halted. But the truth was that new forces with new leaders had come to the battlefield, over which Arafat had little command. The Tanzim, Hamas, Islamic Jihad and others were all stepping up to the mark.

Despite these new players, Sharon still faced mounting pressure to live up to his reputation as a warrior and exact harsh reprisals against the obvious culprits, the increasingly hapless Arafat and his Palestinian Authority. For both sides the talking was all but over. It was time to see who would blink first.

Ramallah, June 2001

It was early morning when the phone rang in my room at the Jerusalem Hotel in the Arab east of the city. 'Meet me at the American Colony Hotel in 15 minutes, he's agreed to see you,' said the voice on the other end of the line. As expected, I was given very short notice of my meeting with Marwan Barghouti. Security had become tighter than ever around the man the Israeli government loved to hate. On three previous occasions already our meeting had been cancelled at the very last moment, with 'security concerns' given by way of explanation. By this stage in the intifada Barghouti was almost constantly on the move. Rarely did he sleep more than one night in the same place, while by day he steered clear of Israeli checkpoints and avoided getting into cars that had not been screened for bombs or electronic tracking devices. Never, never, did he answer his mobile telephone. Too many Israeli assassination 'hits' on Palestinian and other Arab activists had been carried out that way in the past. Sometimes, it was an explosive device in the handset itself, or alternately the phone's signal was used as a positioning transmitter whose coordinates an Apache helicopter gunship or aircraft could lock on to before launching a missile strike at the unsuspecting target. The Israelis had an expression for such deaths, which loosely translated from the Hebrew, was 'a work accident.' At that stage Barghouti had not 'officially' been marked for immediate assassination, but the consensus among many Israeli security people was that it was 'only a matter of time.' They insisted that information was already available to them that Barghouti was not only a coordinator of the intifada, but an actual 'dispatcher' of terror attacks against Israelis.

At the American Colony Hotel located just over the Green Line in Arab East Jerusalem, I ordered a coffee and sat down to wait for my Barghouti 'contact' near the fountain in the cool of the garden at the heart of this famous Middle Eastern establishment. 'The Colony,' as it was commonly known, had in its time been sanctuary to some famous guests visiting this troubled region: Sir Winston Churchill, T.E. Lawrence (of Arabia), John le Carré, Graham Greene and Lauren Bacall among others. A former pasha's palace, the hotel was owned neither by Arabs nor Jews but by Americans, Brits and Swedes. This, however, according to some of my Israeli colleagues, didn't prevent it being nick-named 'The PLO Hotel.' Foreign journalists, UN officers and diplomats all used the place as a rendezvous with Palestinian officials. One Israeli reporter rather indelicately speculated that The Colony was probably so extensively bugged by the Shin Bet security service that 'it would be impossible to fart in the toilets without tipping off someone.' Maybe my Barghouti contact had heard that too, for instead of coming to meet me himself, he had sent a driver to pick me up who wasted no time in ushering me into a car outside. As we drove towards Ramallah the driver seemed edgy, constantly checking the rearview mirror, and making endless calls on his own mobile phone.

'What's your name?' I asked, trying to put him at ease.

The driver threw me a sideways look, pausing just a second longer than I felt was comfortable, before answering. 'My name is Muneer,' he said with a smile, before switching again to mute mode for the rest of the half-hour drive. With small talk clearly not an option, I looked through my notebook at the questions I'd prepared for Barghouti on the course of the intifada, pausing only when an Israeli sentry at the Qalandia checkpoint asked me for identification. Was Barghouti really the mastermind behind the al-Aqsa uprising? Just what was the state of his relationship with Yasser Arafat and his Fatah party? As someone who was instrumental in pursuing the previous peace process, was Barghouti still interested in dialogue with the Israelis? And what did he make of Israel's threat of an impending crackdown?

Ten minutes or so after we had passed the Israeli searches at Qalandia, Muneer pulled over outside a teahouse in the centre of Ramallah. 'Please,' he invited me inside, showing me to a table at the back of the café. Muneer then nodded to a waiter who came over to take my order, before making his way back out to the car and making yet another phone call.

Some time through my second mint tea in an otherwise empty café, Muneer, who had briefly driven off, returned this time in a different car and with another Palestinian man in tow. The accomplice was carrying a machine-pistol at waist level slung from a strap over his shoulder, and he looked seriously heavy-duty. I began to feel a trickle of unease filter through me, even though I knew that security precautions like these were to be expected.

'Please, Mr. David, we must go now,' Muneer insisted. With the three of us now in the new car, we drove around Ramallah for a few minutes until Muneer pulled over to make yet another call. This time though he appeared to be having trouble with the signal or the phone's battery. 'Do you have a mobile that I can use?' he asked me. It was probably a harmless request, but somehow I felt a little apprehensive about handing over my phone to this virtual stranger here in Ramallah. God only knew who he was calling, I thought. And what if the call was monitored in some way and my number recognised? It could make life very difficult for me with the Israelis. Living and working in the Middle East for so long, I knew how easy it was to become a little paranoid, but I also realised how potentially dangerous complacency can be at times like these.

For years, not only in this part of the world, but in various hotspots from Bosnia to Afghanistan and across Africa, I'd learnt that reacting calmly and correctly to that internal alarm bell was the best guarantee against making a fatal error, and if you were lucky, staying alive. I knew that to show any reluctance in handing over my phone would instantly look suspicious. Men like those with me in the car were finely tuned to such things. Over the years in places like Belfast, Beirut or Baghdad, and here in the West Bank, people who have lived on the edge learn to weigh up dangers and make computations in seconds. For Palestinians and Israelis alike, nothing is innocent. Afraid not only of giving off the wrong vibe, but of again losing out on the interview, I handed my phone to Muneer, who jumped from the car and walked a few yards before dialling and making a short call. 'Okay, now we go to Mr Barghouti,' he announced once back in the driving seat, clearly as relieved as I was.

Within minutes we had stopped again, and I was led on foot towards what looked like a semi-derelict office block in a quiet street in the centre of Ramallah. Inside the building, the staircase was ramshackle, badly lit, and smelled of disinfectant. As we got to the second floor Barghouti appeared so quickly I almost bumped into him. Flanked by two young bodyguards, both carrying M-16 automatic rifles, he was casually dressed in denims and a short jacket, and clutching a file full of papers. He looked bleary-eyed and obviously hadn't shaved in some days. Despite this, he appeared younger than a man whose 41 years had been spent honing his revolutionary and political credentials in the bearpit of the Israeli–Palestinian conflict. Even shorter than I imagined, there was something about him that suggested a tremendous amount of pent-up energy, totally disproportionate with his small physique. He reminded me of a tiny tugboat or shunting locomotive, small, compact dynamos, capable of performing way above their weight and size. In a room off the second floor landing I was offered a seat, while Barghouti sat behind a table still flanked by his two heavies and another aide who would act as interpreter and himself take notes of the interview. I had been asked not to bring a tape recorder, presumably for fear of it being yet another potential assassins' weapon, or maybe it was simply a reluctance to have Barghouti's comments electronically documented.

Despite my limited time – I had been given 20 minutes – I began with a question I hoped would ease the tension a little. 'Do you have any special plans to celebrate your birthday?' I put to him, knowing that it was only a matter of days away. The aide taking the notes looked up, and Barghouti himself managed a smile before answering. 'Why ask me this, do you think I have something to celebrate?' he replied, throwing the question back at me before continuing. 'Anyway, these days I try not to tell too many people of my plans in advance,' he joked, his voice now clearly more relaxed. I had intended the question as a harmless icebreaker, and while Barghouti had taken it in good faith, it was obvious that here was a man that took nothing said to him at face value.

Barghouti was born not far from where we sat talking that day in Ramallah, in a village called Kobar, a small picturesque community famed for its olive orchards. The date was June 5, 1960, an auspicious day for the future intifada leader, being almost exactly seven years before the outbreak of the Six Day War, when Israel began its illegal occupation of the West Bank and Gaza. Barghouti was only 15 when he joined Fatah, and was one of the founders of the 'Shabiba,' the Fatah youth movement. From that point onwards his entire life was moulded by the struggle against the Israeli occupation. In 1989 he became a member of Fatah's Revolutionary Council, and its Secretary-General in the West Bank in 1994. Despite rapidly climbing up the Fatah rankings, very early on Barghouti established a reputation for identifying with the grassroots of the movement rather than the formal leadership. He knew for himself what it was like to be on the sharp end of Israeli retribution when he was arrested and charged with being a member of the then banned Fatah, and spent six years in Israeli prisons.

Like most Palestinian students whose education was disrupted due to random Israeli military curfews, closures and imprisonment, it took Barghouti 11 long years to obtain his BA in history and political science at Bir Zeit University. No sooner had he achieved this than he was arrested yet again in 1985. Held under administrative detention for six months without charges, he was banished from the occupied territories by the then Officer in Chief of the Israeli military's Central Command, Ehud Barak. Exiled to Jordan, Barghouti played a crucial role in coordinating the first intifada, acting as a central liaison officer between the PLO outside and Fatah inside the occupied territories. In 1994, at the height of the enthusiasm that reigned after the signing of the Oslo accords, Barghouti was allowed to return to Ramallah and became a pioneer of dialogue with the Israelis. Not only did he build strong relations with those in the Israeli peace camp, but even with some figures on the country's political right who were ready to accept a compromise deal with the Palestinians. However, this détente would not last long. More than anything, it was Israel's insatiable land grabbing and extension of its Jewish settlement programme in the occupied territories that Barghouti saw as a true sign of the deception behind all the empty talk of peace.

'We tried seven years of intifada without negotiations, and then seven years of negotiations without intifada; perhaps it is time to try both simultaneously?' was how Barghouti, the 'intifada man,' as he was by then known, saw future Palestinian objectives. Observations and remarks like these hit the right note at the right time. By now the disappointment over Oslo had aggravated many Palestinians to the point where they felt that Israel must be compelled to act on its illegal occupation. In no time, Barghouti's firebrand oratory and organisational skills ensured that thousands took to the streets to support him on this and other issues. But where had all this left Barghouti today, I wondered, as I sat opposite him that morning in the room in Ramallah? Was his relationship with Arafat and Fatah heading for breaking point as some had suggested?

'Like Arafat, I am a member of Fatah, but that does not mean we have to agree on everything,' Barghouti began by telling me. 'Arafat was active in the struggle when I was still a boy, he has been a leader of the Palestinian people for a long time. But as I have said many times before, I still believe he was wrong to sign the Oslo agreement as it was drafted at that time. Who would dispute that now?' As if on cue, the faint sound of an Israeli helicopter stopped Barghouti in mid-sentence, and one of his bodyguards darted to the window before calling across to someone on the rooftop opposite. After a few tense seconds and satisfied with the reply from whoever was watching the helicopter, the bodyguard returned to his seat and Barghouti announced that it was safe to continue the interview.

Little did I know it then, but on August 4, less than two months from that moment, Barghouti would narrowly escape assassination after two Israeli helicopter-launched missiles just missed his car while he was travelling in the West Bank. As Barghouti resumed talking, he went on to explain how by accepting the Israeli conditions at Oslo, Arafat had pitched Palestinians' lives into misery while making the Israelis more 'comfortable.' 'Arafat arrested many activists, many of our brothers and those from Islamic Jihad and Hamas. It made the Israelis feel better but limited our options in the years just before the present intifada,' he continued. And what about today, did he and Arafat agree on the way the al-Aqsa intifada was planned and was being run? 'As I said, we do not need to agree on everything. The intifada is not run by me or Arafat as individuals, the intifada is a product of collective decision making. We have a central committee made up of all sections of the Palestinian political movement. This committee meets depending on the situation in the West Bank and Gaza. There are also other local committees in Hebron, Jerusalem, Nablus, Jenin and other places, that represent as many as 30 parties. This is what coordinates the intifada,' Barghouti insisted.

By now he was getting into his stride, and both Barghouti's aide and I struggled to write our notes and keep up with the numerous asides and references that came one after another. Jewish settlements, human rights, the role of the United States, and the now virtually redundant peace process were all drawn into his responses. So did he, the man who once advocated dialogue, still think that peace was possible, and what had he made of the findings of the then recently published Mitchell Report? 'Peace is always possible, but not while there is the occupation, that is the heart of the matter. The Palestinian people know all about promises, especially broken promises. I argued for peace, and where did it lead us. . . . I would welcome the findings of the Mitchell Report to be implemented, but the report was only commissioned because the Sharm al-Sheikh agreement itself failed to be realised,' Barghouti explained. He had a point.

It was on 20 May, 2001, less than a month before I spoke with Barghouti, that the Mitchell Report had been released. The document brought together the conclusions of a fact-finding mission requested by President Bill Clinton at the Sharm al-Sheikh summit towards the end of the previous year. Aimed at getting beneath the surface and causes of the continuing violence on the ground, it was chaired by George J. Mitchell, former member and majority leader of the United States Senate. 'Fear, hate, anger and frustration have risen on both sides. The greatest danger of all is that the culture of peace nurtured over the past decade is being shattered. In its place there is a growing sense of futility and despair, and a growing resort to violence,' the report pointed out.

The Mitchell Commission had made recommendations that Palestinians should make 'a 100 percent effort to prevent terrorist operations and to punish perpetrators.' It also asked the Israeli side 'to freeze all new construction of settlements and stop the Israeli army firing on unarmed demonstrators.' The problem was that by the time all this was actually published, it was little more than wishful thinking. Predictably, the report steered well clear of apportioning blame. What's more, most ordinary Israelis and Palestinians were probably right in feeling that it hardly needed a body like the Mitchell Commission to draw the conclusion 'that both sides had to act quickly to pull the region back from the abyss.' Most ordinary people on either side of the divide didn't need to be told that. What they wanted was someone to do something to ensure it wouldn't actually happen.

From what Marwan Barghouti had said to me, clearly he had put little store by the Mitchell Commission's capacity to be anything other than just another talking shop. I remember thinking at the time that if the man said to be the key orchestrator of the intifada believed this, then 'the abyss' was probably far closer than even George J. Mitchell and his commission members had imagined. With Sharon now in harness as Prime Minister, few expected anything less than zero-tolerance when it came to attacks on Israel. On both sides everyone sensed that if the intifada escalated at the speed and direction in which it was now going, then a terrible backlash was inevitable. After all, this was the way things happened in the Israeli–Palestinian conflict, and no amount of recommendations from an international commission would be enough to change that.

I put it to Barghouti that there was increasing concern about an Israeli invasion of the territories to crush the Palestinian Authority, overthrow Arafat and put the intifada out of action for some time to come. 'You are a reporter. Look around you in the West Bank and Gaza. You must have seen it, the Israelis have already strengthened their number of soldiers and tanks. I believe these are not just threats when Sharon talks about invading the territories and trying to break our organisation and resistance. But even Sharon cannot break the will of the people, and the intifada is the will of the people,' Barghouti responded.

Does that mean using guns and bombs as well as stones in this intifada? I asked.

'The use of guns is a new development in this intifada, but we are fighting for our liberation at this moment. Should we rule out armed resistance as part of that? I think that would be foolish. I do not believe attacks against civilians inside Israel are a good strategy, but where there are forces of occupation, yes, of course we must resist with the weapons that are available to us,' Barghouti made clear. Articulate, impassioned, for Marwan Barghouti the intifada was clearly nothing less than a war of independence. In essence it seemed to me that what Barghouti was saying to Sharon and the Israelis was clear. Yes, we recognise the state of Israel, but our intifada will continue to make life difficult and costly for you in the occupied territories until you come to us with an agreement that we can accept. For Barghouti, Israel's 'greed,' as he saw it, was what prevented progress on the negotiating front. To him and indeed the many Palestinians whose political stance he had come to epitomise, it was simply no longer acceptable that the Israelis should have their political cake and eat it. To Palestinians like Barghouti, it wasn't about the Israelis wanting some things. It was the fact that they wanted everything: peace, security, more land, more settlements and a

Palestinian state that would not include Jerusalem. How was it possible to expect so much without our resistance, without the intifada? Barghouti asked

As I got up to leave the room following our interview, I asked how much he worried that when he went to work in the morning he might never see his family again?

'This is something I have to live with. If and when the Israelis want me, I'm sure I'll know about it,' he said with a wry smile.

At least not before your birthday, I joked, as we shook hands.

'Yes, that would be very inconsiderate of the Israelis,' he replied, before disappearing down the staircase to a waiting car, the armed bodyguards trailing in his wake like a ball and chain.

Bethlehem, March 8, 2002

When I arrived on the outskirts of Bethlehem, only the plumes of black smoke snaking over the town hinted at something wrong. Slowly, though, the tell-tale signs of the battle began to appear. It was as if some deadly, invisible pestilence had visited the place. Not a soul in sight, shops shuttered, the streets strewn with the now familiar old cookers and boulders used as improvised roadblocks. As I waited at the Israeli checkpoint on the town's perimeter while my press card was examined, I noticed three Palestinian men who had been detained for questioning, sitting on their haunches in a nearby compound, their hands cuffed behind their backs. They had the look of men resigned to their fate. There was no fear in their faces. Just an expression that said, here we are again, when will all this finally be over?

The young Israeli soldier on the other side of the Perspex partition in front of me said something in Hebrew into the radio mouthpiece around his head, smiled, and nodded in the direction of the eerily quiet street ahead that led into the centre of Bethlehem. I should have known it would not be that easy. After a few hundred yards the only sounds I could hear were my own footsteps, nervous breathing, and the *pop–pop* of desultory gunfire from the maze of nearby streets. Overhead there was also the ominous buzz of a pilotless Israeli drone, taking surveillance pictures of the bloodletting below from a beautiful azure sky.

This was my second visit to Bethlehem in the space of a few days which had seen the bloodiest fighting in the occupied territories in 17 months. The worst of the gun battles had been in refugee camps in the northern town of Tulkarem and here in Bethlehem, where in a large-scale offensive Israeli tanks and troops had entered the holy town from two directions. Already a helicopter had fired on the Aida refugee camp in the town after Palestinians shot at an Israeli outpost. The casualty toll was rising fast, with five Palestinians reported killed and 20 wounded in the attacks. Among the dead were a woman hit by shrapnel from a tank shell that crashed into her home, and Ahmed Sbeih, a hospital administrator whose car was also hit by a tank round.

The huge lumbering Merkava tanks seemed to be everywhere. At a bend in the road I met an Italian TV crew laden down in their Kevlar flak jackets and helmets. They were busy filming a couple of the Merkavas at a junction in the street up ahead. The tanks' turrets turned like tracking radar as their massive bulk churned up the sun-softened tarmac covering the road.

All of a sudden there was a burst of machine-gun fire from one of the tanks, the large rounds slamming into a wall a few yards away. It was clearly a warning to get off the street, and we all scuttled in different directions for safety. Separated from the Italians in the panic, I found myself alone in a dusty alleyway. From a balcony a young Palestinian woman was hanging out washing, proving that for many people it was just another day in the West Bank. She shouted at me in a mixture of Arabic and English. '*Sahafi* [journalist], *sahafi*! Go straight past the toyshop then turn right, it is safer there,' she called, waving her arms in the direction I should go. Within seconds I had lost my way again, only to hear the voice of another woman on another balcony calling out directions while hanging out washing.

In a war of gods and believers, someone up there was clearly watching over me, their messages relayed by an army of Palestinian housewives who had broken off from their chores to steer me through the hazardous frontlines. Not of course that any real frontlines existed in this war, instead it was just a series of no-go areas and no-man's-lands where nothing was ever taken for granted. Places where a sharply honed sense of suspicion and having eyes in the back of your head were the tickets to survival for both Palestinians and Israelis alike. Could the occupants of the car that pulls up alongside you at the traffic lights late at night be driven by killers? Is the nervous-looking young man who got on the bus a suicide bomber? Are the men in the hire car with the letters TV taped to the doors not really journalists but undercover Israeli security men?

Fortunately for me the young Palestinian gunmen I ran into that afternoon in the backstreets of Bethlehem were obviously satisfied at a glance that I was a genuine journalist. Dressed appropriately enough, almost entirely in black, right down to his brand new M-16 automatic rifle complete with telescopic sight, one of the fighters lifted an arm and pointed up the street. 'The funerals are that way,' he said nonchalantly, obviously thinking I had come solely to cover the burials of those killed in the latest battles. Once again I was struck by how different-looking these young militants were from those I remembered from the first intifada. These days those who took to the streets often resembled the hardcore guerrilla fighters from Lebanon's Hezbollah more than the handful of stone-throwing kids that had once been the hallmark of intifada street battles.

Climbing higher towards the centre of Bethlehem, I saw that a few people had ventured out on to the streets sheltered from the fighting to enjoy the unusually warm March sun. Most of them were more than willing to talk about the ordeal of the last few days since the Israeli army had laid siege to the town.

Dressed in an immaculate white shirt and tie, Johnny Lama was a dapper, sprightly 75-year-old. Among other things in a busy life, he had been a chief clerk in the local water department, a farmer in Honduras and a pizzeria owner in Bethlehem. Tourists and pilgrims were few and far between these days though, he told me. 'Why should they come? I spent last night in my basement. The bombing started late and lasted through until dawn,' he grumbled. As he plied me with mint tea and Belgian chocolates it struck me that, despite appearances, he was a lonely and frightened man. Having left his family behind in Honduras, Johnny had returned to Bethlehem to take care of some business and found himself stuck following the outbreak of the al-Aqsa intifada. 'For two weeks now there's been no mail here. From one hour to the next nobody knows what is coming,' he said, his words punctuated by the sound of gunfire from the hillside opposite. 'This house is 100 years old and the walls are very thick, but it will not stop Israeli bombs and bullets,' he told me.

As I left, Johnny pointed across the valley to the Jewish settlement of Gilo and, further in the distance, still under construction, the towering, fortress-like mass of Har Homa. When finally completed Har Homa would provide 50,000 tax-free apartments for Jews from all over the world, especially Eastern Europe and the United States. To build it,

Israel confiscated several hundred acres, or *dunum*, belonging to the neighbouring Palestinian district of Beit Sahour, and destroyed thousands of the village's olive trees to build access roads.

'From Gilo the Israelis shoot back at Palestinian fighters in Beit Jala and Bethlehem. Can you see the wall the Israelis have built to block the snipers?' he asked. I told Johnny that on a previous occasion I had visited Gilo, and that Israelis there were just as frightened as Palestinians here in Bethlehem. 'Yes, but when was the last time they were bombed by planes, helicopters and tanks?' he replied, an air of resignation rather than confrontation in his voice.

It was the explosion of a US-manufactured, 225kg (500lb) MK82 guided bomb that had Suzanne Elias's 11-year-old son vomiting in fear during one of those Israeli air raids on Bethlehem when I had visited a few days earlier along with a journalist from the *New York Times*. Like Johnny Lama, Suzanne was a Palestinian Christian. Her family had moved elsewhere after the first wave of attacks, so her relatives were not there in the pre-dawn darkness when the bombs came again, leaving her home smashed and filled with dusty debris.

'I never believed they would do this,' she said, wandering through her badly damaged house. 'My four children are in shock. Why do they hit us? What did we do? I never dreamed it would reach this.'

It was Suzanne's misfortune that her home sat close to an old police station that dated back to the days of the British mandate in Palestine. Today the building was the headquarters of the Palestinian Authority in Bethlehem, making it the actual target of the Israeli bombing raid that destroyed her house.

Sharon had ordered that attacks on Palestinian police and security buildings be stepped up as a way to punish the PA and force them into action against terrorism. But despite Israeli claims that Arafat had the power to do just that, by now it was clear that the Palestinian leader had diminishing control over many of those who undertook the bombings and gun battles. The tragedy was that few ordinary Israelis seemed aware of the terror and damage Sharon's offensive spread among the innocent Palestinian civilian population. More often than not it was people like Suzanne Elias and Johnny Lama that bore the brunt of the 'precision' air strikes, or seemingly random tank shells that thundered into communities with terrifying destructive power.

At the Palestinian Authority Headquarters, uniformed Palestinian militiamen showed a *New York Times* reporter and myself fragments of a bomb that identified it as a 500lb MK82. With some relish they quickly pointed to a small metal disc on which a serial number and the name TEXAS OPTOELECTRONICS INC were embossed. The militiamen's message was simple. Here is the proof that the Americans supply the weapons with which the Israelis bomb us.

By the time I made my way from Suzanne's house and the PA building to Manger Square in the heart of Bethlehem, the Friday prayer calls of the *muezzin* had given way to political battle cries. The funerals of those killed in the recent fighting that the young street gunman had told me about earlier were about to get underway.

At one end of Manger Square stood the town's main mosque, at the other the Church of the Nativity, in which a subterranean grotto marked the place of Christ's birth. Where every year the square would normally be packed with Christmas pilgrims come to celebrate Christ's birth and life, that afternoon it was thronged with mourners and Palestinian militiamen, there to mark the passing of two martyrs who had lost their lives in the gun battles of the last hours. On the steps of the square, surrounded by thousands of local people, the bodies of the two dead men lay on pallets, wrapped in Palestinian flags, their waxy, nicotine-coloured faces clearly visible. Three male relatives knelt beside them in prayer, gently stroking the dead men's faces, before a masked gunman alongside them pulled a pistol from his belt and fired three shots. The effect was like that of a starter's gun. To the cries of 'Allah o Akbar!' and a crescendo of automatic-weapons fire, the pallets were hoisted up on to the shoulders of pallbearers and carted off through the streets towards the cemetery in the neighbouring village of Beit Sahour.

I remember thinking at the time that this was yet another example of how much the nature of the resistance within the intifada had changed. Here in Beit Sahour during the 1980s uprising, I had covered the famous tax strike against the Israeli government. Now, instead of boycotts, it was bullets that had become the order of the day, and with their use came the inevitable increase in the numbers of dead. I watched as the bodies of the two Palestinians killed in the fighting earlier that morning near the refugee camps of Dheisheh and Aida were laid to rest in a ramshackle cemetery, littered with broken masonry and flanked by overgrown palms. From an adjacent balcony, one local militia leader after another berated Israel and pledged to fight on, no matter how many martyrs it took. Now and again the speeches would be interrupted by volleys of gunfire over the graves and choruses of martial-sound-ing music from loudspeakers rigged up around the burial ground. As the distraught wives and mothers of the dead men filed past, the coffin-sized alcoves that were their final resting-place were already being sealed shut by their male relatives. Their hands smeared in cement, the relatives scratched the names of the deceased and a simple epitaph into the wall.

Ibrahim Mohammed al-Araq and Suleiman Ibrahim Dbis.
They will not be the last.

'Mike's Place', Russian Compound, West Jerusalem, March 9, 2002

I had promised Mike Neri I would meet him that Saturday night for a badly needed beer. We agreed to rendezvous at our aptly named favourite bar in West Jerusalem – Mike's Place. Living as I did in the Arab east of the city, it usually took me about 15 minutes to walk from my hotel near Nablus Road past the walls of Jerusalem's old city to the new downtown area in the Israeli west. As was to be expected in a predominantly Muslim neighbourhood, alcohol was in short supply in East Jerusalem. Although it was possible to drink at my hotel – which had stocks of the wonderful Ramallah-brewed Taybeh beer – I liked occasionally to 'go west' and catch up with the take ordinary Israelis had on whatever was making the headlines. There was never any shortage of political or intifada stories to chew over. Shootings, air strikes, gun battles, suicide bombings, and the political manoeuvrings of Arafat and Sharon were all hot topics. But it was also good to make small talk, to escape the depressing cycle of violence if only for a short time. It seemed a strange luxury to argue about other things like music or sport. Anything but 'the war' as many Israelis now openly called it.

It was a pleasant walk from my hotel at that time of the evening, past the Arab taxi ranks and palm trees outside Damascus Gate, with the last rays of the sun adding an extra glow to the Golden Dome of the Rock. As I climbed the hill up towards the Russian Compound district, I was struck again by how sparse the security seemed to be along this demarcation line between the two communities. As ever there were the Israeli patrol jeeps and police cars moving around, but rarely any fixed checkpoints or ID monitoring along the way. If a suicide bomber or gunman had wanted to walk from the Arab part of the city into the heart of Jewish West Jerusalem there appeared little to stop them. Everywhere else across the West Bank, no matter how short the journey, it was always punctuated by endless watchtowers and barriers where the soldiers checked and rechecked. Why not here, I wondered, where these two warring neighbours shared the same city space? It was as if each side had chosen instead to rely on a mutual stand-off and sharpened sense of alertness that made any intruder stand out like a sore thumb. Even after years of visiting Jerusalem I was always amazed at how two peoples could sit cheek-by-jowl in this way. Sometimes no more than yards or even feet separated them. So near to each other, and yet so far apart.

Gizmo's, my old watering hole from the days of the first intifada and 1991 Gulf War had long since closed down. My friend Ilan Yigal had decided to leave Israel and start a new life on the West Coast of the United States. 'I just couldn't stand living in Israel anymore,' Ilan had told me one afternoon, when by chance I bumped into him in a West Jerusalem street during one of his flying visits from the United States. Ilan's decision had had nothing to do with fear. Liberal-minded and something of a free spirit, for him Jerusalem was just too dour and parochial. Israel, he felt, was so preoccupied with the conflict that the life he sought could never really be achieved there. I missed Ilan's company and the atmosphere in his café, Gizmo's, but had since become a customer at Mike's Place, a little bar on two levels that sat in the Russian Compound district, just a few seconds walk from my old haunt.

The Russian Compound was a strange offshoot of the 19th century. At that time Russian pilgrims visiting Jerusalem far outnumbered those from any other country. Built in 1863 by the Imperial Russian Palestine Society, at the instigation of the last Russian czars, the compound served as an outpost of Mother Russia. A mini-city within a city, full of royal residencies, a cathedral-church, offices, a hospital, hotels, and everything else the 20,000 Russian pilgrims that visited Jerusalem annually might need. After the Russian revolution in 1917 the pilgrims stopped coming and the compound remained empty until it became a British police post. At its heart then stood a courthouse and jail. There was also a gallows where a number of Jewish terrorists found guilty of attacking British targets were hanged in the years 1946 and 1947. As ever, the British seemed to have set the benchmark for so much of what was to follow here. Since then, at the centre of the Russian Compound, right alongside the bars and clubs in which people drink and dance, stands an equally forbidding Israeli detention centre.

Every day outside the jail and adjacent police station, queues of Palestinians can be seen waiting in the hope of seeing or finding out about family members, friends or relatives detained by the Israeli authorities. Among the Palestinian community the jail has an infamous reputation. In Jerusalem today it is not uncommon to hear some Arabs refer to it as 'Israel's Abu Ghraib,' after the prison in Baghdad, where the US military carried out torture and humiliation of Iraqi prisoners. With a capacity to hold over 300 detainees, the jail is divided into two sections: 'criminal,' where both Jewish and Arab prisoners are held, and 'security,' where Arab detainees only are locked up. Over the years, numerous human rights groups such as Amnesty International and Israel's own Physicians for Human Rights (PHR), have documented and severely condemned the regime at the Russian Compound jail. The interrogation techniques employed by the Shin Bet, or Israeli Security Agency (ISA) as it is now known, have been of particular concern.

Inside the jail's walls, literally just yards from the nightlife in downtown West Jerusalem, Palestinian prisoners often sit for weeks, their heads covered with sacks stinking of urine, or caked in the vomit from previous interrogatees. Others would be forced to wear blackened plastic ski masks or goggles over their eyes leaving them in darkness 24 hours a day, week in, week out. Most at some time would be shackled to pipes or tables, handcuffed so tightly that skin was torn or circulation to the arms and legs cut off causing enormous swelling and sometimes nerve damage. Among the most common punishments is 'shabeh,' which means making the prisoner sit in agonising positions for long periods of time. Worst of all is the 'banana shackle' where the detainee is made to lie face down with their arms and legs shackled behind their back, forcing their body into an excruciating arched position. Another method often used involves the sometimes fatal process of violently 'shaking' a prisoner during interrogation. Strapped to a specially designed chair that jerks the prisoner from side to side, the detainee would be prevented from sleeping and quickly become disorientated. Many detainees have told of other interrogation methods where severe pressure is applied to sensitive areas of the body like the throat, neck, genitals and chest. According to human rights activists, the security officers carrying out the questioning are said to be thoroughly familiar with these torture techniques. In one case a detainee said that his interrogator had put Band-Aids on his fingers so they wouldn't slip before he tightly gripped the prisoner's neck, pressing his thumb and index fingers into his throat and lifting him up from the floor.

In October 1991 Israel signed on to the United Nations Convention against Torture. Despite this, and an Israeli High Court ruling in September 1999 to abandon the practice of torturing prisoners, Israel's security services have paid little notice, and human rights abuse against Palestinian detainees remains widespread. To highlight how little had changed following the Israeli High Court ruling, the Palestinian Human Rights Monitoring Group (PHRMG) contacted the fathers and lawyers of three prisoners to help them put together the men's testimonies.

One of the detainees was 19-year-old Ra'ed Ahmad Salem al-Hamri, from Braitha'a, al-Ta'amreh in Bethlehem. Arrested and taken from his home on August 21, 1999, he endured 62 days of interrogation in the Russian Compound. After being beaten, forced to undergo 'shabeh' and enduring burning cigarettes being stubbed on his body, he was hospitalised on September 22, 1999, because his health had deteriorated so badly during his captivity. Ra'ed al-Hamri was accused by the Israelis of being a member of an Islamist militant group, gun-running and throwing stones. Like the two other men whose cases were presented by the Palestinian Human Rights Monitoring Group, he confessed to the charges as a result of the torture he had undergone.

Walking past the detention centre that evening just yards from my rendezvous with Mike Neri, I thought of the chilling stories other Israeli colleagues and friends had told me about passersby sometimes hearing screams coming from somewhere inside the jail. I thought it unlikely, not least given the thickness of the greying limestone walls and because, according to human rights reports, the isolation cells and interrogation rooms were said to be located somewhere deep in the basement.

As ever Mike seemed blissfully unperturbed by any such thoughts as he ordered me a drink, and I struggled to make myself heard against the noise of a band playing in the bar's basement. Mike was a big, bearded Hemingway type, an American Jew who had moved to Israel some years before and now worked as a freelance photographer. While he made a reasonable living covering events inside Israel, he was keen to venture out more into the West Bank to document the intifada.

Some Israeli photographers, mainly those working for the larger news agencies like Reuters and the Associated Press, had always crossed the lines. But unlike the days of the first intifada things had changed. As far as many Palestinian militants were concerned, a Jew was a Jew, and even if found carrying a press card, it was only because they were under-cover agents of the Shin Bet. Understandably many Israeli journalists felt it was simply no longer worth the risk, and confined themselves to working their own beat.

The customers in Mike's Place were a cross-section of Israeli society, though many were Jews originally from the United States or Europe. For most of them the effects of the al-Aqsa intifada had been to harden their position against the Palestinians. In polls conducted by the news-paper *Yediot Aharonot*, only six months after the start of the uprising, 58 percent of Israelis said their opinion of the Palestinians had changed for the worse. Some 37 percent reported that that intifada had caused them to adopt more hawkish opinions as opposed to 13 percent who said they had become more doveish. Israel as a whole had moved to the political right.

Talking to the drinkers around the bar that night in Mike's Place seemed to confirm what the poll figures suggested. In addition, more and more of them were also now supporting the assassination of Palestinian leaders found to be connected to terrorist attacks against Israel. Even those Israelis from the political left who had accorded Yasser Arafat any status in the first place were beginning to doubt his credentials of being a man interested in peace. Meanwhile the Palestinian leader himself appeared to have underestimated this shift in Israeli political thinking.

'Arafat refused to take notice of the impact that the intifada had on Israeli public opinion and politics. . . . Through all my conversations with him, I was struck, time and again, by the degree to which he did not grasp the depth of the shift in Israeli politics and public opinion,' wrote Shlomo Ben-Ami, the Israeli Foreign Minister, about his many meetings with Arafat during that period. It struck me that unlike the first intifada when Israeli society had been strongly divided between the hawks and the doves, the al-Aqsa uprising had galvanised the nation into a no-compromise entity. Like the Palestinians, Israelis were also frustrated about a peace process that had failed to live up to their expec-tations.

It was just before 10.30 that Saturday night as I was about to order one more beer for the road, when the lights in Mike's Place flickered and the bottles on the bar gantry rattled gently. 'A bomb,' Mike announced calmly in the momentarily hushed bar. Almost instantly everyone start-ed punching numbers on their mobile phones. Calls rapidly came and went. Text messages were sent as an alternative when the lines became overloaded with anxious callers. Whether on the Arab or Israeli side, news always travelled fast in this part of the world, bad news even faster. 'It's the Café Moment, in Rehavia!' Mike shouted into my ear after talking to a colleague at Reuters. 'It's only a few minutes from here. Let's go,' he said, grabbing his camera bag and pushing through the door in front of me. Mike was right; it was only minutes before we found ourselves on the scene. So fast were we in arriving that the emergency services fire trucks and ambulances, so efficient in Israel, had only just pulled up.

Sitting on the corner of Aza and Ben Maimon streets in the affluent Rehavia neighbourhood, just across the road from the official residence of Prime Minister Ariel Sharon, the Café Moment was packed that night. It was well known in the city as a hip hangout for Jerusalem's young liberal, secular in-crowd of media types and artists. The sort of café that my friend Yigal Ilan loved, and had used as a model for his own café, Gizmo's. Given its proximity to Sharon's residence, the area was usually heavily watched over by casually dressed men in loose-fitting jackets wearing dark sunglasses and radio ear pieces, the tell-tale signs of a high security presence anywhere in Israel.

Amidst the bedlam the police were already taping off an area around the still smoking black shell of the café. Following Mike, who by now was frantically taking pictures of the carnage, I managed to slip across the cordon into the immediate area of the explosion. It was a scene that stays etched in my memory. Gelled blood and torn clothing lay everywhere across the pavement. I picked my way past a handbag, a mobile phone, pieces of a barstool and a woman's high-heeled shoe still containing her severed foot. On stretchers and along the side of the road outside the café, dozens of people lay shredded by flying glass and timber, doctors working quickly to staunch the bleeding and relieve the pain. Some of those caught up in the blast for whom it was too late had already been zipped up in black body bags. After examining each patient the paramedics would discard their surgical gloves, which lay strewn across the street. Trampled underfoot by the rescue workers or run over by the wheels of passing ambulances, they would fill with air before making a peculiar popping sound. Overhead a helicopter hovered, its floodlight beam and that of the blue beacons on the convoy of ambulances reflected eerily in the pools of blood along the street.

By now the ultra-orthodox Jewish ZAKA volunteer workers had

arrived wearing their distinctive bright yellow vests. Their first priority was to sift through and retrieve the severed body parts of the injured so that the limbs might be rushed to hospitals for possible reattachment. Afterwards, they would patiently scrape all the remaining bits of flesh and blood off the pavements and from inside the café itself, so that the dead could be buried in accordance with Jewish custom.

'My god, there will be another hell to pay after this one,' I heard Mike say, as a woman staggered past me shaking uncontrollably, her clothes and face caked with soot and blood.

Sharon had not been at his residence when the suicide bomber had turned up at Café Moment, mingling with a crowd near the entrance who were waiting for a table. Though the café employed its own guard he unfortunately never noticed the bomber among the crowd. Seconds later the young Palestinian detonated the large quantity of explosives packed full of nails and metal screws that was strapped to his body. Eleven Israelis died that night along with the bomber. Fifty-four others were injured, ten of them seriously. The next day, bleary-eyed and still shaken, I met up with Mike again to mull over what we had witnessed the previous evening.

'Have you seen today's *Ha'aretz?*' he asked, sliding an English-language copy of the liberal Israeli daily across the bar towards me. Mike jabbed at an article by Ari Sharit, one of the paper's columnists who had been a regular customer at Café Moment but fortunately had been elsewhere the previous night. 'This was our café. It was here that we used to come in the morning for our espresso and croissant. In the evening, we would come here for a drink. To cling to what was left of our normalcy, of our secular sanity. To cling to what was left of our way of life,' Shavit had written in his heartfelt piece.

Over the next few days the article would appear again and again. It was quoted like a mantra on television and radio programmes, and discussed in cafés across Israel just like the one in Jerusalem which Shavit had enjoyed frequenting before it was blown to pieces.

When the young survivors start looking desperately for their friends, when the last of the victims with trembling lips are evacuated, and when the police try to restore some sort of order in the chaos that has opened up in the heart of the city, this inconceivable thing coalesces with all the other inconceivable things of the last few months. Will the glaziers and painters really come here in the morning? Will we really come to sit here on the high bar chairs? Will it really be possible to resume our morning routine in a place where bodies are now strewn?

Shavit's commentary had touched a nerve. It expressed something that most Israelis could relate to and feel in the aftermath of the Café Moment bombing and the other attacks that were becoming a terrifying part of their daily lives. Suddenly eating pizza in a restaurant or taking an Egged bus across town could mean coming face to face with the worst excesses and violence that the intifada could generate.

Within hours of the bombing at Café Moment, Hamas had claimed responsibility, and declared that the attack was 'the beginning of retaliatory activities against Sharon's war on Palestinian refugee camps.'

Some six months later, five Palestinians were arrested by the Shin Bet. It was a Saturday night and the men were on their way to plant another bomb in central Israel, said the security service. The bombers were all Hamas members and their cell had been behind the Café Moment blast and another subsequent one at the Hebrew University in Jerusalem. 'Their methods of operation were very intelligent. . . . Their next attacks would have only become more sophisticated,' announced the deputy Public Security Minister, Gideon Ezra, on Israel Radio.

Four of the five Hamas men in the cell held Israeli identity papers and worked in Jerusalem. One, 29-year-old Mohammad Odeh, was a painter for an Israeli contractor, his papers allowing him to move relatively freely in Israel. The alleged leader was from Ramallah. It was strange to think that most of these men lived in East Jerusalem, at most only a little further from Café Moment than the length of the short walk I made on my way to meet Mike Neri that night. Stranger still to imagine that perhaps at some time I might have sat next to one of them in the coffee houses of the Old City's Arab quarter. The intifada was so close to all our lives now, and like everyone else it worried me where it might be going.

Tulkarem, March 26, 2002

It was dark when Abbas Bin Mohammed al-Sayyid arrived at the rundown apartment block in Tulkarem. Everything that was needed had been delivered some hours before: the video camera, a Hamas flag, M-16 rifle and two explosive belts. Already in the building were four of al-

Sayyid's brothers-in-arms, each of them waiting nervously for the start of their secret meeting. Among them was his right-hand man, Muhannad Shrim, who would take care of the posters and video pictures to ensure maximum propaganda value from the operation. Then there was Mu'ammar Shahrouri, a fixer and liaison specialist who had acted as go-between with the other members of the group. Also present was Fathi Khatib, a driver and subsequent eyewitness to the terrible events of the next day that would be executed by the last man in the room, Abd al-Basset Oudeh – the suicide bomber in waiting. Only one of their group was missing, Nidal Qalaq, the second bomber, who had taken ill the day before and was unable to make the rendezvous.

This was the infamous Tulkarem cell, the Hamas men that had initiated, planned and executed the Herzl Street suicide bombing in Netanya less than a year before. It was this cell that had dispatched the young *muezzin*, Ahmad Ayam, who then blew himself up in the town's marketplace killing three Israelis and wounding 50 others. Since that mission, this team of planners and the volunteer bombers at their disposal had also struck again in Netanya. Just a few months after Herzl Street, one of their suicide bombers had detonated his explosives in the Ha-Sharon shopping centre, obliterating the lives of five more Israelis and maiming 86 others.

As deadly as those attacks had been, the cell had now gathered to make final preparations for a far more devastating operation. Like every 'martyrdom cell' the Tulkarem group was tightly compartmentalised within the wider Hamas network and never discussed their affiliation with family or friends. As they mustered that night in their specially rented Tulkarem apartment, few among them could have imagined the subsequent events their mission would trigger. For not only would it incur the wrath of Ariel Sharon, it would bring down the might of the Israeli army on the Palestinian people and change the entire course of the al-Aqsa intifada.

It was back in the early 1990s that a man called Yahya Ayyash, an engineering student and master bomb maker in the West Bank, first proposed that human bombs be adopted in Hamas's military operations. Dubbed 'the engineer' by the late Israeli Prime Minister Yitzak Rabin, Ayyash had written to the Hamas leadership mapping out a strategy he envisaged as capable of inflicting the most pain on the Israeli occupation. In the letter he is said to have pointed out the high price paid by those Palestinians on the streets using slingshots and stones. What was needed, Ayyash insisted, was to 'exert more pressure, make the cost of the occupation that much more expensive in human lives, that much more unbearable.'

It was a strategy that Abbas al-Sayyid, the mastermind behind the Tulkarem cell, had identified with ever since he first joined Hamas while a computer engineering student at Yarmuk University in Jordan. After returning to the occupied territories from his studies, al-Sayyid had quickly risen through the Hamas ranks before being arrested by the Israelis in 1993 for organising riots and other political activities. He was imprisoned for three years, but following his release quickly took up where he had left off within the Hamas infrastructure. Al-Sayyid enlisted recruits, gave political speeches, organised marches and generally worked openly as a spokesman and propagandist for the Islamist movement in Tulkarem. But by now he was also engaged in another much more covert role as the head of the Tulkarem cell, drawing around him his close-knit squad.

Willing recruits were rarely difficult to find in the mosques and refugees camps of Tulkarem. Here, as in Gaza and other Palestinian strongholds, the posters and graffiti on neighbourhood walls often displayed the suicide bombers' symbolic green birds. Like so much iconography of the intifada, the image of the birds is the language of the street but based on the saying of the Prophet Muhammed: that the soul of a martyr is carried to Allah in the bosom of the green birds of paradise. In this, a world where paintings glorify the dead and even calendars show pictures of 'martyr of the month,' it was al-Sayyid's job to keep an eye on the religious young men spending time at local mosques. By asking the right questions, clues might be gleaned as to their suitability as suicide bombers. Just how devout were they? Did they show the commitment and conviction needed? Were they on the Israeli security services' wanted list? Did they have financial worries? Were they emotionally stable? It was a near forensic vetting procedure, aimed at rooting out those in debt, mentally erratic or capable of a last minute change of heart.

What was needed were volunteers who could overcome fear and for whom paradise beckoned and held great promise. Some of those selected are known to have been taken to cemeteries where they would be told to lie in graves to overcome any fear of death. For many it was as if paradise already sat before them, an immediate and close companion to their worldly existence. 'It is very, very near – right in front of our eyes. It lies beneath the thumb. On the other side of the detonator,' was how one volunteer described the feeling of its presence. For those who displayed the right qualities and subsequently participated in 'martyr-dom operations' the spiritual rewards were great indeed. Not only would the shedding of their martyrs' blood during jihad instantly wash away their sins, but on the Day of Judgement they would face no reck-oning. For the martyrs' loved ones too, there were honours, with 70 of them sure to enter heaven on the Day of Resurrection. Outwith the spir-itual dimension, on a purely operational level, the lengthy vetting process also allowed time to check out personal, family or professional backgrounds. The last thing any cell needed was infiltration by those prepared or forced to collaborate with the Israeli Shin Bet. The whole process could take months, if not years, but once chosen the candidate would be given the title, *al shaheed al hayy* (the living martyr).

Abbas al-Sayyid had already found his 'living martyr' in Abd al-Basset Oudeh. In these last days leading up to his mission, Oudeh would have participated in lengthy fasts and spent a great deal of time praying and asking forgiveness for any offences he might have carried out. He would also have made sure that all his worldly debts had been paid off. Failure to do so would mean that the gates of paradise would be closed to him, the same paradise where 72 *houris*, the beautiful vir-gins, would be at his disposal.

Having found his bomber, al-Sayyid and his cell then needed the explosives and other logistical support required to make the operation happen. For these he turned to Hamas's senior operative in the north-ern West Bank, a man called Muhannad Taher, who was based in Nablus. Under Taher's orders the organisation's bomb makers and forg-ers in Nablus were put to work making the explosive belts and coun-terfeit IDs needed for the Tulkarem cell's impending mission. As today's weapons go these human bombs are cheap. Depending on the device's level of sophistication, materials used in their construction might include fertiliser, sugar, gunpowder nails, a battery, light switch and short cable. Rarely would they cost more than a few hundred pounds. Usually the real bulk of the operation's expense would be taken up securing vehicles or identification documents to ensure the bombers' unhindered arrival at the target.

Already it had taken months for the Tulkarem cell and their Hamas counterparts in Nablus to get this far with their plans. Each in turn had carried out their specially allocated tasks, which collectively were about to culminate in the terror of a few final seconds the following day, on the eve of the Jewish Passover holiday.

After greeting each other that night in the Tulkarem apartment, al-Sayyid's men quickly got down to business. While the leader himself began to write the last will and testimony for suicide bomber Abd al-Basset Oudeh, Muhannad Shrim set up the Hamas flag and poster which served as the backdrop for the short video film they would record of Oudeh reading the prepared statement. In the film Oudeh, wearing a green Hamas headband and his bomber's belt, is seen in various poses, pointing the M-16 rifle and declaring that his martyrdom was being carried out on behalf of Hamas's military wing, the Izz al-Din Qassam Brigades. Once finished, the videotape would subsequently be relayed by Hamas operatives via their Nablus network to the Al Manar Television channel run by the Hezbollah militant group in Lebanon. It was scheduled to go on air the day after the bombing. Having read his will for the benefit of the camera, Oudeh went to the bathroom to shave off his beard and moustache, before returning to sit with the rest of the group to receive their final instructions from al-Sayyid. Oudeh would be disguised as a woman and wear a long wig, blue jeans, women's shoes and an overcoat to cover his explosives belt, al-Sayyid told the bomber. Getting to his feet the cell leader then showed Oudeh the switch to detonate the body belt packed with 20lbs of explosives, shredded metal and pellets that would maim and kill their Israeli victims.

At this late stage there must be no mistakes, no small detail left unnoticed that could jeopardise the mission and squander the months of planning and risks taken by the many Hamas activists involved. The top priority was to guarantee that as many of the enemy as possible would be killed. With an explosive belt or carrying a bag, the bomber must always remember that he was in control over location and timing. Al-Sayyid then handed driver Fathi Khatib a brand new, unused mobile phone with instructions that he should use it to keep both him and his superior, Muhammad Taher in Nablus, up to date with the progress of the operation. Turning to both Oudeh and Khatib, al-Sayyid told the men that should they both be captured inside Israel, then Oudeh must detonate his explosives even at the cost of Khatib's life. Never one to miss a propaganda opportunity, al-Sayyid asked Muhannad Shrim to ensure that Khatib was also recorded on video to enable Hamas to release pictures of not one but two martyrs, should the driver also be killed en route to their target. Strange as it might seem, even at this penultimate phase of the operation, none of the cell knew what that target would be. To identify or prearrange one in advance would have been to run the risk of leaking information that might endanger the mission and the whole Hamas network in the northern West Bank. To ensure this would never happen, it had been left up to Oudeh and Khatib themselves, once dispatched, to decide what target best presented itself as an opportunity to inflict the maximum casualties and damage.

It was 2 p.m. the next day – the eve of the Jewish Passover – when suicide bomber Oudeh and his driver Khatib left the Tulkarem apartment and drove to the village of Naslat'Isa. There they switched vehicles, picking up the Renault Express that Khatib had bought for 16,000 shekels, using a fake ID registered in the name of a resident from the village of Taibeh. In this vehicle bearing yellow Israeli licence plates they first headed south to the town of Herzliya in the hope of finding the target they wanted. But nothing there appeared suitable and so the pair continued towards Tel Aviv. The longer they spent on the road the greater their chances of being pulled over by an Israeli army or police patrol. Even with his fake ID, Oudeh had been on Israel's wanted list for over four years, and given any rigorous run through the security service computers, his real identity was sure to be discovered. As they continued to drive around looking for the ideal target, Oudeh told Khatib that he was very familiar with Netanya and had once worked in a number of hotels in the busy coastal city. It wasn't long before they were on Netanya's outskirts and headed west before pulling up near the city's Park Hotel. Their risky round trip had brought them back to less than ten miles from where they had first set out in Tulkarem.

With Netanya having been hit several times before, its security services had been put on full alert during the Passover holiday. But inside the Park Hotel there were over 200 guests about to sit down to the traditional Seder feast, in which Jews commemorate the exodus of the Children of Israel from Egypt. Oudeh and Khatib knew this was the end of the road. Primed and ready to kill, the bombers had found precisely the target they were looking for.

Park Hotel, Netanya, March 27, 2002

Some said the hotel's armed guard was carrying out a security check of the grounds at exactly that moment. Other survivors say the lobby was just too crowded to see Abd al-Basset Oudeh as he walked through the main door just before quarter past seven that Wednesday evening. A few of the mainly elderly guests about to take their seats for the meal distinctly remember seeing the figure of Oudeh dressed in a long black overcoat enter carrying a bag, and looking as if he was searching for his seat. Among those already seated in a private upstairs dining room were Naomi Ragen and her family. Her father and mother in-law, both survivors of Auschwitz, had gone to the bathroom and were due to join them in a few minutes.

'And then I heard it,' Naomi Ragen recalled. 'A sound, like a roar, rolling through the room, making the floor rumble. Then suddenly, there was a deafening crash of sound like no other I had ever heard in my life, a sound that was like an emphatic statement in a language all its own, whose meaning was impossible to mistake for any other, impossible to misunderstand.'

Somewhere near the centre of the packed downstairs dining room Oudeh had detonated the bomb in his belt, just the way Abbas al-Sayyid had shown him the night before in the quiet of their clandestine meeting in the Tulkarem apartment. But that quiet was gone forever. Instead, there was the searing thump of the explosion and its aftershock that bounced off the walls along with the shredded metal and ball-bearings that ripped into the faces, torsos and legs of the hundreds of guests. In such a closed area the bomb's effects were horrific. Oudeh may have gone to his paradise, but for those survivors in the Park Hotel dining room it was a living hell.

'I felt shock waves and was pushed under the table, and everything blacked out,' recalled Itai Donenhirsch, a young Israeli man who was with his 16-year-old sister and 52-year-old mother when the blast hit them. 'There was the smell of smoke and dust in my mouth and a ringing in my ears,' the mother, Nechama Donenhirsch remembered. 'My daughter held me and said to me to calm me, "You are alive, I'm alive, don't worry, we are alive".'

The force of the blast was so powerful that it brought part of the ceiling down on top of the Donenhirsch family and other guests. It blew out walls and windows and hurled slivers of glass and debris into the street outside where shop awnings were buckled by the heat. On seeing the fireball and hearing the sound of the blast, driver Fathi Khatib, waiting outside in the Renault, called Hamas leaders Muhannad Taher in Nablus and al-Sayyid in Tulkarem, to tell them the mission had been accomplished. As Khatib drove off through the night-time drizzle towards the village of Nazlat 'Isa, where once again he would switch back to the bombers' first vehicle, fleets of Israeli ambulances rushed past him on their way to the carnage at the beachside hotel.

A few hours later, once home, Khatib again called al-Sayyid to tell him he was back safely. Already the videotape of Oudeh reading his will had been delivered to Nablus for distribution to the media. In what immediately became known across Israel as the 'Passover Massacre,' 29 Israelis were killed and 155 traumatised and wounded that night. Some of those who died in the Park Hotel had been survivors of the Jewish Holocaust. Naomi Ragen's in-laws, who had lived through the horrors of the Nazi death camps, remarkably survived that night. 'The sound I will never forget, of Abd al-Basset Oudeh detonating the kilos of explosives around his waist in a room full of grandparents and their children and grandchildren, can never be answered in words. It is a language all its own,' Naomi Ragen said afterwards.

Not surprisingly, throughout much of the world, television pictures of scenes from the blast sparked instant outrage. 'This is the time for Chairman Arafat to speak to his people, to tell them that they are destroying their own desire and vision for a Palestinian state living side by side in peace with Israel, behind secure and recognisable borders,' declared United States Secretary of State Colin Powell.

Back in Tulkarem in the hours following the bombing, Abbas al-Sayyid's men organised a march through the town in remembrance of the martyr Abd al-Basset Oudeh. From loudspeakers mounted on top of cars, there were calls to honour his memory by joining Hamas. At Oudeh's family home a three-day period of mourning began, during which an attendant hired by al-Sayyid's aide, Muhannad Shrim, served coffee, juice and sweets to those who came to pay their condolences.

In the months to come, a football tournament for Palestinian boys would be named after Abd al-Basset Oudeh, the man responsible for the worst mass killing of its kind on Israeli civilians since the start of the al-Aqsa intifada. But long before that, Israel would exact a bitter retribution.

Jerusalem, March 28, 2002

For Ariel Sharon, enough was enough. It was some time around 11'oclock when he sat down in the cabinet chamber with Israel's top military and security officials that Thursday night after the end of the

Passover holiday. Less than 24 hours had elapsed since Abd al-Basset Oudeh had walked into the lobby of the Park Hotel with his lethal body belt. A cursory look across the room was all that it took to gauge the mood of the men sitting around Sharon and how serious the government's course of action was likely to be. Among those attending the emergency meeting were Chief of Staff General Shaul Mofaz; Avi Dichter, head of the Israel Security Agency (ISA); General Aharon Ze'evi Farkash, Director of Military Intelligence (DMI); and Efraim Halevy, Chief of Mossad. All were there to discuss, and to quickly approve, what would amount to a massive incursion into the heart of the Palestinian West Bank by the Israeli Defence Forces. It was a time for deeds, not words of prevarication. The tactical plans that had already been drawn up some time before were quickly outlined to the men. Unanimously, they gave the go-ahead for the start of the operation, which they later emphasised was aimed at 'rooting out terrorists.' Only the question of what to do with Yasser Arafat and his Palestinian Authority gave rise to any contention and prolonged debate.

Some hours before Sharon had convened his emergency session, Arafat had made a televised speech in which he expressed his readiness for a ceasefire under certain conditions. Meanwhile, behind the scenes, his own PA officials were frantically conducting intensive talks with Arab states to try and persuade the United States to intervene to prevent drastic Israeli military action. But Israeli officials had already asked their ally to declare that Arafat was responsible for the failure of the recent ceasefire talks and to recall their mediator, General Anthony C. Zinni from the region. As far as the Israeli top brass were concerned, Arafat's conciliatory tone was purely tactical and another attempt to buy time. In short it was a case of too little, too late. Sharon and some of his military staff were in no doubt about what was now needed. Shortly after the meeting began, the Prime Minister made the case for forcibly sending Yasser Arafat into exile. General Shaul Mofaz and other senior officers meanwhile felt that the Palestinian Authority should be designated an 'enemy' and that any incursion should aim to completely destroy its infrastructure.

The international implications of attacking the PA, a body which had been set up under the Oslo agreements, were obvious. It would also effectively mean dismantling the only nominal negotiating partner Israel had on the Palestinian side. Despite these considerations, Sharon argued again and again that his old adversary Arafat must go and that it was dangerous to allow him to remain in his base in Ramallah. Other security officials, among them Efraim Halevy, the chief of Israel's overseas intelligence service, Mossad, felt it better to keep Arafat where his activities could be monitored and his movements restricted, than have him roaming around the world. The session that had started out with a unanimous decision to take forceful military action now dragged on over the issue of Arafat. Throughout the debate, officials came and went from the cabinet chamber until around dawn when a compromise was finally agreed. Arafat would not be forced into exile. Instead, he would be corralled at his Ramallah headquarters, unable to travel inside the territories. Should he travel overseas, his return journey quite simply could not be guaranteed. Arafat was a prisoner in his own land. As Sharon's cabinet meeting wound up, the Palestinian Authority was already evacuating its offices in preparation for the Israeli onslaught.

Israeli military leave had been cancelled. Across the West Bank and Gaza massive numbers of troops were being deployed. Transporters laden with Merkava tanks and Magah armoured personnel carriers were moving to positions outside Palestinian cities. The die was cast. Sharon's 'war on terror' had begun. But as ever, it was the Palestinian people that would bear its awesome brunt.

6

'I HAVE A FEELING THIS IS GOING TO BE VERY BAD'

'The Palestinians must be hit and it must be very painful: we must cause them losses, victims, so they feel the heavy price.'

—Ariel Sharon, March 2002

Ramallah March–April 2002

They came through the wall using sledgehammers. With their faces daubed in camouflage paint and assault rifles and machine guns under their arms they were a terrifying sight for the Hassan family, who huddled together in fear. There were at least ten Israeli soldiers. They took the family's blankets and bedded down. Others came and went throughout the night. When the soldiers left the next morning to continue their house-to-house hunt for 'terrorists' their parting gift was to smash the Hassan's television set – one of the few luxuries enjoyed by this impoverished Palestinian family living in the squalor of al-Amari refugee camp in Ramallah.

'Why did they do that?' asked Ahmed Hassan, bewildered, standing alongside his sobbing wife and their four children, in the shards of broken glass and garbage left by the soldiers in their cramped living room.

A few hours later, less than a mile away at Ramallah's main hospital, I watched and listened as the wailing siren of an approaching ambulance brought dozens of white-coated orderlies on to the streets outside. Braving gunfire, they had come out to help shift the wreckage of cars crushed by Israeli tanks blocking the way to the hospital. 'The Israelis do it deliberately to stop the ambulances. Sometimes the tanks just sit there in the streets and won't let them drive past. Why would people do such a thing?' asked Abdul Rahman angrily, as he watched his colleagues struggle to shift a flattened Toyota while waving frantically at the tank that had stalled the ambulance further down the rubble-strewn street.

Ariel Sharon had the answer to Ahmed Hassan and Abdul Rahman's questions. It was called retribution. The moment had come to teach the Palestinian people and their leaders a lesson they would never forget. Above all it was time to crush the resistance and intifada like never before. The man who had earned the nickname 'The Bulldozer' was doing just that, bulldozing his way into the West Bank in the most massive and brutal Israeli military operation against the Palestinians since the 1982 Lebanon war and the bludgeoning of Beirut. Sharon's government had dubbed it 'Operation Defensive Shield.' At face value it was presented as Israel's almost inevitable response to the series of bomb attacks that had culminated in the suicide strike by the Tulkarem cell at the Park Hotel in Netanya. In reality, it was the long awaited chance to put into effect a secret plan to totally destroy the Palestinian

Authority and put Yasser Arafat 'out of the game'.

'What is happening there is terrible. You will never get in. The soldiers have it sealed off completely,' said the Palestinian waiter at the Jerusalem Hotel that morning on hearing that I was heading for Ramallah. As I sat ruminating over my breakfast coffee, I knew all too well that what he was telling me was true. It would be almost impossible to get past the cordon the Israeli army had thrown up around the city, let alone stay safe in Ramallah's streets should I be lucky enough to get there in the first place. If there was a way in, though, I thought to myself, instinctively reaching for my mobile phone, then my old friend and colleague Mafouz Abu Turk was the one man sure to know about it.

Mafouz was a near-legendary veteran Palestinian photojournalist who worked for Reuters. Small, stocky, balding, with a rolling gait and huge grey moustache, he was a tough operator who had worked the warring West Bank since the early days of the first intifada. We had first met a few years before during some clashes in the alleyways of Jerusalem's Old City. Later that same day he had asked if I wanted to accompany him to cover other fighting he had heard was taking place on the city's outskirts. When we arrived, dozens of Palestinian youngsters were hurling stones from behind an embankment at some Israeli soldiers dug in behind a sandbagged position some yards away. Already there had been casualties among the Palestinians, and live rounds were being used by the Israeli troops. Crouching low as the bullets zipped overhead, I reluctantly followed Mafouz along the length of the embankment. He was determined to get up close, right among the stone-throwers so he could get his shots. At that time I too was working as a photojournalist, and was no stranger to risk taking. To my amazement though, Mafouz happily rose up from behind cover and exposed himself to Israeli gunfire every time a youth prepared to launch a stone. In these situations he was coolness personified. As a photographer he not only had a great eye for a picture but he could be stubborn, tenacious, and had that crucial unerring gift for being in the right place at the right time. Well known among the Palestinian community, Mafouz was able to get places other foreign journalists like myself had difficulty accessing. For that very reason too, he could sometimes be terrifying to be with.

In the first few months of the al-Aqsa intifada, Mafouz had been shot on three occasions. The first and second time in rapid succession was during fierce battles the day following Sharon's walk on Haram al-Sharif in September 2000. Outside the al-Aqsa mosque Mafouz had been taking cover behind a stone column when he was hit in the thigh with a rubber-coated metal bullet. Like the full live rounds used by the Israelis, these bullets regularly killed. It was just a question of where they hit you. Though wounded and in considerable pain, Mafouz continued to take pictures while fleeing towards the mosque. Moments later he was hit again, this time in the right foot. Less than a month later in Bethlehem, while covering riots following the funeral of a Palestinian boy, Mafouz was shot again, this time in the hand as he leaned out from behind a wall to press the shutter on his camera. No sooner had he been taken to Beit Jala hospital where his wound was stitched up, than he was back out on the streets again taking pictures.

Mafouz looked well when he arrived at the Jerusalem Hotel that morning. His face was dark from the sun, highlighting even more distinctly the silver moustache that drooped from his top lip. 'There is a way into Ramallah,' he confirmed, quickly adding that he hadn't used the route for some days and by now the Israelis might have closed it. 'Believe me, David, this time it's different, they have brought in so many tanks and soldiers, the place is full of them,' he warned, pausing momentarily before continuing, 'and they're not in a good mood.' Nevertheless, we decided to give it a try, and less than an hour later, Mafouz's battered car was bumping along dirt tracks off the main road on the outskirts of besieged Ramallah. As we drove, Mafouz pointed to the metal fences, razor wire and watchtowers of the Qalandia checkpoint on the city's edge.

Only a few weeks before, I had gone there to talk to Palestinians about the problems they encountered daily entering and leaving the town. Now, by the roadside, Israeli bulldozers were flattening acres of ground around the checkpoint. 'What are they building?' I asked Mafouz. 'Trenches and earth walls to make sure no-one can skirt round the checkpoint unseen,' he explained.

It was only the beginning. After crossing some waste ground that was exposed, expecting at any moment to be blown to pieces by a tank shell or helicopter-launched missile, we suddenly found ourselves on Ramallah's eerily deserted streets. Everywhere the tarmac and earth were already chewed up by the tracks of more than 100 giant Merkava tanks and armoured personnel-carriers that had come through only a few hours earlier. Some had taken up positions within yards of the compound that served as Yasser Arafat's headquarters, where the Palestinian leader, just as Sharon's cabinet meeting had agreed, would remain under effective house arrest. Lampposts, fences, cars, walls – anything that got in the way of the tanks had simply been crushed, toppled or pushed aside. All around us we could hear gunfire raging across the city, keeping most of Ramallah's 40,000 citizens huddled in basements or trapped indoors. Tapers of thick black smoke, from burning tyres and buildings set alight by shells and missiles, drifted across the city's flat-topped roofs that bristled with the ubiquitous television antennae.

'I have a feeling this is going to be very bad,' observed Mafouz quietly, before suggesting it would probably be smart to pull over and put on our flak jackets and Kevlar helmets that we'd stashed in the car boot. Coming from such a battle-hardened reporter and veteran of this unholy land, it was not what I wanted to hear. In all the years I'd spent covering the intifada, rarely could I remember feeling so uneasy. It was as if I'd had been struck by an almost overwhelming sense of foreboding. The sound of heavy machine-gun fire was deafening as we splashed our way through the raging torrent of a broken water main, burst by Israeli bulldozers digging up the streets to create yet more barricades of earth and broken tarmac, or 'siege works' as the army called them. Geysers of water were everywhere, cutting off supplies to much of the city, which was especially disastrous for the increasingly overcrowded hospitals and civilians imprisoned in their own homes.

Through a warren of narrow backstreets and alleyways, Mafouz led me into al-Amari refugee camp, home to 5,000 Palestinians and what we had been told was a key target of the Israeli onslaught on Ramallah that day. 'A bastion of terror' was what the Israeli Defence Force had called it, just like the Balata camp in Nablus that had been stormed some weeks before. After Balata it was Jabaliya camp in Gaza, then Dheisheh near Bethlehem; now it was al-Amari's turn. On seeing Mafouz and myself kitted out in our body armour, some Palestinians fled, thinking that the first of many Israeli soldiers that would 'sweep' the camp in the coming days could not be far behind. Everyone we met was terrified and expected the worst.

'The Israelis came when it was still dark. The tanks are on all sides. We are trapped,' said Fatima Awad, anxiously. A resident of al-Amari, her tiny sons clung to her legs as she told me how her husband was also trapped somewhere on the other side of town, and she feared the Israelis would arrest him without her knowing what might happen to him. She had every reason to be afraid. By now Apache helicopter gunships shaped like malevolent wasps had opened fire on the camp from the sky. Then loudspeaker announcements ordered all men between the ages of 16 and 45 to gather at a school on the camp's outskirts. As we made our way there, pausing at every street corner to check if we might be exposed to sniper fire, youngsters were already thronging the alleyways, breaking rocks and filling bottles with petrol for Molotov cocktail bombs. None could have been more than 12 or 13 years old. Every so often their mothers or older sisters would appear from doorways to scold them for gambling their lives in these gestures of defiance against overwhelming odds. This was the Palestinian resistance I recognised – the eyeball-to-eyeball, street fighting of the *shebab*. If you are looking for me, then look no further. I'm here, ready and waiting to face off, was their message. This was a daylight world of head-on confrontation, far from the shadowy, stalking existence of the suicide bomber. It seemed a long way too from the threats and double talk of Yasser Arafat's backroom boys. If the Palestinians had a real resistance movement against the occupation, it was this, their enduring civilian population; people who were prepared to put up with the hardship of curfews or take to the streets in demonstrations, but if given the proper chance could be reasonable, hospitable and more than willing to talk. But by now even the remotest chance of any constructive dialogue had evaporated as Sharon's 'Operation Defensive Shield' tightened its grip.

Outside the bulldozed walls of al-Amari school we found hundreds of Palestinian men herded together under guard by soldiers in armoured personnel carriers. As they waited, an old woman, undaunted by the gunfire echoing in the surrounding streets, approached the Israeli soldiers, carrying a white flag attached to a stick, to plead with them on behalf of the detained men. She got within 20 yards before a soldier raised his gun and warned her to return to her home or he would shoot. One by one the men were brought forward, their hands painfully manacled with plastic cuffs, and led into the school compound.

'You can't go there,' shouted one Israeli soldier, pointing his rifle and taking aim at Mafouz and myself as we moved to follow one prisoner inside. Backing off slowly, we slipped through an alleyway behind the school where we were able to peer through a hole in a fence at what was going on. A group of men, about 50 in total, were ordered to line up, take off their jackets and shirts, and empty their pockets. They were then blindfolded, and we watched as Israeli soldiers wrote a number on each of the prisoners' forearms. The men were then forced to sit silently in the baking sun with Israeli guns trained on them, each waiting their turn for interrogation.

The entire operation lasted for hours, and was still underway late in the afternoon when we returned to the school, having by then ventured to other parts of Ramallah. Such methods even outraged some Israelis, as they felt they were reminiscent of the Nazis during World War Two. As increasing evidence of widespread human rights abuse against Palestinians emerged in the following weeks, many Israelis felt compelled to speak out.

Yosef (Tommy) Lapid, a member of the Israeli parliament, leader of the Shinui Party and a former concentration camp victim, confronted Israeli General Shaul Mofaz during a meeting of the Foreign Affairs and Defence Committee, saying that as a Holocaust survivor he found the IDF methods intolerable and shocking. In a letter to Dr. Shevah Weiss, the chairman of Yad Vashem Holocaust Museum, Mohammed Barakeh, an Arab–Israeli Knesset member, put into words the thoughts of many over Israel's tactics during the ongoing invasion of the West Bank: 'In these wretched days, I've asked myself more than once how, within such a short period of history, the victim has become the murderer, and a people who, perhaps, suffered more than any other from arbitrary repression and refugee status, is capable of meting out the same fate to others.'

Figures subsequently gathered by Amnesty International would show that between March and June 2002, during which time there were two other major Israeli offensives as well as Operation Defensive Shield, more than 8,000 detained Palestinians were 'routinely subjected to ill treatment.' Under what was known as 'administrative detention,' a person could be held for an unlimited number of repeatedly renewable six-month periods that were easily extended by military order. 'So far, since the beginning of the Israeli invasion, no Palestinians who have been arrested by the Israelis have been tried. Their detention is just being extended,' Dr. Said Zeedani, the head of the Palestinian Independent Centre for Citizens Rights, told me in the weeks following the start of the operation. Zeedani also confirmed that, like other human rights groups, his organisation had by then received an alarming increase in reports of torture during detention and interrogation. Indeed, by early April Israel would announce that it was reopening the notorious Ansar 3 (Ketziot) military prison in the Negev desert that had been closed since the end of the first intifada.

Even the United Nations – albeit not for the first time – thought Israel's actions unacceptable. In his harshest ever criticism of the country, UN Secretary-General Kofi Annan urged it to stop 'the bombing of civilian areas, the assassinations, the unnecessary use of lethal force, the demolitions and the daily humiliation of ordinary Palestinians.' Annan said that Israel had the right to live in peace and security within secure internationally recognised borders, but insisted it 'must end the illegal occupation.' According to one UN spokesman it was the first time Annan had called Israel's occupation of Palestinian territory 'illegal.' Not of course that any of this mattered to Ariel Sharon and his government. Condemnation from human rights groups, Sharon's own religious and political community, even from the United Nations' itself, would not stop what now was arguably Israel's most extensive military campaign on Palestinian soil since the 1948 war. Sharon, the old warrior, was back doing what he did best.

From very early on it was evident from what I witnessed in Ramallah and elsewhere during Operation Defensive Shield, that the Israeli army's 'tactics' made a mockery of its claim to believe in 'purity of arms.' As Mafouz and I followed Israeli troops around Ramallah's al-Amari camp during those first few days, the house-to-house searches often seemed like little more than excuses for acts of random violence and vandalism. Padlocked doors were hammered or shot off and windows were broken. When an alleyway looked too dangerous to venture into, the soldiers' solution was simply to knock through the adjoining walls of people's homes using sledgehammers. In one block it was like looking through a kaleidoscopic tunnel of living rooms, bedrooms and kitchens. Such tactics, it was said, had been used by the Nazis in World War Two, during their infamous assault on the Jewish resistance in the Warsaw ghetto. The use of Palestinian civilians as human shields by the IDF was also widespread, as documented by the Israeli human rights group B'Tselem, which gathered a number of damning testimonies from individual soldiers.

> Before searching a house, we go to a neighbour, take him out of his house, and tell him to call for the person we want. If it works, great. If not, we blow down the door or hammer it open. The neighbour goes in first. If somebody is planning something, he is the one who gets it. Our instructions are to send him inside and have him go up

to all the floors and get everyone out of the house. The neighbour can't refuse; he doesn't have that option. The neighbour shouts, knocks on the door, says that the army is here. If nobody answers, we tell him that we'll kill him if nobody comes out, and that he should shout that out to the people in the house. The basic procedure was the same no matter who gave the briefing. Maybe the 'we'll kill him' came from platoon, but the rest came from the brigade level or higher.

What amazed me, as we toured the al-Amari camp in the wake of one Israel patrol, was the apparent disregard the soldiers had for our presence as they openly behaved no better than thugs. Clearly hell-bent on doing what they wanted, the fact that a couple of journalists were there watching didn't seem to matter. Only men out of control, or alternatively given free rein by their superior officers, could possibly act with such perceived impunity or disregard for the consequences of their actions.

In one house I watched as they repeatedly kicked the family dog, smashed a glass table with their rifle butts, and kicked over plant pots. This was no search for weapons or militants. It was nothing more than malicious, crude vandalism. The family home of Wafa Idris – one of the first Palestinian women suicide bombers, who killed herself along with an Israeli and wounded more than a dozen people in a Jerusalem street in January earlier that year – was given a very special going-over. That the other family members knew nothing of her involvement with a suicide cell until after her terrible attack made no difference to the half-dozen soldiers who took great relish in wrecking their home.

Whatever Ariel Sharon and his military commanders said at the time, Operation Defensive Shield was no straightforward knee-jerk response to an escalation in suicide bombings and other attacks on Israel. Rather, it was the evolutionary outcome of a series of strategic blueprints designed to incapacitate the Palestinian Authority and various armed militias, while simultaneously striking fear into the Palestinian population as a whole. The precise nature, extent and intensity of such an operation had been left open and fluid since it first appeared in draft form, long before the end of March 2002 when Operation Defensive Shield finally swung into gear. At different stages in its development, the plan had taken on various names and titles, but what mattered most to the Israeli government was not what it was called, but finding just the right time for its implementation. Indeed, some analysts argue that the original blueprint was drawn up even before Ariel Sharon's election as Prime Minister in February 2001. In its initial form they say it was known as the 'Dagan Plan,' having been drafted by General Meir Dagan, Sharon's security advisor during his election campaign. In essence the Dagan Plan's objectives were simple. By ratcheting up a massive military operation of increasing intensity, the Israelis hoped to systematically isolate Yasser Arafat and the PA both domestically and diplomatically.

Writing in the Israeli right-wing daily *Yediot Aharonot*, security correspondent Alex Fishman claimed the Dagan Plan was based on two unalterable premises: 'One, Arafat is a murderer, and one doesn't negotiate with a murderer. Two, the Oslo Accord is the greatest evil that has ever fallen upon Israel, and everything should be done to destroy it.'

Following Ariel Sharon's election as Prime Minister, General Dagan was given a key government position as Israel's go-between with the US special envoys in the region, Anthony Zinni and Senator George Mitchell. Some Middle East observers have speculated on just how much Washington knew at that time about any Israeli plans to invade the West Bank and dismantle the Palestinian Authority. Given the close consultation between US and Israeli military and intelligence officials, many believe it would be inconceivable that the Bush administration would be unaware of such an invasion blueprint. According to some commentators it was even possible that a deliberate stalling of the peace process and implementation of the Dagan Plan, or some variation of it, was all part of an agreed agenda between Washington and Jerusalem. Rather than it being a case of Israel having to secure a green light from Washington, was it in fact doing its bidding, many began to ask? With an escalating Israeli–Palestinian conflict increasingly frustrating US plans to attack Iraq, a punitive military blow might have suited some in Washington keen to obtain quiet in one part of the region in order to stir things up in another. Israel, along with its many supporters in Washington, had calculated that once such an operation was underway, Arafat would either have to surrender or be quietly removed with the help of some within his regime who had been cultivated over the years by the CIA and Israeli intelligence. The very fact that CIA director George Tenet had been put in charge of so-called 'peace negotiations' was surely evidence enough that dodgy deals were being done, insisted sceptics. As part of that process, getting rid of Arafat and the PA would no doubt have to be factored into any potential strategy.

In his panoramic and incredibly detailed book *The Great War for Civilisation – The Conquest of the Middle East*, Robert Fisk recounts a warning made by George Tenet to Yasser Arafat at the very end of the Camp David talks. 'We can make new borders, we can make peoples, we can make new regimes,' Tenet is said to have told the Palestinian leader after Arafat had refused to accept Clinton's and Barak's terms. Whatever the truth about how much Washington knew or was involved with any Israeli advanced plans to invade the West Bank or destroy the PA, by July 2001, according to one media report, those blueprints for action had been firmed up. During that month, IDF Chief of Staff General Shaul Mofaz is said to have presented the government with an updated version of the plan for an 'all-out assault to smash the Palestinian Authority, force out leader Yasser Arafat and kill or detain its army.'

Mofaz, it should be remembered, some eight months later would be among the most strident voices in favour of launching military action to destroy the PA during the emergency cabinet meeting held the night following the Park Hotel suicide bombing.

But back in July 2001 according to the London-based 'Foreign Report' published by the specialist defence and geopolitics information group 'Janes,' Mofaz presented the then-updated plan which now had two new titles: 'The Destruction of the Palestinian Authority and Disarmament of All Armed Forces' and the more succinctly titled 'Operation Justified Vengeance.' The Israeli generals were now said to envisage a military offensive of up to one month's duration, which would result in deaths of thousands of Palestinians and hundreds of Israelis. The assault would begin with intensive air raids using F-16 and F-15 warplanes and helicopters against all the main PA installations in Ramallah and Gaza. Israel would then deploy more than 30,000 troops and hundreds of tanks and armoured vehicles. The operation was to be launched at the government's discretion following the next big suicide bomb attack in Israel. The need to 'root out terrorists' would be cited as justification for the assault.

Sharon's Likud–Labour coalition government quickly denied the claims in the 'Foreign Report' article. Foreign Minister Shimon Peres told Israeli radio that he was 'happy to see that such an important journal has such a fertile imagination,' and that General Mofaz's presentation of the plan 'simply didn't happen.' The US State Department also denied any knowledge of the strategic blueprint or that Israel had told them anything about it. Washington remained content with repeating again that 'there is no military solution to this conflict.' But according to 'Foreign Report' the details in the assault plan even took into consideration any potential regional and international response to the invasion. Mofaz dismissed the possibility of any serious response from Israel's Arab neighbours. Israeli military intelligence was said to have doubts that Egypt, Jordan or Syria would go to war on behalf of the Palestinians. The international community would likely make a fuss, but it would be minimal and probably come too late to make any substantial difference to what by then would be a consolidated Israeli military position on the ground. According to then Palestinian Planning Minister Nabil Shaath, both President Bush and French President Jacques Chirac had spoken 'very clearly to Sharon about this issue and warned him against the great dangers of such a policy.' Other Palestinians who had the ear of the United States and the CIA in particular, like Mohammed Dahlan, head of the PA's Preventive Security in Gaza, also confirmed that Israel was seriously weighing up plans to remove the PA. So far advanced were they said to be that there was even talk of a list of potential successors to Arafat having been drawn up. Among them was his deputy Abu Mazen and others who might prove more flexible in peace negotiations.

What had started as the Dagan Plan had now become Operation Justified Vengeance. Perhaps Alex Fishman, the security correspondent for the daily *Yediot Aharanot* had been right, back in 2001, when he suggested that none of this had happened by chance. Instead, Fishman insisted, it had all been part of a calculated strategy by Sharon from the outset. 'Coldbloodedly, with the patience of an old hunter who knows the weak points of his prey, Sharon threw out his snares from the moment he became Prime Minister. The prey (Arafat) managed to save himself and slip away, but this week he got caught in the nets.'

By early March 2002, following a wave of Palestinian suicide bomb attacks, Sharon was already implementing some of his plan's measures under its latest title 'Operation Security Imperative.' The net was indeed closing on Arafat. Addressing the Knesset on March 5, Sharon made it clear that by now Israel had discarded any pretence that it was simply engaged in conflict management designed to reduce the levels of violence. 'Israel is at war,' Sharon declared, emphasising that the Palestinians 'must be dealt a heavy blow, which will come from every direction,' and that Israel would 'inflict heavy losses on their side.' Within 72 hours of his statement the West Bank and Gaza Strip were subjected to their single bloodiest day since June 1967.

On March 8, a day known by Palestinians as 'Black Friday,' the real onslaught began with armoured columns moving into a number of Palestinian towns and refugee camps. Barely a few weeks later, the Park Hotel suicide bombing provided the perfect pretext that allowed Operation Security Imperative to ultimately metamorphose into the full-blown Operation Defensive Shield.

The longer I spent in Ramallah with Mafouz, the more we realised that Sharon and his generals really meant business this time. By now ominous comparisons were being made between Defensive Shield and the Israeli assault on Beirut in 1982, a campaign out of which Sharon of course emerged discredited after the Sabra-Shatila massacre. Following the punishing Israeli action against the al-Amari and Qaddura refugee camps in Ramallah, the offensive began to extend across the entire city. Faced with overwhelming firepower, Palestinian resistance at first amounted to little more than groups of rock throwers. But slowly militia fighters began to take to the streets and confronted the huge tanks that smashed through neighbourhoods with their rotating guns. Around the central Manara Square, hundreds of spent bullet cartridges littered the alleyways. Hooded Palestinian gunmen leapt from behind walls to fire Kalashnikovs and M-16 automatic rifles, while others sat loading bullets into fresh clips before rejoining the gun battles. Behind their masks the militiamen's eyes sometimes seemed to betray a fear or frustration about a fight they knew they could never win.

With Mafouz I would make my way across the city in a nerve-wracking series of dashes across open ground. Staccato bursts of gunfire rolled over the olive trees in the surrounding rocky hills and in the main streets of the city centre. We cowered next to walls and peered round corners for the guns of snipers or barrels of stationary tanks that might mistake journalists for fighters. On the few occasions when we plucked up enough courage, we walked openly to avoid suspicion, hoping the bright yellow letters TV taped to our flak jackets and helmets would identify us as reporters. I hated those walks, when every instinct in your body told you to run or take cover, but I knew that to panic was to look suspicious, and virtually guaranteed you would be shot by increasingly jumpy Israeli soldiers, who rarely paused to check if you were a reporter before opening fire.

The image of what could happen still haunted me from a few weeks before when another colleague, Italian photojournalist Raffaele Ciriello, had been killed. Nobody really knows whether the Israeli tank-gunner that killed Ciriello made a mistake or not. 'We came to Manara Square and took a sidestreet because we heard raised voices,' explained Amedeo Ricucci, one of Ciriello's colleagues afterwards. 'Out of a corner an Israeli tank appeared some 150 yards away. It was going in the opposite direction but stopped. We started to film, then hid behind a building. I told Raffaele to get under cover because it was dangerous. He got behind the building but he leaned out with a small camera. They got him with a burst of gunfire,' Ricucci recalled.

Mafouz and I had been working nearby when we heard that Ciriello had been hit, but moving around had become so dangerous that it was much later when we finally got to Ramallah's Arabcare Medical Centre. At the entrance to the hospital, trolleys came in waves with the wounded from the gun battles that were raging just a few yards away on the streets outside. Everywhere inside the hospital, orderlies, doctors and nurses, overwhelmed in bloodstained gowns, dashed backwards and forwards. Mafouz managed to stop one orderly and ask if he knew where the foreign photographer had been taken. We had no idea then whether Ciriello was alive or dead. Perhaps he had been working alone, and if so it was best to check if there was anything we could do for him.

'I'm sorry to tell you he is dead, but I will take you to him,' the orderly replied with a gentle smile. His voice was almost drowned out by the cries of pain and orders being shouted, as yet more wounded were ferried in from an ambulance that had screeched to a halt outside. I suddenly felt uncomfortable. What's the point of going to him if he's already dead, I thought to myself? It wasn't as if we were family members or close colleagues who had come to confirm his identity. Fear of what I might encounter didn't come into it. Over the years I had seen countless dead in wars here and around the world. There just seemed no point. I really didn't know Raffaele Ciriello that well. On a few occasions I'd spoken to him in passing, while covering some street clashes, demonstrations, or renewing our press accreditation at the Beit Agron centre for foreign journalists in Jerusalem. But beyond that I didn't know where in Italy he came from, if he was married or had children, or even who he worked for. Yet something about the orderly's voice and manner suggested all that didn't matter. At this precise moment in time he seemed to be saying it was our sacred duty to pay homage to our colleague. He's one of your own, his voice implied, a *sahafi* like you, who has come all this way to witness these painful times. It was as if by seeing what had become of Raffaele Ciriello, then all of us – hospital orderlies, journalists, Ramallah's citizens, Palestinians, Israelis – would somehow collectively realise just what was happening here. That each and every one of us might be bonded by some common experience, which would help make sense of the madness on the streets outside and across this troubled land.

We followed the orderly up a narrow staircase, the sounds of gunfire echoing from outside now louder than ever. On the third floor he introduced us to Dr. Mohammed Luai, who told us that Ciriello was in cardiac arrest when he had been brought in. There had been some Italian journalist colleagues with him, but they had since gone, hoping to get through the Israeli army cordon back to Jerusalem to take care of the necessary formalities. 'We tried to revive him but he had lost too much blood,' Dr Luai explained. The body of the dead photographer lay on a trolley in front of us, the exit wounds from the six bullets having left gaping holes in his back. Though his flesh was a ghostly white, Ciriello otherwise looked at peace. Even though his colleagues had been there, it seemed a lonely way to die. To end up here in this rundown ward cut off from the outside world and far from home.

Like all war reporters, Mafouz and I had faced moments when death seemed almost certain. It went with the job. War could be exotic, high octane. In that sense it was like 'drinking from a very dangerous cup,' as Jeremy Bowen, the BBC's great foreign correspondent once put it. Sometimes it could be an addictive cocktail of adrenaline, horror and fun. Afterwards, just like any hangover, the bitter nausea of fear was quickly forgotten and only the excitement of the party remembered. It'll never happen to me, was the prevailing outlook. It's probably safe to say that Raffaele Ciriello thought the same way.

That same day after we left the hospital, Manara Square where Ciriello had been shot was the scene of a killing of another kind, when angry Palestinians strung up the corpse of a young man said to have collaborated with the Israelis. With blood staining his face and bare chest, the body of Raed Naem Odeh dangled upside-down from a metal pylon for hours before it was finally taken down. A resident of al-Amari camp, the young Palestinian had been shot dead by al-Aqsa Brigade militiamen who suspected him of being an informer for Israeli forces in an operation that targeted a senior Brigade member.

Ciriello and the young alleged Palestinian informer had been dead a few weeks by the time Operation Defensive Shield began to fully descend on Ramallah; two early casualties and an ominous warning of the bloodletting to come as the assault cranked up to full speed. Perhaps remembering Ciriello and seeking safety in numbers, but also because Mafouz was by now desperately needing to file his pictures from al-Amari, we decided to try and make our way to the Reuters office that occupied the fourth floor of a tower block in central Ramallah. Getting there was a series of heartstopping cat-and-mouse sprints between tanks and APCs parked at intersections. By now I had become almost obsessed with the threat of snipers; it seemed like only a matter of time before one of us would be hit by the countless bullets that seemed to criss-cross between the buildings that we passed.

At the Reuters office, where Mafouz was well known, we found clusters of journalists hunkered down having also decided to seek sanctuary from the dangers outside. But even here it wasn't entirely safe. No sooner had Mafouz started to edit and transmit his pictures than Israeli soldiers fired volleys of machine-gun fire at what the army later claimed were Palestinian snipers in the building. For over an hour reporters, camera crews and photographers found themselves crawling around on the floor or kept their backs to the thickest walls as bullets crashed repeatedly off the building. At no time while we were there did we see any evidence of snipers. One cameraman attempting to film from the building was shot at by soldiers whose powerful binoculars could have left them in no doubt that photographers, not snipers, were inside. At one point during a lull in the rounds whacking against the office walls, we tentatively peered out and saw a Palestinian woman below us being shot at as she attempted to cross the street, despite carrying a white flag. Had she also been mistaken for a sniper?

Later a senior officer insisted that no journalists had been targeted. What he said was clearly untrue. What's more, if the army was prepared to brazenly lie about this, then what else, we wondered, were they also willing to distort? A case in point that came to light in the following days were the circumstances surrounding the deaths of five Palestinian policemen whose bodies were found in a third-floor room of a building that housed the Cairo Amman Bank in Ramallah. The Israelis insisted that the men were victims of a gun battle that ensued around the building in which two of their own soldiers had been wounded. But eyewitnesses who made it into the building, like reporter Anthony Shadid of the *Boston Globe*, found a scene that suggested a very different take on events: 'Three had been shot in the head at close range – one of them had two bullet wounds to the back of his skull. Blood and bullet holes about three feet off the floor lined the walls behind them, the height of someone kneeling.' Palestinian Red Crescent paramedics, who took the bodies away and had seen more than a few gunshot victims in their work, told Shadid what they thought had happened. 'They were shot point-blank,' said Mohammed Awad, one of the paramedics. 'This is an execution.'

Shortly afterwards Anthony Shadid was himself shot as he and his Palestinian colleague Said al-Ghazali made their way in the direction of Arafat's compound from Ramallah hospital. Both were wearing flak jackets with TV displayed prominently in red tape on their backs. Despite this, Shadid believes an Israeli soldier who mistook him for a Palestinian shot him. The sniper's bullet entered Shadid's left shoulder, tore off part of his vertebrae, and exited through his right shoulder, leaving 12 pieces of shrapnel lodged in the journalist's upper body.

Along with similar eyewitness accounts, again testimonies gathered by human rights group B'Tselem from Israeli soldiers themselves provide some of the most telling insights into the behaviour and actions of those troops deployed on the ground at the time.

> The town was under curfew. The troops on guard duty saw a person moving about 100 metres away from them. It was 7.30 p.m. and was dark outside . . . the troops reported that he was holding something large in his hand; one of the soldiers claimed it was a weapon. From that distance and in the dark, it was impossible to tell for sure. . . . They waited a long time, almost a minute. Then the commanders ordered them to fire eight rounds at the guy. . . . One of the soldiers saw the person lying on the ground. He was clearly dead. When we came down, we realised that what we had thought was the ground was actually the roof of a two-and-a-half-storey house. We went onto the roof and saw a man lying there with a wrench in his hand.

Across Ramallah, as the Israelis began to enforce a blanket curfew, ordinary Palestinians became the target for the soldiers' anger. It was early morning on March 29 when Ahmad Nimer was woken by Israeli soldiers raiding his apartment block and ordering everyone in the building to gather in the top-floor apartment.

There were eight of us in the small room, including an eight-month-old baby and an eight-year-old child. The soldiers refused to allow us to make phonecalls and ordered us not to speak. They threatened that if there was any movement around the building we would be shot dead. We were kept in the room for two days without electricity and prevented from making contact with the outside world. During this time, around 20 soldiers used the house as a base. Snipers were placed on the roof. I discovered later that the snipers had killed my neighbour as she tried to cross the street to collect her baby from a nearby house.

Belongings smashed, rooms used as toilets covered in urine and excrement, jewellery, mobile phones and money stolen, including in one instance 50 shekels from a child's pocket money piggy bank – Israeli troops might have been there to 'root out terrorists' but they were also on a rampage of looting, wanton destruction and terror. Not that those in the corridors of power from Washington to London and elsewhere took much notice. All eyes after all were focused on the fate of Yasser Arafat, as tanks and giant Israeli army D-9 armoured bulldozers smashed their way into his compound and pitched battles raged in the surrounding streets.

From the beginning, the grey-green Merkava tanks had kept up a barrage on the compound from different sides. Some in Irsal Street fired on the western wall, while others closer to Manara Square lobbed shells onto the southern end of the 'Moqata'a,' as Arafat's compound was known. Having destroyed the two outer walls, the tanks lumbered over the rubble into the compound itself. As Israeli soldiers poured in and began searching the main building room by room, there was no sign of Arafat.

Along with some close associates the Palestinian leader had retreated to a windowless room in a limestone three-storey building to the north of the main structure. From inside this virtual tomb, Arafat could only sit, wait and listen to the boom of the Israeli tank shells slamming into the building around him. Yet still the wily old operator managed somehow to get out a message which was broadcast on al-Jazeera and other channels. 'They want me a prisoner, an exile, or a dead man, but I tell them I want to be a *shaheed*,' the 72-year-old leader insisted. Then he repeated the last word three times with dramatic effect, his voice tailing off slowly: '*shahid, shahid, shahid.*'

As Arafat remained under siege and his message was aired, Israeli soldiers would mockingly singsong 'shahid, shahid, shahid.' As curfew was called each evening, they would mimic Arafat's familiar address to the Palestinian people providing their own version of the message: 'O heroic people, curfew is declared. Those who violate it will be shahid, shahid, shahid.' The curfew lasted almost a week before there was any temporary lifting of the restrictions on movement. Palestinians, who had been under round-the-clock incarceration in their homes, came out to grab what food they could, bury their dead and try to comprehend the levels of destruction around them. 'Is the curfew over, have they really gone?' other journalists and I were asked time and again as people began to venture out onto the streets. Both Mafouz and myself had spent many days unable to venture out. Most journalists had decided to stay inside Ramallah rather than leave and have no chance of returning while the curfew was in place. Now that it was temporarily lifted we went out to meet Ramallah's citizens who had lived in terror for days. Even now, there was the occasional desultory pop–pop of small arms fire, causing the hopeful shoppers to visibly wince, as Israeli mop-up operations continued against the last remnants of resistance from Palestinian militiamen.

Slowly the full extent and scale of the Israeli military whirlwind that had passed through Ramallah's communities was being realised. Above all else the myth of Israel's 'restraint' had been exposed by the viciousness of its army. The soldiers had left no stone unturned or missed any opportunity to cause as much damage as possible to the infrastructure of civilian life. 'It's a scene that is repeating itself in hundreds of Palestinian offices taken over by the IDF for a few hours or days in the West Bank,' reported the Israeli daily, Ha'aretz. 'Smashed, burned and broken computer terminals heaped in piles and thrown into yards, server cabling cut, hard disks missing, telephone exchanges that disappeared or were vandalised . . . and it's all in rooms full of smashed furniture, torn curtains, broken windows . . . and here and there the soldiers left obscene graffiti or letters full of hatred.'

The IDF admitted that its troops had engaged in overly destructive behaviour in Ramallah but denied that they had been ordered to do so from the top. One senior Israeli military source, however, was not so convinced, as he admitted to a reporter from Ha'aretz: 'It was not an order from above, but that's how it was understood in the field. The infantry, both the conscripts and the reservists who accompanied the intelligence teams, understood they were allowed, indeed expected, to destroy the property in the offices.' Given such an understanding it was hardly surprising that the thin line between officially sanctioned seizing of the spoils of war and outright looting was frequently blurred.

During the siege of Arafat's compound, the commander of an elite Israeli unit transferred 23 Land Rover jeeps from the courtyard of the compound to a base set up to collect the spoils from the campaign, and from there on to his own unit's logistical base. The IDF denied all this was looting, claiming instead that the taking of the jeeps was justified on the premise that they were being used to conduct 'criminal activities.' At Ramallah city hall, also ransacked and its second floor burned, tax receipts, building permits and other documents vital to governing the city disappeared. That many important land deeds were destroyed was not by chance. Successive Israeli governments had after all been able to confiscate Palestinian property on the grounds that the owner possessed no written records or papers verifying possession. Without vital civil records the Israeli government would again claim that the Palestinians were incapable of governing themselves. But if the material cost to Ramallah and other West Bank communities was bad enough, then the human cost was appalling.

At Ramallah hospital, the temporary lifting of the curfew meant other priorities, like the digging of a mass grave in the car park as fast as possible so they could bury the dead that had piled up after days of siege. The mortuary had not been big enough to hold all the dead of the last five days. Until then, the Israeli army had prevented proper burials from taking place, perhaps realising that the funerals could turn into yet more riots and resistance.

We watched as 18 bodies were carried into the hospital car park in white plastic bags smeared with blood. Each was marked with an identification number and name in the hope that their families could give them a proper burial some time in the future. One was a woman shot in the neck by a sniper just the day before, 50 yards from the hospital. Abu Ali, one of the gravediggers, said he didn't want to use the precious time during the lull in fighting to restock food supplies for his family because the *shahid* came before anything else. As the corpses were carried out they were put on the ground in rows for traditional Muslim burial prayers. Just before they were moved to their temporary grave, one woman arrived and started to open the white bags to see the face of her son for the last time. Another woman was looking for her husband, until one of her children shouted, 'Here it is, I can read his name on the bag.'

So much death in such a short time – and it was far from over. As the base for Yasser Arafat and the PA, Ramallah had predictably been the first to take a pounding under Operation Defensive Shield, but already even worse stories were beginning to emerge from other besieged towns and refugee camps – places like Jenin and Bethlehem.

From Jenin in particular, which had always been a bastion of the intifada, resistance had been fierce against the Israeli assault, and truly terrible things had gone on there. 'Don't talk to me about the intifada. Those days are over. This is not an uprising, this is now a war. We may not have tanks and planes, but we have our blood, and with that our victory is certain,' a young Palestinian had insisted to me one afternoon during a lull in a gun battle around Ramallah's Manara Square.

So much blood had already been spilled. How much more would it take, and just what did he mean by victory? There were other questions too that needed answers, not just about the tactics employed by the Israelis, but about the failings of the Palestinian leadership. Why had they not acted to prevent the mass suffering of their people? Where were they when their people needed them most? If resistance was what they wanted, why then leave a few lightly armed PA men to hopelessly fight it out in a running battle? If preventing a rise in the violence and avoiding civilian casualties was their intention, why no concerted political attempt to make that policy clear and consistent among those same Palestinians active in the streets? The intifada seemed rudderless, driven by a momentum of its own, without direction or objectives. It was a dangerous vacuum, easily exploited by the Israelis and those Palestinians who saw killing Israelis as the intifada's sole objective.

During another temporary lifting of curfew in Ramallah around that time, I watched one afternoon as Palestinian policemen fired in the air as the latest victims, wrapped in flags, were carried on stretchers from a mosque to the local cemetery. Nearby, just visible in the sea of faces, was a toddler sitting on his father's shoulders, holding up a toy gun. 'This can only mean more martyrs, more suicide bombers, perhaps even my own son's life in the name of the intifada,' the man told me. His voice was not angry, but resigned. 'What did Sharon achieve by sending the tanks here, except to cause more pain?' the man asked. 'Why did they bother to come at all?'

Manger Square, Bethlehem, April 2002

They appeared suddenly from a doorway. The menacing click of their rifles being cocked and pointed in our direction stopped us in our tracks. 'Get in here, move now, or we will shoot,' shouted one of the Israeli soldiers as they pushed Mafouz, a Japanese photographer, and myself inside the narrow stairwell of a dilapidated building in Bethlehem's Manger Square. Haggard and hollow-eyed, there was no mistaking the soldiers' fatigue and edginess. About a dozen khaki-clad young men moved nervously around the building, their boots crunching the broken glass and rubble littering the floor as they peered out of windows, weapons at the ready. Most had their guns trained on the Church of the Nativity 50 yards away. It is said Jesus was born there. But that day when we arrived it was where up to 200 people, among them armed Palestinian fighters as well as civilians, remained barricaded inside after the Israelis had stormed into Bethlehem days before.

'Put your cameras on the ground, hands behind your heads and face the wall,' a young fair-haired Israeli captain ordered us abruptly. I knew that for myself and the Japanese photographer things would probably work out fine, but I was worried about what might become of Mafouz. He was Palestinian after all, and fairly well known to the IDF as a man forever slipping into places and documenting things they would rather the world didn't see. As we faced the wall, hands on our heads, I turned slightly to see Mafouz give me a knowing look that said, 'you do the talking.' The more I could keep the officer's attention, the less chance they would ask Mafouz anything, and with any luck we might be quickly sent on our way. After a few minutes of questioning to which I gave most of the answers, and some cursory searching of our camera gear, the young captain's tone changed and we were invited to sit down. 'We have to be careful. The terrorists sometimes pretend to be journalists, and this is a closed military area off limits to you,' he warned, with that now familiar refrain. 'Can I offer you something to drink before we escort you out?' he asked almost apologetically, before his words were drowned out by the clatter of machine-gun fire from a soldier crouched at a nearby window. The belt of bullets feeding the soldier's gun jumped furiously as a confetti of spent cartridge cases fell to the floor. 'You see, the terrorists are still around. You're lucky that they or we didn't shoot you,' the officer said nonchalantly, as he placed three cans of Coca-Cola in front of us. Five minutes later, having drunk the Coca-Cola in record time, the three of us were escorted by some of the Israeli soldiers away from Manger Square and the besieged Church of the Nativity.

Our failure to get inside the church to cover what had become the big story of the moment, and the latest chapter in Operation Defensive Shield, had become something of an obsession. The encounter with the Israeli unit was just the latest in a series of touch-and-go moments since we'd slipped into Bethlehem's streets a few days before. As ever, journalists had officially been forbidden from entering the city, but you would never have guessed it from the small clusters of reporters edging their way nervously around the stone-paved lanes full of crushed family cars and the tell-tale signs of tank tracks. 'Bethlehem tours departing daily. Rachel's Tomb, Manger Square and, if you're really lucky, the Church of the Nativity,' joked one TV cameraman as we arrived one morning at the rendezvous point on the city's outskirts from where it was possible – if risky – to slip past the Israeli patrols into this famous biblical arena.

Until a few years before, a real army of tour guides had worked Bethlehem's historic sites and shrines. It was a place I had visited many times in the past, without ever really falling for its reputed charms. To me it was rather nondescript and had something of a forlorn air about it. It struck me as sad and shabby, like a spaghetti western town, complete with the tacky tourist trappings you would expect of what was said to be the birthplace of Christ – although historians and archaeologists disagreed over the veracity of that claim. During the years of the first intifada, tourists undaunted by the stone-throwing had come by the busload, stumbling off the coaches into the bright sunlight and chased by packs of Palestinian street urchins selling picture postcards. Souvenir shop owners would usher the dazed pilgrims into their cavernous little stores laden with battery-lit baby Jesus figures and mother-of-pearl Nativity scenes, while offering coffee or tea and a seat in the shade away from the sapping heat of the sun. But slowly Bethlehem began to die. The tourists would continue to come and look around the Church of the Nativity, but afterwards they would quickly return to their buses and leave. They no longer wanted to browse the trinket shops, didn't have time for a meal, or to stay overnight in a local hotel. Bethlehem had become just too edgy and the town's tourist industry and Palestinian economy earned less and less. The final nail in the coffin came with the eruption of the al-Aqsa intifada, as Bethlehem gradually became a battlefield. Flanked by the Omar Mosque at one end, and the Church of the

Nativity at the other, Manger Square by then had the feel of Snipers'
Alley in war-torn Sarajevo.

It was in the half-light just before a chill dawn on April 2, when
Israeli armour and infantry fanned out into Bethlehem's old city in the
latest phase in Sharon's invasion of the West Bank. Waiting for the
Israelis in the narrow streets were a few dozen fighters from the al-Aqsa
Brigades and Tanzim led by Ibrahim Abayat and Jihad Ja'ariea, armed
with Kalashnikov and M-16 rifles. Realising they had neither the
weapons nor manpower to resist the advancing tanks and armoured
carriers, 29-year-old Abayat ordered his Tanzim gunmen to spread out
across the old city in a harassing action aimed at picking off the Israeli
infantry. Hugely outnumbered, the Palestinians' rearguard tactics rapidly turned into a running retreat, the Tanzim guerrillas scurrying through
the old city's deserted marketplace pausing only to return fire at the
Israelis in pursuit. Weary and wet through, the gunmen tried to regroup
in Bethlehem's Syrian Orthodox Church, where one of their fighters was
shot dead by the Israelis as terrified nuns and priests looked on.
Strategic options were running out for Abayat, who ordered his men to
move towards the Church of the Nativity. There they found the door
lock on the Franciscan cloister had already been shot off and the Tanzim
men pushed their way in. 'Please put down your guns,' the priests inside
urged, asking that the fighters respect the sanctity of the church.
Though angered by such an infringement, the monks and Christian clergymen were under a religious obligation to allow Abayat's men to stay.
Within minutes the Tanzim were ensconced inside the basilica alongside
fighters from Hamas and the PA, as well as many civilians who had
sought refuge from the fighting. It would be 39 days before most of
them would be able to step into the sunlight again, during which time
everyone from the Vatican to the CIA would be involved in the protracted negotiations over what to do with them.

Little had changed it seemed since back in the fourth century when
Emperor Constantine the Great had built the first basilica around the
grotto marking Christ's birthplace. Almost from that moment, the
fortress-like site became one of the world's most fought over holy
places, involving a succession of armies including Muslim and Crusader
forces. In the end it was these schisms that finally led to a shared custodianship of the building between the three Christian communities: the
Armenian, Roman Catholic and Greek Orthodox Churches.

But even with this arrangement in place, spats between clergymen from the three denominations over such trivial things as cleaning rights and ownership of keys continued to break out. According to an 1852 Ottoman diktat, all three communities had to be given a key to the lock on the front door of the church. In 2002 the Greeks upset the others when they changed the lock one night under cover of darkness. They argued that the diktat granted the others keys but not the right to use them. By now though such petty disagreements over custodianship were the least of Bethlehem's worries. The birthplace of the 'prince of peace' had become the backdrop for a much more serious confrontation, pitching Palestinian guerrillas against the might of the IDF as it rolled into the town. Bethlehem was now fixed in the Israeli crosshairs, and the stand-off at the Church of the Nativity was already a few days old when Mafouz and I arrived.

The weaponry deployed by the Israelis was staggering. Apart from the heavy tanks, sophisticated surveillance equipment like airborne drones fitted with powerful cameras, and remote-controlled sniper rifles fixed to cranes overlooking Manger Square, gave them complete tactical superiority over the few lightly armed Palestinian gunmen. As the hours, days and ultimately weeks passed, those inside the church could only sit and wonder what would become of them should they step from behind the cold stone walls of the basilica. Only the religious symbolism of the site stood between the Palestinian gunmen and an all-out Israeli assault. Already the bodies of seven Palestinians – alleged collaborators – lay strewn around the streets in central Bethlehem along with other victims of the Israeli attack.

Among them was Samir Ibrahim Salam, the Church of the Nativity's bell ringer. Bethlehem's residents are said to have always known by the tolling bells when a mass was underway, when a couple was getting married, or when somebody had died and was to be buried. Samir Ibrahim Salman had a different chime for each one. According to those who knew him, the quietly devout 45-year-old Palestinian Christian was only interested in taking care of the church and spent most of his time in its gloomy interior. It was only a few days into the siege when Salman had run from the basilica. No one really knows why, but almost instantly he was shot in the chest by Israeli snipers, his body slumping onto the street just a few steps from the church. 'He was a simple man. He never harmed anyone,' said a relative, Anton Salman, who spoke by mobile telephone from inside the church after the shooting.

While the Israelis had cut off the electricity supply, they ensured that mobile phone networks continued to operate in an effort to keep open some channel of communication with those sheltering in the basilica. In every other way, however, the IDF was determined to keep up the pressure, often using psychological warfare techniques to wear down the gunmen and those civilians who had chosen to sit it out with them. Loudspeakers were set up and a barrage of sounds, including the thump of explosions, rumble of tanks and bizarre animal noises all added to the terror of those besieged.

Outside, things were not much better for Bethlehem's 150,000 citizens also under lockdown in the city centre, two surrounding villages and three refugee camps. In the town's Al Fawaghreh quarter, around the narrow Najajaragh Street leading to the central market, some of the fiercest battles were still being fought between Israeli soldiers and the handful of Palestinian gunmen still on the loose around Bethlehem. The labyrinthine streets felt claustrophobic, and inching our way along them towards Manger Square it seemed impossible not to collide head-on with an Israeli patrol.

The constant thump of metal shop fronts and gates being blown open by the soldiers, and their warning shouts to anyone inside during their house-to-house searches, echoed off the buildings like surround-sound. Row after row of cars parked in these neighbourhoods, including one bearing the UN insignia, had been crushed by advancing tanks that had squeezed through the lanes. With only inches to spare between their armour-plated sides and adjacent walls, the tanks had shorn off shop fronts, doors and anything else that protruded. In what until a few days ago had been a busy marketplace, red tiles blown from the roofs lay strewn across the wooden stalls. The hissing sound of water escaping from burst pipes and the smell of rotting, uncollected rubbish wafted down the streets on the breeze.

'Stay well clear of that canister,' warned Mafouz, pointing to an old propane gas cylinder lying on its side just off Manger Square. 'I've heard that some are rigged as booby-trap bombs,' he explained. Nothing, it seemed, had escaped the bullets, including many religious statues peppered with holes like target figures in a fairground shooting gallery. Here and there, I occasionally spotted Palestinians furtively peeking out from behind the curtains billowing from the smashed windows of their homes. 'I'm afraid to let you come inside because the soldiers might see you and come back later,' cried Ratibah Abdullah from the flat where she, her husband and four children had been stuck for a week. Eventually plucking up the courage to open her front door, she led us into a dark, damp, communal staircase that was littered with mattresses and blankets. 'This is where we have been sleeping. Now we have run out of food and the water is bad. What are we to do?' Ratibah asked, her eyes moist with tears. Inside her apartment the carpet was covered in broken glass and plaster, the walls pockmarked by bullets and shrapnel. 'How can we sleep here? We never know when the shooting will start again, all we can do is wait and pray,' she said.

Suddenly from the street outside there was the sound of soldiers' voices. For what seemed an eternity they inched their way past. Standing on the staircase we all held our breath, and I watched as Ratibah turned ashen with fear. Instinctively her children picked up on their mother's nervousness and cowered closer together on some sodden blankets draped over the stairs. After the soldiers had gone, Mafouz and I quickly returned to the streets outside. The crackle of gunfire reverberating across Bethlehem and the occasional thump of a heavy shell landing nearby were further reminders of Israeli determination to crush any resistance without mercy.

As in Ramallah, the Israeli soldiers engaged in the Bethlehem operation also seemed preoccupied with destroying or damaging as much Palestinian Authority property as possible. According to one soldier's account, referred to by Josh Hammer, the Jerusalem bureau chief for *Newsweek* magazine and author of the powerful book, *A Season in Bethlehem: Unholy War in a Sacred Place*, Israeli reservists vandalised cars and ransacked offices belonging to the PA. Car tyres were slashed or shot out, and office windows were smashed. The soldier also claimed that thousands of toys gifted by a humanitarian organisation and destined for Palestinian children were stolen by the IDF.

For those journalists, human rights activists and aid workers trying to make sense of what was going on inside Bethlehem, their own wartime tour of the beleaguered town usually began with a visit to Beit Jala hospital on its outskirts. As the only public hospital in the district, Beit Jala had around 20 fully qualified doctors but no chest or neurosurgical specialists. Hardly ideal at the best of times, this lack now posed a serious problem given the kinds of wounds the hospital's doctors were having to treat. As if that wasn't bad enough, according to local Palestinians it was only the perpetual presence of international TV crews that had so far deterred the army from raiding the hospital premises.

At nearby Beit Sahour medical centre, a little more off the beaten track, it was a different story. Already the IDF had made numerous 'visits' to the clinic to identify or arrest men taken there after being wounded. By now staff at both centres were increasingly shocked at the wounds sustained by those the ambulance crews had managed to bring in. 'It is difficult to look at such things,' Murad Amro, a 24-year-old volunteer nurse at Beit Jala hospital, admitted to me one afternoon, as we passed a trolley on which lay the body of an elderly man. It was indeed a terrible sight. A heavy calibre bullet had blown off almost the man's entire head from the nose upward. 'Here in normal times in the casualty department, we have more than 100 patients a day, yet now when we are at war, it is almost empty because the ambulances can't get to most of the wounded inside the town,' explained Amro, who was a fourth-year nursing student at Bethlehem University.

'The drivers only managed to get two casualties into the hospital yesterday by hiding them under some corpses the Israelis had given them permission to recover.' He told me how the hospital had opened a telephone medical helpline for those with wounded or sick who were unable to leave their homes. 'One woman called us after her husband had been shot and was bleeding badly from a femur wound, but later she called back to say he had died,' Amro continued. 'Now with the electricity cut and people unable to recharge their mobile phones we have fewer and fewer calls. Who knows how many people out there are in desperate need of help,' he added, shaking his head in disbelief. The young nurse was right, it was impossible at the time to tell how many of Bethlehem's citizens were suffering in this way.

Slowly, though, their desperate stories began to filter out. One account involved a family who had been forced to lock their six children in the bathroom to protect them from seeing the rotting corpses of a 60-year-old woman and her 38-year-old son. Both had been killed by Israeli gunfire and the army had subsequently refused permission for medical personnel to remove the bodies.

As I talked with Murad Amro, some of the latest victims fighting to survive gunshot wounds arrived by ambulance. One man was wheeled in surrounded by paramedics working frantically to keep him alive. There was a gaping hole in his lower abdomen and what looked like part of his intestines hung in a bloody knotted lump down his left side. From a nearby bed another patient, hooked up to a series of drips and also recovering from a bullet wound, clasped her boyfriend's hand and watched the Palestinian man's fight for life as he lay on the blood-soaked trolley.

Kate Edwards was not a Palestinian, neither was that her real name. An Australian now living in Manchester in the UK, her first ever week in the Middle East had come to a painful end a few days earlier while she was protesting on Bethlehem's streets with the pro-Palestinian International Solidarity Movement (ISM). 'It probably doesn't make much difference now, but I don't think it would help me with the Israelis to have my name all over the newspapers,' she told me, before going on to describe how she had been wounded. 'We were marching to some of the areas under curfew, trying to take food and medicines to people, when the Israelis opened fire,' she recalled. 'They were using stun grenades, which make a loud bang. When I felt the pain I just thought it was a splinter; it wasn't till I was dragged clear I realised I had been shot in the stomach,' she said.

Back outside on the streets, more and more local Palestinians under curfew were taking their own enormous risks to feed their families. In the Al Fawaghreh quarter other journalists and I would often watch citizens of all ages run the gauntlet of Israeli fire. Laden with bottles of water and thin blue plastic carrier bags stuffed with bread and other basics, they would hesitate on street corners waiting for what they felt was the right moment to dash across the exposed street as bullets whizzed past them. It was impossible not to think of Sarajevo and those other Balkan towns and cities where years earlier I had similarly watched ordinary people forced into such extraordinary rituals in order to survive. Why was this happening again? Was the world really that impotent when confronted with such desperate and shameful images? How could we let people face a life and death lottery like this, all for the sake of a few things to eat? I don't remember much about it now, except that I was making my own dash across Bethlehem's streets one afternoon when that gamble almost lost me everything and the world suddenly went black.

It was just off Pope Paul VI Street after I had launched into a short sprint that I heard a second or two of gunfire and an enormous crash above my head. The next memory I have is of lying propped against a wall looking at the figures bending over me through what seemed like the distorted glass of a goldfish bowl.

'David, David,' I heard someone call me, before telling me to 'lie still' and 'take it slow.' I was probably unconscious before I hit the ground, those that witnessed what happened told me afterwards. I had just started to run when a burst of heavy 50-calibre machine-gun fire from an Israeli tank slammed into the wall of the building above me. Hugh chunks of masonry gave way under the impact of the armour-piercing bullets, tumbling to the street below, where a sizeable lump hit me on the left side of my head and knocked me out cold. Fortunately, almost instantly, a few colleagues rushed forward and dragged me out of sight of the Israeli gunners. Among those that helped bring me round was Ben Wedeman, CNN's Cairo Bureau Chief, who had been filming nearby.

Wedeman was a well known face around the Middle East's hotspots. I had met him a few times before while working in the occupied territories and South Lebanon, and I would later bump into him again while covering the fall of the Iraqi cities Kirkuk and Mosul, during the first few weeks of the war there. A few years earlier, in October 2000, Wedeman himself had fallen foul of crossfire that resulted in a far more serious injury, when he was hit in the back near the waist by a live round at the Karni border crossing between Gaza and Israel.

'You sure you're okay?' he asked, a short time after I unsteadily got back to my feet in the Bethlehem street that day. The size of the lump on my skull was of cartoon character proportions, but remarkably the skin hadn't been broken and left little bleeding. 'Get it checked out, you've got to be careful about delayed concussion,' he advised, as just on cue I felt a wave of nausea course through me.

Back in Jerusalem later that day, I called the *Sunday Herald*'s foreign desk to let them know when I would be filing my copy, and mentioned to Louise Shannon, the Deputy Foreign Editor about the bang on the head. 'Probably best not to mention it to the boss,' I suggested, worried that I might be grounded, or worst still told to come home in the middle of what was the biggest story in the Israeli–Palestinian conflict for years.

Unable to sleep that night back in my room at the Jerusalem Hotel, I lay propped up in bed flicking through the television channels with my head pounding. One of the satellite channels was showing Fashion Television (FTV) which ran an endless parade of beautiful models strolling up and down the catwalks of Milan, Paris, London and elsewhere, dressed in the most elegant and sometimes bizarre clothes. It was a humid night and having opened the window instead of running the noisy air conditioning, the sounds from outside drifted into the room.

Every so often, just audible in the distance, came the dull thud of an explosion. Leaning out from the second-floor window it was just possible to see the occasional flash or tracer trail light up the sky somewhere over towards Bethlehem. Closing the window, I turned to find the fashion models still strutting their stuff on the catwalk. Not for the first time I thought to myself what an incongruous world we live in. For a moment I imagined those trapped at home in Bethlehem or in the Church of the Nativity. For them right now the simple pleasure of watching television or being able to sleep in peace without fear of snipers or the crash of bullets and shells, would have seemed like the ultimate luxury. Yet, here I was barely a 20-minute drive away, able to do just that.

The next day I was back in Bethlehem with Mafouz. We had come to cover the arrival of a small relief convoy of vehicles from the International Committee of the Red Cross (ICRC), who were evacuating civilian wounded and sick, as well as delivering basic essentials to families who had been trapped indoors under curfew for over a week now. 'We've had so many requests for assistance, but obviously conditions inside the church are an increasing cause for concern,' said Graham Leman, a straight-talking Liverpudlian ICRC delegate. We watched as the Red Cross workers helped load stretchers into an ambulance. On one stretcher was a local woman suffering from renal failure and in need of kidney dialysis, and on another a woman who was pregnant.

There was a sad and desperate moment when the menfolk from two Palestinian families who had always been good neighbours began fighting each other over the foodstuffs the Red Cross were distributing, before Leman managed to calm the situation and reassure them that there would be more coming soon. 'We're trying to gain access to the church but so far it has been a no-go,' admitted Leman when I pushed him for more information. 'You probably know as much as we do.'

It wasn't until April 23 that the first round of face to face negotiations to end the stand-off at the church began across the road in Manger Square's 'Peace Centre.' The Israeli negotiating team was led by Lt. Colonel Lior, the Palestinians by former PLO commander Salah Taamri. At that stage the two sides were far from any compromise deal, and the Israelis simply reiterated Sharon's demand that Ibrahim Abayat, his Tanzim and other Palestinian gunmen on Israel's wanted list face either trial in Israel or deportation. In the coming weeks, the two sides would meet many more times to try and come up with a solution to the crisis.

Their wrangling invariably took place at the Peace Centre, just a few yards from where Mafouz and I had briefly been held by the Israeli soldiers some weeks earlier.

I remember asking the young Israeli officer, just before his men escorted us away from Manger Square, what he thought would happen to the 200 or so Palestinians holed up inside the Church of the Nativity. 'We Israelis understand the importance of religious sites like the basilica,' he answered. 'Yes, but what about the people inside?' I asked him again. 'Those who are innocent, I'm sure will come to no harm, but I cannot vouch for the safety of terrorists. Israel has had enough of terrorism once and for all,' he said with a shrug.

7

ROCKET THE CASBAH

'I had lots of satisfaction in Jenin, lots of satisfaction. It was like getting all the 18 years of doing nothing into three days.'

—Moshe Nissim ('Kurdi Bear'), D-9 bulldozer driver

Jenin, April 2002

For days the heavy, grey storm clouds had hung over the West Bank town like some omen of things to come. It was cold, damp and dark at 3.30 a.m. on Wednesday, April 3, when Brigadier-General Eyal Shlein relayed the order for the tanks and infantry to move in. Unlike a smaller operation a few months before, this time the Israelis would come from three directions. From the southeast and southwest, units from the elite Nahal and Golani Brigades trundled forward, their tank tracks chewing up the sodden ground. From the north, the 5th Infantry Brigade, comprised mainly of reservists and accompanied by a commando section, began their own cautious advance.

Ten days later, as the world still reeled in horror from the events that unfolded in the wake of their assault, I was to meet some of those Israeli soldiers in the ruins of their objective – Jenin refugee camp.

'I'm an old soldier, a paratrooper. This is my third war, including Yom Kippur and Beirut in 1982. The last 11 days of fighting here have been the worst I have ever seen,' Israel Caspi murmured as he sat down wearily among the other dirty and exhausted men of his reservist unit. Caspi was from the Israeli town of Herzlia. At 48 years old he was indeed an old soldier compared to those in their late twenties and thirties who made up the bulk of the reservists in the 5th Infantry. Whatever their age though, none of the men I met that day was typical of the Israeli soldiers I had so often encountered in the past. Gone was the usual swagger and confidence. Now I found sombre, introspective men, men clearly marked by the things they'd seen and done inside Jenin camp. The Israeli army would not forget the battle of Jenin in a hurry.

As for the Palestinians who lived, fought and died there, the struggle for the camp would quickly enter the annals of intifada folklore. 'This is the most terrible situation I can remember in my entire life,' said Khaled Amoudi, an 80-year-old Palestinian grandfather, who had lived in Jenin camp since his family was first made homeless during the 1948 Arab–Israeli war. As we spoke, standing on Jenin's outskirts, Israeli Apache and Cobra helicopter gunships clattered overhead on their way to pound more missiles into the crumbling camp. The old man told me how he and his wife Suda, along with some of their children and grandchildren, had decided to flee as the fighting intensified in their neighbourhood. 'Believe me when I say there were many dead in the street, and after a few days the smell was choking. What else could we do but leave?' Khaled said with a shrug. 'In 1967 we lost the West Bank, but now it's worse because we are losing so many of our people and everything we have,' the old man continued, barely able to hold back the tears. Khaled said that not a single house escaped the Israeli soldiers, describing how they blew them apart with grenades or shells without checking whether people were inside. Other houses he said were simply bulldozed. 'Who knows how many people were killed like this? For days now we have been worried about my daughter Lena and her family who are all missing. I can only pray they did not die this way,' Khaled said, his voice beginning to quiver. 'Many of our friends are missing, no one knows what happened to our neighbours. You can smell the dead, the whole camp is destroyed,' the old man went on, determined to make sure I fully understood what he had witnessed. 'We hear it is like Sabra and Shatila. Can you imagine what it was like for these people waiting days to die? At least in Sabra and Shatila the wounded were taken to hospital, but in Jenin they die because the Israelis deny them access to the hospital,' he said angrily.

The Israeli army had always known that crushing resistance in the Jenin refugee camp would be no pushover. According to an internal Fatah document seized by the Israelis the previous September, the camp's people were said to be 'ready for self-sacrifice with all their means.' The fact that the camp was home to the likes of Khaled Amoudi's family and 15,000 other Palestinians mattered little in the context of Ariel Sharon's Operation Defensive Shield. To Sharon, Jenin was nothing more than a 'nest of cockroaches' that needed to be cleaned out.

The 'capital of martyrs,' as some Palestinians called Jenin, was for the Israeli government a cancer on their doorstep. It was a sanctuary where the most wanted Palestinian bomb makers or 'engineers' of Islamic Jihad, Hamas and the al-Aqsa Martyrs' Brigades thrived and recruited. It was a bolthole for men like Mahmoud Tawalbe, who when not working in a record store, headed the local Islamic Jihad cell. Other senior Islamic Jihad activists, including Ali Suleiman al-Saadi and Thabet Mardawi, who had been the masterminds behind numerous strikes on Israelis, also lurked within the camp's confines.

It was the need to root out terrorists like these, Sharon insisted, that led him to deploy over 1,000 Israeli soldiers into the cauldron of Jenin camp that drizzly April morning. Among them were infantrymen Israel Caspi and Yoni Wolff. 'The camp was ready for war,' insisted First Lt.

Yoni Wolff, a 26-year-old reservist and platoon commander whose men were among the first to sweep down a hillside and enter the enclave from the south just after dawn. 'Every alley we walked down was booby-trapped, wires were connected to cars, rubbish bins, doors, closets, chairs, fridges, sports balls and weapons that were left behind,' Wolff recalled. Some of the bombs were massive, containing as much as 250 lbs of explosives, almost ten times the size of that used by the average suicide bomber.

It was the kind of situation every soldier dreads, fighting in a built-up area full of narrow passageways and flat roofs from which snipers and bombers could operate. 'The place was just one big bomb – women and children were sent out to put explosive devices on the streets, throw them at us, or act as spotters so the terrorists could fire at us. They were waiting for us everywhere,' Israel Caspi told me.

Wary of giving the Palestinians the 'propaganda coup' of mass civilian casualties, Major General Itzik Eitan, Israel's Chief of Central Command, had decided against air strikes and was confident his troops could take control of the camp in 48 to 72 hours. The General would quickly be proved wrong. Within hours the fighting became ferocious, often at very close quarters, house-to-house, window by window. Palestinian fighters moved from one building to another through a warren of tunnels they had dug in preparation for the Israeli attack. It was as if at times the men trying to kill the Israelis seemed invisible, Caspi said. Sometimes it took the Israelis a whole day to advance 100 yards. According to the infantrymen, the camp had become like a living malevolent creature, whose weapons were snipers and suicide bombers barely out of boyhood.

'Three times after killing Palestinians, men from my unit had to continue shooting at their bodies for 10 to 15 minutes to detonate the bombs they were carrying,' Caspi said, shaking his head in disbelief.

Like Khaled Amoudi and his family, much of the camp's civilian population had fled as the fighting closed around them. But even four days into the battle as many as 1,300 ordinary Palestinians remained trapped or unwilling to move. Around the camp Israeli soldiers using loudspeakers would order families to leave. 'People in the house get out now. We are coming in, get out now or we will shoot.' Sometimes those who ventured onto the street were shot anyway.

'My father came out of the house – he is an old man of 80 – and they shot him in the hand and leg,' said Jamal Ali Fayed, a 34-year-old science teacher. By the time Fayed had managed to get his wife and two children safely out of the camp and tried to return for his wounded father, he was unable to reach him in the chaos and panic. Hundreds of other families were also separated in the tumult.

At the Jenin Charitable Society's offices on the edge of the city those who had escaped the fighting were sleeping in corridors and on the floors of the building. On improvised notice boards messages from the new arrivals had been scrawled in the hope of reuniting loved ones. Once again here was another generation of Palestinians dispossessed and rootless, just as they had been so often throughout their history. Everyone that had fled had a tale to tell of what had gone on inside the camp. 'The Israelis gave us no opportunity to come out before they started going from house to house – burning, arresting men and shooting those trying to escape. I saw one man almost coming apart after being shot, even though he had his hands in the air and was giving himself up,' claimed Khaled Amoudi's wife, Suda.

For some of Jenin's inhabitants, the traumas of those first few days on top of years of repression and hardship quickly proved too much and psychologically tipped them over the edge. Writing in the Cairo-based English-language weekly *Al-Ahram* online, British journalist Jonathan Cook recounted the story of one man called Jamil Wardin, who was found wandering through fields in his underwear shouting aggressively at anyone who approached him.

> 'Crazy,' someone said. But what sent him crazy? Could it be the three nights he and his heavily pregnant wife, Areej, spent as the tanks wrecked the streets outside and Apache helicopters fired missiles from overhead? Or maybe it was his wife going into labour at midnight as the shelling reached its peak. Or was it trying to explain his wife's condition to the soldiers pointing their guns at him and screaming at him to go back indoors? Or perhaps it was watching his wife grow sicker through the night? Or carrying his wife, white flag in hand, out to the tanks at dawn to try to persuade them to let them go to hospital? Or maybe it was being made to strip in the street and lie on the ground with his wife, while soldiers discussed the significance of the 400 shekels in his trouser pockets. Or being separated from his wife and unborn baby at the time they needed him most. Or possibly it was the humiliation of sitting at the interrogation centre stripped to his underwear for many hours while waiting to be ques-

tioned. Then again, maybe it was the realisation that he had lost everything that was precious to him.

As the hours and days went by, the distinction between Palestinian fighters and petrified civilians became increasingly blurred as Israeli helicopters and tanks rained withering fire on the camp's central district.

By Thursday and Friday, April 11 and 12, eight days into the assault, I had made my way to a hillside farm overlooking the camp, from where I watched pairs of Israeli helicopters deliver their deadly salvoes. 'Be careful,' warned Moustafa Abdullah, a farmer, as we hid beneath the cover of some olive trees on the slopes around his land, watching the silhouettes of the gunships bank over the beleaguered camp and return in our direction. 'Yesterday when they passed over low they shot at us,' Moustafa said. Beneath us, explosion after explosion rumbled as rockets and tanks shells sent clouds of dust into the clear blue sky. Everywhere fires raged across neighbourhoods. What, I wondered, must it be like for those trapped under such an onslaught? It was impossible to imagine anyone surviving such a barrage.

According to the Israeli military, these helicopter strikes were carried out based on maps created from aerial photographs on which each building in the camp was numbered. Platoon commander Yoni Wolff said the helicopter-fired missiles were carefully guided to their targets in an effort to avoid civilian casualties. 'We would identify a room where snipers were and tell the helicopter pilot which house to hit. I would tell them to fire in the third window on the left and they would fire at the exact window they were firing from,' Wolff insisted. While it might all have sounded clinical and incisive, it was anything but. At the heart of the camp, in an area the size of several football fields, virtually every building was pulverised. If the first four days were a round-the-clock hell of helicopter missiles and tank shells, then the second phase of the assault relied on the awesome destructive power of the gigantic D-9 bulldozers that ploughed their way through whole neighbourhoods.

The Caterpillar D-9 is a fearsome machine. Towering 20 feet tall, and complete with armour weighing in at 60 tons, they were bigger than most of the concrete shanty houses they were sent in to destroy. As many as a dozen had been unleashed in the camp, cutting swathes through buildings and streets, crushing cars like cigarette packets and trundling over explosive booby-traps that would barely dent them.

It was the exploits of one Israeli army D-9 bulldozer driver called

Moshe Nissim – nicknamed 'Kurdi Bear' – that provided the most revealing insight into the real nature of IDF tactics inside the camp.

'The moment I drove the bulldozer into the camp, something switched in my head. I went mad. All the desperation, caused by my personal condition, just vanished at once,' admitted Nissim. Nissim was a self-confessed fanatical soccer fan and supporter of Jerusalem Beitar, the most politically oriented team in Israel and often associated with the country's right-wing and anti-Arab sentiments. By his own admission his life had been a mess for almost two years before he arrived in Jenin on active duty. Not only did he drink heavily, but he had been in debt and was suspended from his job as a senior inspector with the Jerusalem municipality after allegations that he and colleagues had accepted bribes from contractors and other business owners. A military reservist for 18 years, during which time he was 'constantly in jail' and 'just messed around,' Nissim had never operated a D-9 or demolished a building before he arrived in Jenin.

Having been shown by a friend how to 'drive forwards and make a flat surface,' Nissim then begged his battalion commander to give him a chance manning one of the bulldozers as the IDF pushed their way into camp. 'First thing I did was to tie on the Beitar Jerusalem soccer team flag. I had it prepared in advance. I wanted the family to be able to identify me. I told the family and the kids, you will see my bulldozer on television. When you see the Beitar flag that will be me.'

Nissim's first mission was to deliver food to some infantrymen who were under such intensive fire from the Palestinian resistance that a D-9 was the only way of reaching them. 'You couldn't tell where the charges were. They (the Palestinian fighters) dug holes in the ground and planted charges. You would just start driving, and you would hit a three-inch pipe, welded on both sides. As you touch them, they go off. Everything was booby-trapped . . . I saw a birdcage blow up in some pet shop where we opened a track. A flying birdcage. I felt sorry for the birds.'

On Tuesday, April 9, 13 Israeli soldiers – reservists from Yoni Wolff's and Israel Caspi's infantry unit – were blown to pieces in an elaborate ambush in one such booby-trapped building. That same day a Golani Brigade soldier was also shot dead. It was the deadliest single day of Israeli combat casualties since the end of the Lebanon war in 1985 and the mood among the IDF troops battling on the camp's streets hardened even further. Fuelled by whisky he had smuggled into the D-

9's armoured cabin, Moshe Nissim began a straight 75-hour-long
marathon of destruction. 'I had no mercy for anybody. I would erase
anyone with the D-9, just so that our soldiers wouldn't expose themselves to danger,' Nissim said.

While the bulldozers were meant to rumble up to a house and give
it a small thump to shake it and wait for those inside to come out before
tearing it down, this rarely happened. 'They were warned by loudspeaker to get out of the house before I came, but I gave no-one a
chance. I didn't wait. I didn't give one blow and wait for them to come
out. I would just ram the house with full power, to bring it down as fast
as possible,' Nissim said.

Like many Palestinians I spoke with who had fled the camp, Arwah
Abdullah, a 30-year-old mother of three young children, said there often
wasn't even any loudspeaker warning before Nissim and other drivers
crashed the 60-ton mechanical monster into their homes. 'They didn't
call out to us at all, but when the bulldozer rammed the house next to
ours, we just ran. I was crying, shouting for my babies, my mother.
Everything collapsed,' she said.

As the D-9s ground their way further into the heart of the camp they
levelled an area 200 yards square. Moshe Nissim would later jokingly
refer to it as building the 'Teddy' football stadium, a reference to the
ground at which his beloved Jerusalem Beitar team played in the Israeli
capital. 'Others may have restrained themselves, or so they say. Who are
they kidding? I didn't give a damn about the Palestinians, but I didn't
just ruin with no reason. It was all under orders,' Nissim insisted.
According to Human Rights Watch, under those orders the bulldozer
drivers levelled more than 140 buildings and severely damaged another
200 in the camp.

'I found joy with every house that came down, because I knew they
didn't mind dying, but they cared for their homes. If you knocked down
a house, you buried 40 or 50 people for generations. If I am sorry for
anything, it is for not tearing the whole camp down,' Nissim later boast-
ed. Though Moshe Nissim would never individually receive any medals
for his actions in the camp, his unit would later be awarded a citation
for 'outstanding service.'

Some Israeli soldiers did express concern as to how the Jenin operation was conducted and would go down in terms of international opinion. 'When the world sees the picture of what we had wrought, it will
be immensely damaging for us. The Palestinians in the camp are under-

going their own Masada battle,' an Israeli officer was quoted as saying in an article in *Ha'aretz*. Ever since the Jewish revolt against Rome in the first century a.d., Masada has been a symbol of freedom and courage to Jews. During the battle at Masada surrounded Jewish fighters held out for three years against the Romans before choosing mass suicide rather than surrender. For the hundred or so armed Palestinian fighters inside Jenin camp, however, their own determined resistance was finally beginning to falter against the sheer might of the Israeli assault. Like the Jews at Masada many of the Palestinians would also refuse to surrender.

Mahmoud Tawalbe, the Islamic Jihad leader on Israel's most wanted list, is said by Palestinians to have killed a number of Israeli soldiers during the street battles. Along with 50 other Islamic Jihad fighters Tawalbe held up the Israeli advance yard by yard, until he was crushed to death by falling masonry while trying to get close enough to a tank or D-9 bulldozer to plant explosives on its armour. Like many other Palestinians who died in the fighting his body was buried in Jenin's Martyrs Cemetery. Only a handful of fighters who survived made it out of the camp after slipping through the ring of Israeli tanks and troops. Among then was an Islamic Jihad 'engineer' who would only give his name as 'Omar' to journalist Jonathan Cook who interviewed him at a safe house while the young Palestinian was still on the run.

Omar told Cook that he was one of only a few dozen fighters not to die or 'emerge in plastic handcuffs' from the battle. Having lost his right arm while trying to throw a *kwa* – homemade bomb – at a tank during the earlier smaller incursion of Jenin by the Israelis some weeks before the main assault, Omar was only able to fire a revolver with his left hand during the latest street battles. At one stage towards the end of Cook's interview with the young Palestinian, Omar asked the reporter whether he thought doctors would be able to give him an artificial arm with fingers he could operate. When Cook replied that he didn't know and asked why, Omar's answer revealed much about how the endless cycle of violence in the Palestinian–Israeli conflict finds its own eye-for-an-eye dynamism. 'Because I want to be able to hold a heavy rifle again. That way I can kill more Israeli soldiers. It's that or become a suicide bomber,' Omar told him.

As Jenin's fighters ran out of ammunition and the Israelis consolidated their grip, I stood one afternoon on the outskirts of the camp watching the last Palestinians to emerge from the rubble being rounded up by Israeli troops. Most were filthy; many were gaunt and haunted-looking. 'same shit, different day' read the slogan on the T-shirt of one young Palestinian man as he yanked it up to his shoulders to prove he wasn't carrying a bomb underneath.

Rifles at the ready, the Israeli soldiers crouching some distance away behind an armoured personnel carrier were taking no chances, and ordered him to kneel by the roadside with his hands on his head. Behind the man, waiting in line for the call to come forward, were perhaps 30 more Palestinians.

A few days earlier during a similar round-up, the Israelis' inability to distinguish between combatants and civilians once again ended tragically. Sixty-three-year-old Fatih Shalabe told *Time* magazine reporter Matt Rees how he, his son Waddah and a neighbour's son, Abdel Karim Saadeh, were ordered by the soldiers to stand against a wall and raise their shirts. As they did so the Israeli soldiers immediately panicked, thinking the medical support corset that Abdel Karim wore to strengthen his bad back was in fact a bomb belt. Instantly the two young Palestinians were gunned down, while the elderly Fatih also fell to the ground for cover. Drenched in his son's blood he lay pretending to be dead until the Israeli patrol had moved on. 'I would have been luckier if I had died,' Fatih later told *Time* reporter Rees.

Any battlefield is a terrifying place. For those who have never encountered such a thing it's hard to imagine the effects fear can have. Even with the best trained soldiers in the world it often simply boils down to personal survival. 'You must be realistic and understand the dangers that existed in Jenin. These were people trying to kill us like they kill our wives and children in the centre of Israel,' Israel Caspi told me that day when I encountered his unit at the end of ten days fighting. 'On Thursday I took part in the capture of 36 of the most militant and dangerous fighters among the Palestinians, including the leader of Hamas in this part of the Samaria area,' said Caspi.

For days before their capture, Caspi claimed, the Palestinians were afraid the Israelis were going to kill them, and had been in touch with political pressure groups and human rights organisations outside in an attempt to save their own lives. 'In the end the 36 surrendered and 36 are now safe. We made them take off their shirts and trousers when we were looking for bombs, and we tied their hands and blindfolded them. But that was it, no one even hit them,' Caspi insisted.

If indeed that was the case, such kid-glove handling was rare. By April 15, a few days after the last shots from the resistance had died away, the Israeli army was forced by an Israeli Supreme Court decision to allow the Palestinian Red Crescent Society to enter the Jenin camp for the first time to retrieve bodies. The Red Crescent teams entered at around 7 a.m. and immediately encountered a body hanging out of a window of a smashed house. Then they found the body of a militia commander wanted by Israel and a woman in her fifties near the central square, followed by two more bodies of men on the northern edge of the camp. Close to a UN building, they found three corpses but could only remove one because the other two were wearing belts of explosives. The level of destruction and stench of the decomposing dead shocked even those team members used to such horrors. 'This is unbelievable. At least 75 percent of the camp has been destroyed, houses have been demolished, turning alleyways into wide streets to allow tanks to roll through them,' said Khaldoun Uweis, a Red Crescent worker with the team.

Tentatively, Palestinians began to emerge to assess the damage and look for missing loved ones. By now, journalists including myself had managed to slip into the camp, and I watched as many Palestinians stumbled aimlessly through the main square, their faces frozen in blank shock as if unable to believe what they were seeing. Where homes once stood, there were scenes resembling an earthquake epicentre. Slabs of concrete hung precariously from spiky steel girders. Bedding and clothing fluttered crazily from blasted balconies. In Jenin town the devastation was widespread, but not on the scale of the camp. There, the worst hit buildings were little more than pancaked heaps. Others had gaping holes with the tell-tale spatter marks of rockets scarring the smoke-blackened walls. Twisted pylons, rubble and spent bullet and shell cases littered the streets. The crushed carapaces of cars run over by tanks and bulldozers – now a trademark of Israeli incursions into the West Bank – bore testimony to the power of the Merkavas and D-9s. Standing in the camp, every so often the breeze brought the nauseating smell of the decomposing dead. Once encountered it's a smell you never forget. Sickeningly sweet and cloying, it seems to cling to your nostrils and clothes for hours afterwards.

As happened elsewhere during Operation Defensive Shield, those few homes almost untouched by fighting appeared to have been ransacked. As in Ramallah, Bethlehem and elsewhere, Jenin's residents said money, jewellery and other valuables had been stolen. Here and there in what remained of some rooms I saw Jewish Stars of David spray-painted on some walls and mirrors, and one resident showed reporters the shredded pages of a Koran. In one area I came across some Palestinians crowded around as a civilian bulldozer deployed to unearth bodies began to edge into the side of a hill. Whispers began that a dozen people had sought refuge inside a cave and that Israeli D-9s had toppled a house over the entrance while clearing the area, trapping everyone inside.

As the bulldozer bit at the dirt, a woman ran screaming to block its path. 'You are putting more earth on top of my brother!' she screamed, pointing to where the bulldozer had piled the debris it had taken from the hill.

In one alleyway we came across some Palestinian Red Crescent workers clearing away chopped-up human remains. The pieces of bone and mangled flesh, covered in flies and worms, were lifted gingerly by the masked workers and deposited inside a white plastic bag, before being loaded onto a trailer containing other similar bags. Bodies continued to turn up. On one afternoon it was the charred remains of an old woman from the top floor of a building. At one point the corpse slipped onto the road from the blanket workers had wrapped around it and children watching nearby began to scream.

At the hospital, Palestinians walked through to a car park at the back to see where their relatives were buried. During the siege – just as in Ramallah – the hospital grounds had been turned into a temporary graveyard. I watched other burials in the camp, including one where Palestinians held their hands in prayer while others stumbled away in tears, supported by their friends.

By now, an Amnesty International team, including University of Dundee forensic pathologist Professor Derrick Pounder, was on the scene gathering evidence of the fate of those who died. 'What we saw before us easily paralleled anything I had witnessed while working in Grozny after the Russian offensive,' he said. 'There are two urgent tasks. The first is the humanitarian task of gathering evidence to identify the dead so that the bodies can be given to the families. The second is to obtain forensic evidence about the causes and circumstances of death, which will clarify what has been happening in Jenin camp.'

Slowly but surely the word 'massacre' began to be used by many to describe what had happened inside Jenin, not least by the Palestinian leadership itself. One senior advisor to Yasser Arafat claimed there were more than 3,000 people missing. Other Palestinian officials put the death toll in the hundreds. Part of the problem was that early on in the assault the IDF had alluded to 'hundreds of dead.' This, combined with talk of removing bodies and the deployment of refrigerated trucks to Jenin, had sent the rumour mill into overdrive. Adding even further to the growing suspicion was the Israeli army's near obsession with preventing journalists from gaining access to the camp or even Jenin town. Among those of us who did, many were arrested, among them a CNN TV crew and a *Time* magazine photographer. It almost became something of a joke when I would repeatedly run into my colleague from *The Observer*, Peter Beaumont, as we separately circled Jenin and the camp looking for a way to sneak in under the Israeli cordon to get our story about 'what really happened.'

Some weeks after the end of the siege, Peter would write an invaluable piece headlined not a massacre, but a brutal breach of war's rules, which would put in perspective and accurately sum up what did take place within the camp. 'Whatever crimes were committed here – and it appears there were many – a calculated massacre of civilians by the Israeli army was not one of them,' wrote Beaumont. Often of course a precise definition of just what constitutes a massacre is a difficult thing to determine. As Robert Fisk, the British correspondent who revealed to the world the story of what happened during the Sabra and Shatila camp massacre in Beirut in 1982, later wrote about Jenin: 'So when does a bloodbath become an atrocity? When does an atrocity become a massacre? How big does a massacre have to be before it qualifies as a genocide? How many dead before a genocide becomes a holocaust?'

Fisk had a point, but if there was one thing certain about Jenin, it was that even before the dust from the rubble had settled, anger-filled rumour gave rise to exaggerated stories of the numbers of dead and their identity. As time passed, evidence clearly showed that the majority of those bodies recovered were fighters from Islamic Jihad and other groups including Hamas and the al-Aqsa Martyrs' Brigades. Subsequent investigations and reports by the United Nations, Amnesty International and Human Rights Watch documented that approximately 30 Palestinian fighters, 22 Palestinian civilians and 23 Israeli soldiers were killed in the fighting, and concluded that there was no massacre. But even if a massacre had not taken place, the same investigators concluded that terrible breaches of human rights did occur. As Peter Beaumont later rightly pointed out, 'the true crime of Jenin is the act of physical erasure.'

Under the Fourth Geneva Convention's Article 147, the laws of war state that an attacker must attempt to distinguish between military targets and civilians and their property. If he does not, he is guilty of the war crime of 'indiscriminate attack.' If that attack also results in extensive, unnecessary and willful damage then he is also guilty of 'wanton destruction.' Article 147 also mentions other crimes of which the Israelis were guilty, according to Human Rights Watch and Amnesty, including the taking of hostages for human shields, the army's refusal to allow medical and humanitarian organisations access to the camp, and the deliberate targeting of civilians. In all the clamour over allegations of a massacre and the inaccuracies in the numbers of dead presented by Palestinian officials, these facts tended to be forgotten.

In the longer term the massacre claims did little more than deflect attention away from the real war crimes charge sheet against Israel, charges for which many human rights groups insisted the country's government should be held responsible. Many Israelis knew this to be the case and thought the hairsplitting over whether there was a massacre or not was to miss the real point. One of them was journalist Arie Caspi, who expressed just that in a powerful article in *Ha'aretz* magazine:

> Okay, so there wasn't a massacre. Israel only shot some children, brought a house crashing down on an old man, rained cement blocks on an invalid who couldn't get out in time, used locals as a human shield against bombs, and prevented aid from getting to the sick and wounded. That's really not a massacre, and there's really no need for a commission of enquiry . . . whether run by ourselves or sent by the goyim. The insanity gripping Israel seems to have moved beyond our morals . . . many Israelis believe that as long as we do not practice systematic mass murder, our place in heaven is secure. Every time some Palestinian or Scandinavian fool yells 'Holocaust!' we respond in an angry huff: This is a holocaust? So a few people were killed, 200, 300, some very young, some very old. Does anyone see gas chambers or crematoria?

Many Israelis of course vehemently disagreed with Arie Caspi's assessment, insisting that the luxury of such a 'liberal' viewpoint did nothing more than undermine the tough job being done to ensure Israel's security. As if to reinforce their case and just around the time the IDF imposed its grip on Jenin, a Palestinian teenager called Shadi Tobaci left his small village of Sila Harithia a few miles away and headed towards Haifa. Strapped around Tobaci's waist was a belt of explosives, just like those found on the bodies of many dead fighters inside Jenin camp. Stepping aboard a bus in Haifa, the youngster detonated the bomb, killing himself and eight Israelis, wounding 14 others.

The day following the bombing I watched as most of Tobaci's village took to the streets to commemorate his martyrdom. Chanting support for Hamas and Islamic Jihad, the crowd gathered outside the dead boy's house. Volleys from a Kalashnikov were fired into the air as a photograph of the young *shahid* was held aloft. The image was of a bespectacled, intellectual-looking boy, the sort you would expect to find at home in front of a computer, not the latest martyr from what had virtually become a human assembly line of 'ticking bombs.'

'We don't regard Shadi or those like him as suicide bombers, but as our defenders. Can you ever understand that?' said a man standing next to me in the crowd, his voice desperate, almost pleading.

The following day, a Friday, and clearly timed to coincide with US Secretary of State Colin Powell's visit to Jerusalem, another suicide bomber struck in the city's central market district. Powell had been dispatched by President George W. Bush on his 'urgent peace mission' and would spend eight days in the region, during which time he virtually ignored what had happened in Jenin and submitted no request to visit the town once it was secure. The latest bomber had struck in a busy marketplace in what was a mainly Orthodox Jewish community. Around the neighbourhood a furious crowd gathered carrying banners that read: LET THE IDF ROOT OUT THE TERRORISTS – BUSH DON'T PUSH.

At the scene of the bombing, an angry Israeli spokesman was in no doubt who was guilty of ordering such terrorist outrages and those in the global community who were complicit in appeasing them. 'As long as Arafat is here there will be no peace. That's why I was angry when journalists visited him in Ramallah. He used their mobile phones to get in touch with his cronies and give orders,' claimed Daniel Seaman, Director of the Israeli Government Press Office (GPO), as I spoke with him on the street. 'The Palestinians' problem is not what Israel does, their problem is that Israel exists,' he told me, while nearby the ultra-orthodox Jewish ZAKA volunteers sifted for the remains of the bomb victims.

I had met Daniel Seaman a number of times over many years, but never had I seen him this angry. 'As long as the Palestinians' position is accepted by Europe this is going to continue. Israel is not going to behave just to be liked by the Europeans or lay down and play dead. We are going to defend ourselves,' he continued. Seaman pulled no punches and called it as he saw it, berating whatever country or organisation he felt 'appeased Palestinian terrorism.' He even included the United Nations Palestinian relief agency, UNWRA, accusing it of turning a blind eye to weapons stored in its food warehouses. 'So I'm asking you, what are these organisations doing when they criticise Israel? All Israel is doing is defending itself. Eight years ago we set out on the Oslo process and we tried to sign a treaty with Arafat. Now we have the evidence that Arafat has used these eight years to create an abomination on our border,' claimed Seaman, who was now fully fired-up.

'The Europeans haven't said a thing against terrorism for over a year and a half, but the moment the Jews stand up to defend themselves, they're the ones screaming bloody murder instead of telling Yasser Arafat this is unacceptable.' Seaman's anger reflected not only the mood of many Israelis, but that which had given rise to Operation Defensive Shield and the events I had witnessed in the preceding weeks inside Ramallah, Jenin and elsewhere. This was the voice of an Israel that had lost patience with anyone or anything that didn't see things its way regarding the Palestinians. It didn't matter whether it was European governments, the international media, United Nations or anyone else; if you weren't with us, then you were against us, was Seaman's message.

For what it was worth, George W. Bush had already called for Israel to withdraw from the West Bank, while UN Secretary General Kofi Annan described the crisis as 'an affront to mankind.' 'The situation is now so dangerous, and the humanitarian position so appalling that a force should be sent in to create a safe environment,' insisted Annan. But as so often was the case, the United Nations talked but remained politically impotent. And Israel wasn't for listening anyway.

Less than two hours' drive from the scene of the latest suicide bombing and Daniel Seaman's angry denunciation, Palestinians in Jenin were meanwhile trying to come to terms with what had stormed through their lives. Along with Jenin, seven other Palestinian cities were now under siege, and Israeli tanks and troops were still on the move. Operation Defensive Shield was not quite over yet. While Jenin, and the sieges of Arafat's compound and Bethlehem's Church of the Nativity had caught the world's attention, in the West Bank's most populous town, Nablus, some of the toughest battles were being fought.

Nablus, April–May 2002

Lt. General Shaul Mofaz, Israel's Chief of Staff, left no doubt about the importance of the fight for Nablus when he personally briefed paratroopers before they were sent into the winding high-walled warren of the city's casbah in what was the biggest deployment of the West Bank invasion. 'This war should be called the "war for the home",' he told them. 'This is a very critical time. Each one of you understands the great responsibility on your young shoulders,' he said, as the paratroopers listened, crammed together in a hushed hall. Every one of these Israeli soldiers knew that Nablus was another stronghold of the intifada's 'hard men.' After all the city was home to the al-Aqsa Martyrs' Brigades.

It was back in October 2000, sometime after midnight, when five Palestinians sat in an alleyway in Balata refugee camp in Nablus drinking small cups of coffee, that the al-Aqsa Martyrs' Brigades were conceived. It had been a long deadly day of confrontation with Israeli troops, and the five exhausted men were taking stock of where best their own future role lay within the intifada. All of them were frustrated at the way Fatah, the organisation to which they belonged, was attempting to battle the Israelis. Among the fighters were Yasser Badawi, his brother Nasser and their long-time friend Nasser Awais. 'We have to form a strong, fearful group to put an end to the continuous Israeli attacks and settler occupation,' Yasser Badawi suggested to his comrades, his brother Nasser later recalled in an interview. Nasser Awais agreed, and he and Yasser Badawi, each about 30 years old and trusted by their friends, became the leaders of the group they named after the Jerusalem mosque where the al-Aqsa intifada had first sparked into life.

In a series of operations the brigades quickly challenged the notion of Israeli invincibility and became known as the militia wing of Yasser Arafat's Fatah movement, albeit created by and under control of local commanders. Indeed, from the outset there were always questions as to just how much control Arafat had over this new generation of fighters who had a habit of doing things their way and were often openly critical, if not confrontational, with Fatah's 'old guard'. 'Most of the people that founded the Brigade, people that joined the Brigade, were well trained before they joined it,' Nasser Badawi would later say. 'Some had experience in the old intifada, or were wanted or experienced in military work. Some were taught outside,' the former sociology student now turned Brigade commander confirmed.

Adding to the Brigades' power was the wide base of support from which it could draw. Unlike Hamas or Islamic Jihad, and their desire for a religious state, the Brigades were able to tap into and recruit from that large cross-section of the more secular Palestinian community represented by Fatah.

Speaking in an interview in early 2002, just weeks before the Israelis launched Operation Defensive Shield, and less than a year after his brother Yasser was killed by a car bomb, Nasser Badawi once again reiterated the al-Aqsa Brigades' independence from the Fatah old guard. 'You have to understand something. The al-Aqsa Brigades were not formed by a leadership decision and will not be disbanded by their decisions,' he pointed out. 'The Brigades were created by the people, created from the womb of the intifada, nourished and cherished by the people, and it will die only when the occupation vanishes,' he insisted.

Barely had Badawi spoken these words than Operation Defensive Shield rolled into action. Along with other prominent al-Aqsa leaders on Israel's most wanted list he was clearly in the cross-hairs as IDF paratroopers fought their way into the old city of Nablus. As in its northern West Bank neighbour Jenin, Palestinian resistance in Nablus was ferocious. At the entrance to the casbah, home to 30,000 residents, sat a vast crater gouged by a D-9 bulldozer. This was the demarcation line beyond which lay a labyrinth of vaulted alleyways where fighters had spent weeks preparing their defences.

Reporter Philip Sherwell and photographer Julian Simmonds of the *Daily Telegraph* were the only British journalists to make it into the casbah just hours before the Israeli tanks and troops surrounded it. In his dispatches Sherwell described being given a night-time tour of the city's Palestinian positions that included a mass of sand bag and oil drum barricades, behind which a few hundred armed Palestinian fighters had taken up positions in an effort to stop the Israeli advance. Booby-traps, trip wires and hidden mines were everywhere. Unlike Jenin's crumbling refugee camp the buildings were too solid and close together for the D-9s and Merkavas to simply shove their way through. The Israeli paratroopers would have to do it on foot after heavy barrages of tank shells and helicopter missiles had been lobbed into the old city to 'soften up' the resistance and make the Palestinians think again.

But the fighters inside were not for turning and remained defiant, with Nasser Badawi pledging to turn Nablus into 'a cemetery for Israeli soldiers.' 'We will resist until the last bullet and the last fighter,' Badawi told Sherwell. As if to show they, too, meant business, one of the first things the Israelis did at the start of the Nablus operation was to blow up four houses near the entrance to Balata refugee camp, one of which belonged to Nasser Badawi's family. Few doubted that this was yet another act of 'collective punishment,' in this case for having two sons that were founders of the al-Aqsa Brigades, whose fighters were now showing their true mettle in the defence of the city.

By the time the Israeli paratroopers began pushing their way into the casbah, the scene resembled something from the 1960s film *The Battle of Algiers*, when French airborne troops entered a similar warren of streets in an effort to flush out Algerian resistance to France's colonial occupation of the country. Very quickly, the casbah began to fill with the stench of blood and rotting corpses, and the green Jamal Bek mosque at its heart became an improvised casualty centre overwhelmed by wounded Palestinian fighters and civilians alike. For five days the fighting raged, before the Israelis finally agreed to let Palestinian Red Crescent workers in to evacuate the wounded. Some reporters, among them Suzanne Goldenberg of *The Guardian*, took the opportunity during the lull in the fighting to see for themselves conditions at the heart of the casbah and the Jamal Bek mosque.

> Most of the dead and wounded were men, cut down as the Israeli army blasted its way through the labyrinth of narrow lanes, raking the pavements with heavy machine-guns. The ground underfoot was littered with tank shells. Water gushed from smashed pipelines, a child's lace-up black shoe lay abandoned. The corpses were stacked in a courtyard of the mosque. Some faces were blackened and pitted, apparently by an explosion. Blood curdled around mouths, and seeped from gaping chest wounds. One wore the green bandana of Hamas around his neck, the face of another was masked with a black and white chequered *keffiyeh*, but it was impossible to say in the chaos how many of the dead were Palestinian fighters, and how many were civilians.

There were 26 Palestinian bodies inside the mosque, where local doctors had fought to save the wounded, working without blood supplies, proper surgical tools or antibiotics. As the Red Crescent workers gently lifted more than 60 casualties on to stretchers, they left behind the bloodstained mattresses on which the injured had lain in agony for

days. Relays of stretcher-bearers moved the wounded and dead to
ambulances waiting outside the casbah, passing silent Israeli soldiers
who by now had taken control of much of the city. The medical workers moved fast, eager to evacuate as many of the wounded as possible
before the Israeli army re-imposed its curfew.

Just a few days previously, despite a coordinated agreement between
the IDF and the Red Crescent, four ambulances had come under fire
from the soldiers, their bullets hitting the vehicles' tyres and engines.

As in Ramallah and Jenin, the use of Palestinian civilians as human
shields was another breach of the 'rules of war' that in the close house-
to-house fighting inside Nablus became commonplace.

On April 7, 25-year-old Anan Abu Dahar remembered the moment
when, despite Israeli soldiers threatening to shoot him, he refused to
cooperate during their search of a building.

> I sat down on the step and grabbed the water pipe. The soldiers
> ordered me to continue, and not to say a word. They tried to loosen
> my grip on the pipe, but I held on with all my strength. They hit me
> in the back, head and legs with their rifle butts. They slammed my
> head into the wall and ordered me to keep quiet so that the
> Palestinians wouldn't know that soldiers were in the building. . . .
> One of the soldiers sat me down by the window with my head stick-
> ing out. He rested his rifle on my head and started to shoot. Every
> time he fired, it felt as if the bullet had penetrated my head.

As the casbah increasingly fell under the relentless Israeli advance,
the last vestiges of Palestinian resistance, mainly al-Aqsa Brigades fighters, found themselves cornered among the ancient stone buildings of the
Al-Yasmina (Jasmin) Quarter. Faced with Israeli heavy weaponry the
siege was all but over for the Palestinian fighters. Many had been killed,
among them according to initial reports, Nasser Awais, the life-long
friend of the Badawi brothers and a founder of the al-Aqsa Brigades.
But while the Palestinians had pronounced Awais dead during the final
stages of the battle, they did so to throw the Israelis off the scent while
the young fighter slipped out of the city.

Finally, on April 13, 2002, Awais was tracked down to a remote village in the Jordan Valley where the Israelis took him into custody, and
to this day he remains held in isolation in the Beer Saba prison.

Many others who had taken up arms or were simply in the wrong place at the wrong time were not so lucky. One woman from Nablus described the battle's aftermath in a diary account:

> The 78 martyrs in Nablus were kept in a refrigerated truck belonging to al-Safa milk factory. They were not allowed to be buried until two days before the Israel soldiers left the city centre. They were buried in mass graves. No funeral was allowed. All families of martyrs received condolences at the same spot. Bereaved mothers, sisters, wives, daughters wore a badge with the name of their beloved ones. Some of them wore more than one badge. Members of the Shu-bi family wore six badges.

Just as in Jenin, where Islamic Jihad had been the Israelis' prime target, the al-Aqsa Brigades' cells had now largely been routed from Nablus. Indeed, across the West Bank the toll of dead and detained among the three main Palestinian armed factions – the al-Aqsa Martyrs' Brigades and the Islamist groups Hamas and Islamic Jihad – had been substantial.

Perhaps more important than numbers for the Israelis, however, was the calibre of arrests. High-profile activists like Nasser Awais of the al-Aqsa Brigades, Thabet Mardawi, an Islamic Jihad leader, Sheikh Ali Safuri of Islamic Jihad, Jamal Akhuil of Fatah, and Bilal Barghouti of Hamas had all been caught in the net the IDF had trawled in the wake of its West Bank invasion. But by far the biggest catch of all was the man I had interviewed in Ramallah the year before and who many recognised as the leader of the al-Aqsa intifada – Marwan Barghouti.

People around Barghouti had always warned him that his time would come. By now the Israelis had assassinated a number of high-profile figures of the intifada, including Abu Ali Mustafa of the Popular Front for the Liberation of Palestine (PFLP). Barghouti, after all, was the real deal. No ordinary activist, he was in effect the day-to-day orchestrator of what by then was an uprising that had lasted the best part of two bitter years. By now his reputation had spread far beyond the borders and boundaries of the West Bank, and his name was often mentioned at an international level as the potential successor to Yasser Arafat. Almost from the moment Israeli tanks and troops had advanced into the West Bank, Barghouti had gone into hiding and kept on the move.

'He kept moving from one place to another, both inside and outside

Ramallah,' said his wife Fadwa. 'But when the curfew was lifted for a few hours he wanted to change his place after meeting one of his colleagues. But the Israeli forces were either after his colleague or else they got him by monitoring his cellular phone,' she explained in an interview to *Al-Ahram*. It was strange to think that perhaps Barghouti's mobile phone had led to his capture. I couldn't help thinking back to that day in Ramallah, when my own phone was the object of so much attention by Barghouti's driver and bodyguard.

It was on Monday, April 15, that the Israeli army received intelligence that Barghouti was hiding in the house of Fatah official Ziad Abu Ain, in the El Birreh neighbourhood of northern Ramallah. Initially the Israelis had deployed a reservist unit to surround the house before then bringing up a Special Forces team.

'Are you going to kill me or arrest me?' Barghouti reportedly asked the Israeli soldiers in Hebrew, before he was taken into custody rather than killed in some shoot-out as many anticipated. For some time it had almost been a given that Marwan Barghouti would most likely die in an Israeli helicopter missile strike, mysterious car bomb explosion or the like. Why didn't Israel simply assassinate its number one Palestinian enemy, many asked? It wasn't as if it had hesitated in the past when the need arose to 'take out' troublesome Arab militants. Many Middle East analysts believe the answer to the question is simply that Prime Minister Ariel Sharon did not want Barghouti dead. Instead, here was a perfect opportunity for the Israeli leader to bring Barghouti to trial in a civilian court. In itself such a move presented an ideal public platform on which the Israelis could effectively criminalise and defame any future Palestinian leadership and reveal them for the terrorists they believed them to be. With Barghouti in the dock, it would be easy for the Israelis to reiterate their point about having no one within the Palestinian ranks they could genuinely do business with. Is this really the kind of man you want us to negotiate a peace deal with, they would argue?

Barghouti's arrest was further proof of what really lay behind Operation Defensive Shield. Yes, the Israelis wanted to crush the Palestinian 'terrorist infrastructure,' but they were also determined to ensure that no popular party, group or individual leader might conceivably challenge them in the future. Having worked so hard during the West Bank invasion to incapacitate the Palestinian Authority, the last thing they wanted was to see it fully resuscitated.

Immediately following his arrest, Barghouti was moved first to the

Russian Compound Detention Centre in Jerusalem where the General
Security Service (GSS) interrogated him. Just over a month later, on May
26, he was transferred to the Petah Tikva Detention Centre. Again it
was disconcerting to think that the man I had interviewed not long
before was now being deprived of sleep and subjected to other torture
in a Russian Compound isolation cell just yards from the bar in which
I often still drank. Curious too that it should be the same place where
photographer Mike Neri and I had been the night of the Café Moment
suicide bombing, an attack that helped push Israel that much closer to
launching their invasion in the first place.

Just a few days before the Israelis advanced on Jenin, American
journalist Thomas Friedman made the case in the *New York Times* that
Israel needed to deliver a military blow 'that clearly shows that terror
will not pay.' In the aftermath of Operation Defensive Shield many people around the world asked themselves just whether such an objective
had been achieved. Even some Israelis had their doubts about its effec-
tiveness in keeping them safe. 'Though Israel could be said to have won
tactically the war of the intifada, she could by no means claim a strategic victory, for she was incapable of turning her military superiority into
a strategic breakthrough,' Shlomo Ben-Ami, former Israeli Foreign
Minister, would later reflect.

In the course of the operation the Israeli army invaded and re-occu-
pied every West Bank city except for Hebron and Jericho. As many as
250 Palestinians were killed, thousands wounded and over 8,000
imprisoned in arrest sweeps. But polls conducted in Israel a little over a
month after the operation found that 50 percent of Israelis felt no safer
than they had before it started. Indeed, even as Operation Defensive
Shield was still underway, Israeli Defence Minister Ben Eliezer admitted
that the country would gain at best only a few months respite.

Israelis I met remained as nervous as ever about the potential threat
on the streets around them. During the upsurge in violence not only had
the economy floundered even further, but also the only growth industry
seemed to be in the private security sector, which cost a fortune but produced nothing. Banks, offices, cinemas, and all but the smallest cafés
and stores, seemed to have Uzi-wielding guards lurking somewhere.
Newspapers even featured a 'guard of the day,' complete with a personal picture of the lucky custodian. Countless hours every week were
spent inspecting bags, backpacks or rubbish bins for bombs.

Among Palestinians, meanwhile, there was a realisation that the momentum of the intifada had been dealt a serious blow. It wasn't the knock-out blow some Israelis had hoped for, but it was enough for certain Palestinian leaders to stop and think again about where armed resistance might ultimately lead their cause.

A few weeks after the operation had officially ended, I came across a group of Palestinian prisoners being held by the Israelis following some street clashes outside the West Bank town of Dura near Hebron. Sitting in the baking sun, bound and blindfolded, with their faces badly cut and bruised, the prisoners had clearly been beaten. All were in a terrible condition, but there was something unbowed and determined about the men. Nothing had changed, I thought to myself. Still they fight, still the Israelis arrest them, and yet still more take to the streets.

Across the West Bank as the weeks passed, fighters from the armed factions began again to march. Carrying pictures of their comrades who had died in defence of their towns and cities, they would fire defiantly into the air with their Kalashnikovs and M-16s and vow to continue the intifada. In the ruins of Jenin's refugee camp and in the Nablus casbah, the remnants of Islamic Jihad and al-Aqsa Martyrs' Brigades' cells were already regrouping.

While Israelis by now talked about Operation Defensive Shield in the past tense, the IDF incursions continued daily in what the army often referred to as 'pinpoint operations,' usually in response to suicide bombings. But the suicide cells too had learned new tactics and now rarely revealed the identities of the 'martyrs,' making it difficult for the Israelis to accurately target their reprisal raids. In the basements and backrooms a new generation of 'engineers,' 'ticking bombs,' gunmen, counterfeiters, runners and street fighters were gathering to take revenge and continue the fight against the occupation.

'I am not like the traditional Arab leaders who change defeat into victory. We were defeated – but in this battle only, not the war,' said Hussam Khader, a legislator in Balata refugee camp expressing the thoughts of countless other Palestinians. While Operation Defensive Shield might have failed to decisively break the 'terrorist infrastructure' and the intifada, on the political front it had other much wider long-term implications for the Palestinians. Most importantly, Ariel Sharon had ended any pretence of Palestinian self-government functioning on its own terms. In Ramallah and elsewhere, his soldiers in their systematic destruction of everything from computer databases to handwritten land deeds ensured that the administrative mechanisms and institutions

Palestinians needed to govern were no longer available.

On the one hand Sharon had called on the PA to rein in or combat Palestinian militant groups, at the same time depriving them of the police and security apparatus needed to do so. What's more, while PA-linked 'organisations in the field,' in the shape of the Tanzim and al-Aqsa Brigades had been badly mauled by the Israelis, Hamas by contrast had weathered the onslaught better. In short, by concentrating their military campaign on the PA and militant groups linked to it, the Israelis ironically may have handed Hamas something of a 'get out of jail free card' and ensured them a freer hand in the future. Indeed, by the end of June 2002, Hamas had emerged as an independent force in the occupied territories, rapidly filling the resistance vacuum left after Israel's crushing of the PA related groups.

Meanwhile on the broader political front, it was clear that should any resurrected PA or its equivalent rise from the ashes of Operation Defensive Shield, it would most likely be on Israel's terms and be manned by Palestinians who had been suitably groomed.

In some ways Sharon had achieved his long sought return to the status quo that had existed prior to September 1993 and Oslo; a situation that not only relied on the destruction of the PA's infrastructure and institutions, but the creation of a new West Bank geography whereby each of the eight Palestinian areas was territorially separated by encompassing Jewish settlements and army buffer zones.

Significantly Gaza had not featured as a target of Operation Defensive Shield. Palestinian bases there had largely escaped unscathed. Ever since the first intifada, there had been an intensifying consensus for getting out of Gaza emanating from within Israel's corridors of power. It was a feeling that would grow, and it sat nicely alongside Sharon's longer-term game plan. By Sharon's own definition, Operation Defensive Shield had been a declaration of war on the Palestinians and their uprising. But many Israelis felt he had not gone far enough. The killer blow to Arafat and his PA cronies had not been delivered.

For his 'restraint' Sharon's military victory was quickly crowned with a diplomatic one when on June 24, 2002, George W. Bush finally delivered his vision of a Palestine living side-by-side in peace and security with Israel. It was in effect the initial sketch for what would become the road map for peace. But as ever the devil was in the details. From the outset, in close negotiation with Sharon, Bush would lay down conditions on everything, ensuring that the Palestinians would elect a new

– and most importantly – acceptable leadership, the sort of regime that was sufficiently malleable and out of which they could squeeze maximum concessions. Manufacturing such a body would be easier said than done. Certainly there were some among the Palestinian leadership who saw the militarisation of the intifada as the kiss of death for the survival of the PA. They at least could possibly be brought on side. But while individual Palestinians like these – among them veteran Fatah leader Mahmoud Abbas – might be wooed into such an arrangement, out on the streets ran a new younger breed of militant who would have no truck with such a central leadership. To this 'young guard,' leaders like these were little more than Israeli lackeys and yes-men not worthy of their support. The intifada had reached a strategic impasse.

Unlike most Israelis and Palestinians worn out by events of the last months, I at least had the opportunity of some real respite by returning home briefly to Scotland to catch my breath and ponder what might happen next. Relaxing among the crowds in Edinburgh's Charlotte Square Gardens, the setting for the city's International Book Festival, could not have been further removed from the suicide bombers, curfews and killings of Israel, the West Bank and Gaza. 'At the moment I'm just inhaling this new experience of being able to sit among people and not be afraid,' Israeli writer David Grossman told me. I had met him that afternoon, just before a discussion I had been invited to chair on the theme: 'The Middle East: What Next?' Along with Grossman was fellow Israeli author Amos Oz and Palestinian writer Raja Shehadeh, who had sat out Operation Defensive Shield in besieged Ramallah and would later publish a lyrical diary account of that time entitled *When The Bulbul Stopped Singing*.

Yet for all the apparent tranquillity of the evening, even here in distant Edinburgh, the shadow of the violence that wracked the writers' homeland lurked in the background, with additional security and a police 'sweep' of the venue before the discussion got underway. Not that any of this spoiled what was a remarkable discussion, during which three of the most eloquent literary voices of the Middle East resounded against the bitter rhetoric of a conflict Amos Oz described as 'not one of good guys and bad guys, but more like a Greek tragedy.'

It would have been all too easy to dismiss what was said that evening as nothing more than a talking shop, a comfortable intellectual exercise in the cosy confines of an understanding and informed audience. In reality, though, what surfaced was a remarkable insight into the mindset and culture that the Israeli occupation and intifada had created.

'At some point both sides are going to undergo major surgery that is going to hurt like hell. Deep down in its heart of hearts the patient knows already what is going to happen. The patient is essentially ready – but the doctors are cowards on both sides,' Oz insisted, in an undisguised attack on both Sharon and Arafat, or 'Sharafat,' as he liked to call the duo.

As the discussion closed that night and the writers made their way from the platform, surrounded by autograph hunters and others still keen to hear their views, it was curious to think of them returning home to Jerusalem and Ramallah and such an uncertain future.

'Right now, at home, I feel like we are in a hermetic bubble. It is a vicious cloud that is enveloping us all and we need help to get out so we can breathe again,' said David Grossman, as we all shook hands and said our good-byes.

The ability for both sides to breathe again was the last thing on Ariel Sharon's mind. For the moment he had taken the initiative and was not about to throw it away. Already two new Israeli strategies were beginning to take shape. One was an attempt at systematic control over the movement of Palestinians. The other, inextricably connected to it, was an effort to restrict international support for the Palestinians, both financial and political.

Palestinian areas within the West Bank would be divided into cantons, or *bantustans*, as the South African apartheid regime used to call them, making it impossible to travel without permission. 'With no political solution in sight, the spectre of an apartheid bi-national state of South African characteristics, but with no conceivable South African solution to it, was suddenly no longer a hollow threat,' Shlomo Ben Ami, former Israeli Foreign Minister, noted later.

The war of economic attrition was now underway, and a massive wall that Israel would call its 'security barrier' began to take shape. Back in the occupied territories, Palestinians were still trying to sort out their own house. Those who had survived the invasion of the West Bank would be slow to forgive and forget what the Israelis did in the course of Operation Defensive Shield.

Whether an apocryphal story or not, news that in the wake of the battle for Jenin, doctors in Gaza City delivered three baby girls all called 'Jenin' by their parents, seemed to poignantly capture the Palestinian mood.

Israel had suffered too, of course. It has even been suggested by some Israeli human rights groups like B'Tselem that the intensity of pain and anger felt by Israelis following the wave of suicide bombings in their cities had perhaps led their soldiers to forget just who the real enemy was. Whatever the reasoning, the one thing certain is that the most powerful army in the Middle East attacked more than two million civilians while the international community stood back and did nothing.

Looking back now on those dark days in Ramallah, Jenin, Nablus and other West Bank cities, I can't help thinking again about a question put to me by Khaled Amoudi, the 80-year-old Palestinian grandfather I had met on the outskirts of Jenin. 'Why does the world not understand and Sharon gets away with anything he wants?' he asked, having spent another day making fruitless enquiries about the fate of his missing daughter and her family. 'At the end of the day, the world sees us only as terrorists. There is no truth in this world. All we want is an identity and a Palestinian state. Is that really so much to ask, when this is the alternative?'

8

ANOTHER BRICK IN THE WALL

TO EXIST IS TO RESIST

—graffiti on Israel's 'security barrier'

West Jerusalem, September 2004

'These are a way of life here,' said Alon Tuval, loading bullets into the magazine of his Beretta pistol. Feet apart, arms locked, one eye closed, he took aim. After a few minutes he put down the gun and took me forward to check the results of his shooting. 'One dead terrorist,' he said smiling, the paper target showing three good 'head shots' and a cluster of ripped holes 'well grouped' around the chest.

Having passed with flying colours, Alon returned to the main gun shop attached to the shooting gallery, where the owner renewed the licence for his Beretta and sold him a fresh box of bullets. 'Winchester – full metal jacket' said the writing on the box. In the display case beneath the counter was an assortment of other guns, saw-toothed 'special forces' knives, knuckle-dusters and telescopic batons for sale. Next to us an elderly Israeli woman, who a few seconds earlier was going though her own locked-and-loaded routine like a veteran SAS man, was now perusing a selection of 'discreet gun pouches' which the manufacturer's slogan on the outside insisted was the best home your weapon will ever find.

'Be sure to wash your hands before lunch, you don't want to get lead poisoning,' Alon told me as I picked up one of the tiny copper-coloured bullets from the table to take a closer look.

I had met Alon Tuval at the Beit Agron Press Centre in Jerusalem where I had gone to renew my accreditation as an overseas visiting correspondent. Housed in a dirty yellow stone building with the surrounding grounds littered with broken glass and smelling of stale urine, Beit Agron was home to the offices of most foreign newspapers and the Israeli Government Press Office (GOP). Whenever the intifada raged, or during other times of political crisis, reporters, photographers and TV crews from overseas would invariably pass through Beit Agron, presenting their own national press cards in exchange for one issued by Israel.

These days, some of them heading into a volatile Gaza or West Bank might also stock up on new body armour from a specialist retail company supplying flak jackets and helmets that sold its products from a stand on the ground-floor entrance foyer. Inside the building's gloomy corridors foreign journalists could also find Israelis like Alon Tuval more than willing to work as fixers, translators or stringers while any big story was unfolding.

Though himself a journalist and fixer by profession, Alon, like many Israelis, had long since carried a pistol. 'Ever since I was in the army I've tried to practise regularly. These days you never know when you might need it,' he told me that afternoon as we walked to the gun shop and shooting gallery nearby, where he was scheduled to undergo his gun licence 'refresher course.' Inside the shooting gallery, Alon suggested I try a few shots myself using the Beretta pistol. I wasn't keen on the idea. Not because of any ideological or ethical objection, but simply because after years of being around weapons of all types, I was happy enough for guns to be in the hands of those who knew exactly what they were doing with them.

A few times in the past while working in some war zone I had been asked to try using a weapon. Usually the reason for the invitation was for those standing nearby to crack up laughing at my expense, or as some kind of acceptance ritual into the ranks of whatever militia or guerrilla group I was accompanying. I should have learned my lesson after the first time such a situation arose.

It was in the early 1980s, while travelling clandestinely as a reporter in the mountains of Afghanistan with *mujahideen* guerrillas fighting the Russian invaders of their country. 'Shoot, shoot, Mister Daoud,' insisted the commander of my rebel hosts for the umpteenth time, as we rested in a remote craggy valley one afternoon. With his holy warriors looking on, the commander slotted a full clip of the familiar boat-tailed bullets into a Soviet-made AK-47 and thrust the weapon towards me. The time had long since passed for acceptable excuses about journalistic ethics and my non-combatant status. Judging by the looks of the fighters around me, this had simply boiled down to an issue of initiation and acceptance; a very Afghan thing about loyalty and brotherhood. To refuse now would have made my presence at best uncomfortable and, at worst, untenable.

A battered plastic bottle was set up some distance away as a target. As I squeezed the trigger and the first rounds cracked against some rocks reasonably close to the bottle, the gawping bearded guerrillas who had clustered around began to grin. It wasn't a question of them ever expecting me to fire in earnest, just about passing some strange macho muster.

Once again for some reason that afternoon in Jerusalem with Alon, I reluctantly agreed to go along with a 'shooting lesson.' After a few minutes of instruction from one of the trainers in the gallery, I pulled down my ear protectors and raised the Beretta, squeezing the trigger in the gentle double action way I had been shown. Though clearly I was no sharpshooter, there was something disconcertingly easy about the whole process. How simple it was to lift this small piece of metal and fire these rounds. How comparatively easy to have them hammer home at least accurately enough on target to achieve what the Beretta was made for – killing people. As I watched Alon go through his paces with all the expertise you would expect of a trained soldier, I couldn't help wondering what it must be like feeling the need to carry a gun daily, never knowing when you might be expected to use it. Then it would not be about punching holes in the 'menacing' silhouette of an armed figure in a paper target, but through real flesh and bone, knowing that you were taking someone's life.

'Look, David, it's them or us, you have to understand that,' Alon tried to explain, as we tucked into a sandwich in a West Jerusalem café. 'Them or us. Them or us.' How many times now had I heard that phrase, I asked myself? It was back in the days of the first intifada that it had initially struck home, when my Israeli photographer friend Zeev Ackerman explained how he'd once been 'sympathetic to the Arabs,' before it had come down to being a case of 'them or us.' Alon, perhaps sensing that such thoughts were going through my head, pressed home his point. 'Just remember what happened at the Sbarro pizza place up the road from here,' he said, nodding over his shoulder in the direction of the café. For a moment in my mind's eye I could see the suicide bomber walking into the crowded pizzeria on the corner of King George and Jaffa Street, around the same time of day as now, just a few years back. 'You think it would have made a difference if someone had been armed?' I asked Alon.

'Maybe yes, maybe no,' he shrugged. 'But we Israelis need to take whatever measures we can to guarantee our security now,' Alon insisted. Life here and now had become all about that one word – security. But just what had this desperate need for Israel's security meant, I wondered, for the security in the lives of ordinary Palestinians who in the wake of Operation Defensive Shield had perhaps never felt so vulnerable.

Sitting discussing these issues with Alon, it was hard to imagine that it was now four long years to that very week since Ariel Sharon had gone for his now infamous walk across Haram al-Sharif, and the al-Aqsa intifada had erupted in response. As yet another year of killing loomed, many on both sides were becoming ever more concerned as to where it was leading them. According to an Israeli Defence Force estimate in the autumn of 2004, the following 12 months were expected to be a critical period for the Palestinian people and the intifada. 'This year will be the year that will shape the Palestinian struggle. The Palestinian leadership will have to decide whether to aim towards a peace agreement with Israel or to continue with the armed resistance,' was how one senior IDF officer had put it.

In the past, particularly in the years following the first intifada, anniversaries of the uprising had often been opportunities for Palestinians to endorse resistance to the occupation through street demonstrations or an escalation of attacks on Israeli targets. But that year somehow the mood felt different. By now the suicide bombings – like the latest one just a day or so before in the busy French Hill suburb of Jerusalem – had lost the intifada some of its worldwide sympathy. Added to this, a leadership crisis had led many to predict that what really preoccupied Palestinians by then was not the intifada, but an 'intrafada,' an uprising not against Israel but against elements of Yasser Arafat's Palestinian Authority, now widely seen as corrupt and politically out of touch. Also having an impact on the intifada and lives of those Palestinians living in its shadow was the slow severing existence of Israel's latest 'security measure,' the massive barrier it was busy building across the West Bank.

Later that afternoon, following my meeting with Alon Tuval, I travelled the short distance across Jerusalem's Green Line towards my old home away from home, the Cliff Hotel, and the nearby village of Abu Dis. I wanted to see for myself just what impact the 'them or us' mindset and Israel's craving for security meant for ordinary Palestinians who were living inside the noose that seemed to be tightening around their lives, choking whole communities into paralysis and perhaps extinction.

Abu Dis, September 2004

Hassan Akramawi was a Palestinian shopkeeper based on what used to be the main Jerusalem to Jericho Road. When I met him he was suffering from flu, worried about who would pick-up his kids from school, and the effects on his grocery shop of what was simply referred to in this neighbourhood as 'the wall.' 'My business is dead because this wall has cut the street, cut people off from each other and their own families,' he said, his voice shaking with emotion. Perhaps it was the effect of the flu, but I felt a real sense that this was a man hovering on the edge of breakdown.

Outside Hassan's shop the wall ran right across the road. Twenty-five feet high, it sliced through the community, severing Jerusalem from the West Bank village of Abu Dis. In doing so, it had also divided the old road that dropped down into the Jordan Valley. On a clear morning with a wonderful view across the Dead Sea and surrounding hills, I used to love travelling this road. Such was the drop in altitude, to what is the lowest point on earth, you could often feel the pressure change in your ears and the temperature rise noticeably, especially in winter time. Now, because of the wall, the route from East Jerusalem down into the valley would never be the same again. Likewise the lives of countless Palestinians who lived along its path had also perhaps changed forever.

'If you want security for your house you build the wall in your own garden, not in your neighbour's,' Hassan complained, increasingly fired-up and distraught, as we talked about the impact the wall had made on the local community. As he spoke I couldn't help thinking of the lines in a poem by American writer Robert Frost:

> Before I built a wall I'd ask to know
> What I was walling in or out,
> And to whom I was like to give offence.
> Something there is that doesn't love a wall,
> That wants it down.

Outside Hassan's shop, the wall's ugly grey cement was pockmarked where rocks had been thrown at it in anger. In bright red painted letters someone had daubed 'from warsaw ghetto to abu dis ghetto.' Someone had inscribed that it was 'paid for by the usa,' while another asked 'is this the work of a man of peace?' A few children, negotiating an Israeli check-point that allowed access from one side of the wall to another on their way home from school, stopped by Hassan's shop for some sweets while we talked. 'This is all I sell now, for a shekel or two to the kids. I even take the lightbulbs out because I have to save some money. Life is too difficult to live any more.'

To anyone who has never seen the wall, it's hard to over emphasise the sheer injustice of this concrete scar that gouges its way across olive tree orchards, family homes, grazing areas, places of work, schools and anything else that, frankly, the state of Israel has decided to confiscate. Its sheer physical presence bears down when you are near it. Walking beside it, on either side, you can see Palestinians trying to live their lives under its weight.

'This used to be a beautiful place, now I live in the shadow, no sun, no light, even the air seems bad,' one local Abu Dis farmer would tell me later that day, struggling to make himself heard against the deafening sound of bulldozers working on the next stretch of wall nearby.

The degradation and humiliation of the Palestinians is made all the worse by the employment of some of their men by private Israeli security firms to guard other Arab labourers who work on the wall's construction. 'I know they blame us for this,' admitted one guard, when I asked what he thought of the Palestinian villagers who stood nearby watching as a bulldozer dug up their back garden to lay cables used for high-powered security lights and electrified fencing. 'I know the bitterness they feel, but my family has to eat,' the guard repeated, clearly wrestling with the guilt that came from feeling complicit in such a perceived betrayal. As we spoke, barely a few hundred yards away, I could just make out a few figures hurriedly clambering through unfinished gaps in the wall. They too were Palestinian men, part of an army of 'illegal' workers who daily ran the gauntlet of Israeli military patrols. Once across the wall, Israeli employers waiting for them in cars would pick up the workers. Among these unscrupulous Israeli businessmen, the issue of security clearly mattered less than ensuring they had an endless supply of cheap labour.

The hypocrisy struck me as unbelievable. Time and again I had listened to ordinary Israelis warn of the dangers in their lives from lapsed security. Yet, here were some of them more concerned with making a buck than worrying about the possibility that these Palestinians whom they were willing to 'employ' might just be suicide bombers or gunmen. A few Palestinians taken on as workers no doubt exploited their own role in this capacity to attack Israelis. But for the vast majority, whether employed legally in jobs like security guards and labourers on the wall, or illegally at the bidding of shady Israeli middlemen, it was largely undertaken out of economic necessity. Taking on an illegal job was not something to be considered lightly. On the one hand it meant running the risk of being arrested by the Israeli army or police, and on the other of being called a 'collaborator.' Largely abandoned by the international community, life for many Palestinians caught in this situation had simply boiled down to survival. As the construction of the wall slowly engulfed their lives, they were left to earn a crust as best they could. Not for the first time Palestinians found themselves asking that familiar question, succinctly put by one Abu Dis resident in a documentary film made about the impact of the wall: 'Where is the world? Where is the world?' Why, most wanted to know, had the outside world been so quiet in its condemnation of the wall despite the International Court's ruling that its construction was illegal? Why was it called a 'security' wall at all, they asked, when instead of just separating Israel from the West Bank, it separated Arab from Arab? Indeed, how could a people whose history is full of terrible ghettos now themselves be building one?

Leaving Hassan Akramawi to the worries of his failing grocery business and the effects of his worsening flu, I walked the short distance that skirts the route of the wall from the main road up the hill to the Cliff Hotel overlooking Abu Dis. As a struggling freelance correspondent covering the first intifada in the 1980s, the Cliff had been the closest thing to home off and on during the years I worked here. In its restaurant or around its pool table, I had whittled away many a day under curfew listening to the crackle of gunfire as yet another riot ensued outside. Then there were those uncertain winter nights in 1991, at the start of the Gulf War, lying in the darkness of my room, gas mask at the ready, as the sound of Israeli air raid sirens warned of an imminent Iraqi Scud missile attack. At the Cliff I had met fellow journalists and aid workers, celebrated Christmas, held an engagement party, and made friends from among the Palestinian community and around the world. Some of the memories of my time spent at the hotel are among the fondest of my life.

For those reasons alone it was difficult to take in the scene I discovered on nearing the hotel that day. Not only had the wall cut right through its grounds, but the building itself was now used as an Israeli army base and checkpoint. On the roof where I once sunbathed or just took in the spectacular view across the Jordan Valley, a Star of David flag fluttered above a sandbagged watchtower from which two Israeli soldiers peered out through binoculars across Abu Dis. In the gardens where in the evening I would sit reading or listening to the *muezzin*'s call to prayer reverberate across the hills, or watch the sunlight soften on the al-Aqsa mosque, Israeli soldiers lolled around with their M-16 rifles littering the flowerbeds with the remains of their ration packs. Just for a moment my heart ached, and I felt fleetingly a mixture of sadness and resentment that 'my place' had somehow been violated. After many years of working here, it was the closest I had ever come to any real understanding of what most Palestinians had long since lived with – occupation. While in its day the hotel and its owners were no strangers to 'visits' by the IDF, now it had become the army's stronghold in the district.

According to one local Palestinian who asked to be called 'Abu Hamid,' just a few days before my visit following the suicide bomb attack in Jerusalem's French Hill suburb, many Palestinians carrying green West Bank ID cards and returning from the capital were arrested and detained at The Cliff. 'Abu Hamid' said that one man was badly beaten by soldiers, who then urinated in his mouth before pushing him from the second-story roof where I used to spend time relaxing and taking in the view.

As I wandered dazed around the neighbourhood next to the hotel, watching the bulldozers, workmen and soldiers, I came across Ali Ayad, whose cousins were owners of The Cliff as well as my old friends. 'We have been here since 1958. First they confiscated the hotel when we would not sell, and now they cut us off from the rest of our family just over the other side,' he explained, pointing towards Abu Dis. Already, Ali Ayad had paid the equivalent of £1,700 to a lawyer to take up his case with the Israeli authorities, but admitted it was probably hopeless, given that a military confiscation order had been signed, over which Palestinians rarely had any right of appeal. Knowing this, I asked, why then did he pay the lawyer money? 'Like a blind man who cannot move you take whatever guidance you can get,' he replied. Again it was all about trying to survive. Doing what one could, though the odds were heavily stacked against success.

Now, to visit the rest of his extended family, Ali had to travel 10km of Israeli checkpoints and undergo harassment for the sake of the few hundred metres that separated him from his in-laws. Did he think that one day he might see the wall come down? 'If the Europeans and international community stand with us, it will come down. The Berlin Wall fell and who would have thought that possible?' he answered, with that perennial Palestinian optimism.

Most Israelis of course had a very different reaction to the significance of the security barrier. Many, like the country's prominent military historian, Professor Martin van Creveld of the Hebrew University, firmly believed that 'walls worked.' Indeed, it was van Creveld who more

than 16 year earlier, while giving a lecture to Israeli military commanders at a training college, first proposed the idea of a wall around the
West Bank to separate Palestinians from the Jewish state. Van Creveld
has freely admitted that he drew his inspiration for this proposal from
the Berlin Wall, after he and some colleagues made a visit to the barrier
during a year's sabbatical he spent in Germany in 1980–81.

'At first we all said it was terrible, it was inhuman, until our guide
stopped us and said, "You don't know what you are talking about. This
wall is the best thing that ever happened to this city",' van Creveld
recalls. 'He was a native Berliner and he said that before there was a
wall, there was an incident every week. And after the wall was built it
had become the most peaceful place on Earth.' Van Creveld was quick
to recognise the 'psychological deterrent' that his guide claimed was the
Berlin Wall's greatest strength.

'They know that one inch further and they are dead – so 99.9 percent don't even try,' his guide had told him. Dismissed as it was all those
years ago during his lecture at the military college, by now van Creveld's
idea had not only gained legitimacy but the actual wall was being constructed across the West Bank. Despite this, he was far from satisfied,
and remained worried that under political pressure over such a contentious policy, Ariel Sharon would not go far enough in building a wall
to be reckoned with.

'I just don't want to see a security fence. It is not good enough,' the
historian insisted in a *Sydney Morning Herald* interview published just a
few months before I returned to Abu Dis to see the result of his 'vision.'
'I want to see a concrete wall, because concrete walls are much more difficult to breach, because the effect will be largely psychological,' said
van Creveld unequivocally. 'In theory, if I could, I would build a concrete wall so tall that even the birds could not fly over it. And, above all,
so the people cannot look each other in the face – complete separation.'
Van Creveld need not have worried: Ariel Sharon would later take the
building of the wall to heart. But the historian's remarks said much
about Israel's obsession with security and the lengths it was prepared to
go to achieve it. Whenever questions about the legality of the wall were
raised, Israelis invariably responded with the same answer: 'It stops the
bombers and that's all that matters.' For Israelis such as these there was
simply no debate to be had. As far as they were concerned the crushing
effects of the wall on the lives of millions of Palestinians was a small
price to pay for this relative – if somewhat imaginary – guarantee of

their own personal security.

'They had their chance, many chances, to rein in the crazies within Hamas, Islamic Jihad and the Tanzim, and Arafat blew it,' one Israeli friend summed up, when asked about the legitimacy of shuttering in whole communities behind the concrete and barbed wire rising up across the West Bank. Deep down most Israelis knew that the extent of Arafat's reach and leverage wasn't as long or effective as they imagined, especially among the Islamist groups. But to call it that way made for a convenient defence of a policy they also knew was pretty indefensible in terms of international law. Certainly, the wall's existence helped reduce the number of suicide bombings and other attacks. But it would never stop them entirely so long as the occupation continued, and Palestinians suspected that the motive behind the barrier's construction was nothing more than another land grab. While such suspicions were not far off the mark, they only partly explained the rationale behind Israeli strategy.

It was back in February 6, 2001, the same night that Ariel Sharon was elected Prime Minister, that another leading Israeli academic was called to a meeting with Sharon's aides and told to 'bring the maps.' Professor Arnon Sofer was a geographer at Haifa University, who just a few months earlier had given a lecture at the Herzliya Conference on the 'Arab demographic danger.' During the presentation Sofer had illustrated his talk with a series of maps illustrating how 'new borders' should be created, that he claimed would safeguard the Jewish State from being swamped with Arabs. According to an article in the Israeli daily *Yedioth Aharonoth*, both Sharon – then opposition leader – and Sofer talked at the conference, during which the professor outlined how the West Bank should be cut into three sections or 'cantons'. One canton would stretch from Jenin to Ramallah, the second from Bethlehem to Hebron, and a third smaller area created around the city of Jericho. Once an 'electric fence' – as envisaged by Sofer – surrounded all three, Israel's worries would effectively be over. Sofer was to stay in touch with Sharon until his election as prime minister, and subsequently insisted that the final map outlining the route of the separation wall was almost identical to his original blueprint. But others believe that Sofer should not have been so quick to take the credit, insisting instead that the idea for the separation barrier had been fermenting in Sharon's mind from perhaps as far back as the mid-1970s. Whatever the truth, Sharon at first was slow to push the idea of the wall any further, even if the wider Israeli public increasingly thought it time for action to be taken.

'The first intifada destroyed the credibility of the greater Israel movement. The second intifada destroyed the credibility of the peace process. People were desperate for something that would get us out of this. They thought if only we put up the fence, things would be better,' said Daniel Seidemann, an Israeli lawyer and civic activist in Jerusalem.

Like the settlers on whose behalf he had long fought, Sharon feared that any physical divide built along the pre-1967 Green Line between Israel and the West Bank would eventually consolidate into the permanent future political border. To concede this amount of land to the Palestinians was unthinkable, but slowly it dawned on the old campaigner that appeasing his public and holding on to what he believed rightfully belonged to Israel were not mutually exclusive policies. Certainly, by 1999, Sharon is said to have openly spoken of the proposed wall to former Italian Prime Minister Massimo D'Alema, during a brief visit he made to Italy. Even more significantly perhaps, it was the first time Sharon had publicly referred to it as 'the Bantustan plan,' explaining to D'Alema that the South African apartheid model offered the most appropriate solution to the Israeli–Palestinian conflict. The term 'Bantustan' harks back to the so-called 'independent' homelands created under apartheid for black South Africans. Far from being 'free' and separate, however, these homelands possessed no genuine sovereignty or outside recognition by other states. In effect they were little more than fragmented chunks of land in which the white authorities and apartheid regime forced people to live. In drawing up the Bantustan boundaries, the regime usually ensured that areas of valuable natural resources and arable land fell outside their demarcated area. In short, the Bantustan policy kept anything of value in white hands and the blacks 'in place.'

As a peculiar historical footnote to these proposals, some years ago, during a dinner in my home town of Glasgow hosted for a visiting delegation of veteran African National Congress (ANC) members who had been in the forefront of the struggle against apartheid, one of the delegates told me how Israel and Taiwan had been the only countries that had sought to take up business relations with the Bantustan 'governments.' Historically, at least, it seemed Israel had no political difficulty in accepting the Bantustan model. As grotesque a means of control and oppression as it was, Ariel Sharon now also appeared to have no qualms about adopting the Bantustan approach for the West Bank and Gaza, despite the warnings the South African experience had ultimately delivered about the dangers of corralling a people into such a system.

By the mid-1980s, unrest in South Africa's Bantustans had descended into widespread rioting, terror and near anarchy. So bad did the situation become that by January 1994 they were finally dismantled. Some Israelis could see the potential for these long-term dangers arising at home, and a few, especially on the far left, opposed the barrier, recognising that it would likely set back any hope of a negotiated peace with the Palestinians. These opponents were few and far between, however, when set alongside the vast majority within the political mainstream, who heartily embraced the wall as their first line of defence against the intifada, and the best means of keeping 'terror' out.

The simple reality of course was that the building of the separation barrier was just another – albeit enormous – brick in the labyrinth of walls and fences Israel had for years been constructing in its attempt to contain the Palestinian population and its uprising. In effect it was the most tangible evidence yet of what Jerusalem-based human rights activist Jeff Halper has called Israel's 'matrix of control.' What Halper meant was Israel's extensive use of settlements, confiscated land, planning laws and checkpoints to herd Palestinians into the spaces it allocates. All of which was aimed at eroding the national consciousness of the Palestinian people, chopping and separating their identities into Gazans, West Bankers, refugees, Israeli Arabs or East Jerusalemites. Almost always this was done in the name of Israel's 'security' but its real goal has been to hinder the growth of a popular Palestinian leadership and at the same time weaken the intifada. Destroy Palestinian identity and you destroy Palestinian resistance to the occupation, was the Israeli government and military's working maxim.

Livelihood is central to any people's identity, and almost from the start the wall began to deprive many Palestinians of an income as it swallowed up their land. In Abu Dis the collapse of Hassan Akramawi's shopkeeping business or loss of the Ayad family's hotel was only the tip of the iceberg. Across the West Bank there were countless similar personal tragedies, most of which, as ever, were invisible to much of the Israeli public. As the Israeli journalist Meron Rappaport wrote in *Yedioth Aharonoth*:

Who here cares about farmers like Nimr Ahmed, who in one day lost access to his lands, which he and his fathers had worked for generations? Who cares about a shepherd like Naji Yousef who was forced to sell his sheep because the fence blocked access to pasture? Who is upset that the principal of a high school like Mohammed Shahin of Ras a-Tira was forced to use donkeys to bring textbooks from Kalkilya since all the roads were blocked by the fence?

Who cares about a doctor from Tulkarm who drives five hours every morning from his house to his job in Kalkilya, a distance of 15 kilometers, because he is forced to go by way of Jenin, Nablus, the Jordan Valley, Ramallah and the trans-Samaria road? This kind of occupation perhaps doesn't kill. Not right away, anyway. But it does destroy the soul.

For Palestinians living in Israel and the West Bank this systematic destruction of the soul boiled down to a life where everything was colour-coded and segregated. Blue car licence plates, green or blue ID cards; special border crossing points away from the eyes of tourists who might find the endless searches and questioning distasteful; 'Arab rooms' at Tel Aviv airport where the interrogations and rummaging through bags and belongings lasts for even longer. Like prisoners in any jail subjected to long periods of confinement and control, such a day to day existence leads to a virtual conditioning of individuals.

The Palestinian writer Raja Shehadeh once told me a story about when he and his wife Penny – herself not even Palestinian by birth – were travelling from their home in Ramallah through Jordan on their way to Europe and the United States on business.

'We were at Amman airport and our baggage had just been checked and cleared by the airport security officials,' recalled Shehadeh. 'Suddenly Penny asked the security man why he hadn't put any stickers on our bags, because at Tel Aviv airport the stickers were compulsory as a sign that you had been cleared and were able to board the plane.' The security official tried to explain to Shehadeh's wife that at Amman airport they only put stickers on those bags that needed more rigorous scrutiny and that the couple's bags were fine and didn't need stickers. 'Just for a moment I could see the look on Penny's face that told me she couldn't quite equate that things were different here, she had become so used to the Israeli way of doing things and the terrible problems it would cause us if we did not have the right stickers.'

Problematic as it was for Raja Shehadeh and his wife to leave their home in the West Bank and venture into the world outside, for them at least it was possible. For countless other Palestinians such a journey would have been like contemplating a visit to the moon.

For as the separation wall grew, the restrictions on movement and economic plight of many worsened daily. Given this, it seems strange that for a country so preoccupied with history, Israel seemed so quickly to have forgotten the lessons of its own recent past.

After all, it was a little less than two decades ago following years of claustrophobic containment and economic deprivation, that the giant prison that was Gaza boiled over into the first intifada.

Given the obvious parallels between then and the economic conditions the wall has inevitably created today, just what might Israel be stoking up for the future by imposing on the Palestinians this latest massive extension to its 'matrix of control'? Much of what the Israeli government insisted were its real motives behind putting up the barrier were more myth than reality. First among these myths was that Palestinians were informed about the wall's construction and given the opportunity to contest the Israeli government's decision. The truth is that while Palestinians were told about the wall's construction, all protests sent by lawyers to the Israeli Supreme Court were flatly rejected with 'security' cited as the reason. Another myth was that the Israelis were building the wall to protect its citizens by preventing Palestinians from crossing into Israeli areas. The reality was that any security wall could have been erected on the international border or even inside Israel and still have met the same objectives.

As it stood, the wall was going up on average six kilometres to the east of the international border, and in some places much deeper into Palestinian territory. What's more, this deviation meant that the wall would be almost double the length of the border. Away from Sharon's maps and Israeli myths, it's worth stopping to consider some of the hard facts. Running for 420 miles, the wall consists of reinforced cement, razor wire, electrical fences, trenches, electronic motion sensors, fortified watchtowers and up to three security roads. One road would be used to trace infiltrators, another for army patrols and a third wide one for tanks. All this costs money, lots of it. At around $1.6 million per kilometre the ultimate cost is virtually incalculable, but one Israeli analyst has put the final price tag at perhaps $1 billion. Not that everyone at the heart of the Israeli military establishment believes it is money well spent. 'I don't think the fence will solve all the problems. If I were given that money I would invest it elsewhere,' admitted Moshe Ya'alon, the Israel Defence Force Chief, in an interview in August 2003.

While Israel's wall, like that of its more famous counterpart in China, can now be seen from space, up close it has meant Israeli bulldozers clearing 11,500 square metres of Palestinian land, damaging or wiping out 83,000 olive trees and destroying greenhouses and water networks in more than 39 villages. According to the United Nations Office for the Coordination of Humanitarian Affairs, an estimated 10 percent of the West Bank, home to nearly 50,000 Palestinians, will be incorporated into Israel. Coincidently – just as with South Africa's Bantustans – much of the land to be taken is the richest agricultural territory in the West Bank, and includes the aquifer system that provides 51 percent of the West Bank's water resources. Far from outlining the wall's route at the outset, the Israelis have consistently altered its direction, keeping the Palestinian Authority guessing, with decisions taken on an almost daily basis.

On the ground, meanwhile, the line of the barrier takes a looping route to ensure that it encompasses the settlements accounting for about three quarters of the 240,000 Israeli settlers in the West Bank, mainly those in Ariel and Maale Adumin. This snaking route has inevitably meant the creation of isolated Palestinian enclaves such as the town of Qalqiliya where the 40,000 residents are completely surrounded by the barrier with only one way in and out through an Israeli checkpoint. Cut off from farmland and wells, Palestinians in Qalqiliya are reduced to seeking permission from the Israeli army to access what by right belongs to them. Those who don't can pay a heavy price, as in October 2003 when a few farmers from the village of Jayous, near Qalqiliya, crossed from the West Bank side of the wall through to the Israeli side with their families to gather their crops. Later that day when they tried to return, soldiers stopped them from getting back to their village. Eventually the women and children were allowed to cross, but some 70 Palestinian farmers were forced to stay outside the wall by their land for almost nine days. All the time Palestinians were paying such a punitive price, the Israeli government was insisting that the requisition of property in the occupied territories was legal according to Article 23(g) of the 1907 Hague Regulations, which states:

> In addition to the prohibitions provided by special Conventions, it is especially forbidden to destroy or seize the enemy's property, unless such destruction or seizure be imperatively demanded by the necessities of war.

In other words, in building the wall and appropriating Palestinian land, Israel says it was entitled to do so 'by the necessities of war.' However, as international lawyer and former war crimes investigator Paul Troop, in an article entitled 'The Reality and Legality of Israel's Wall,' points out, Articles 46 and 55 of the same Hague Regulations clearly state that private property must be respected and that the occupier is regarded only as an administrator and therefore must safeguard such properties. In addition Israel – despite being an actual signatory to the document – is clearly in breach of articles 53 and 147 of the Fourth Geneva Convention, which forbids the destruction of property and confinement of persons by an occupier. Indeed, under the Fourth Convention the taking of such property can amount to a 'grave breach' which potentially could leave Israel open to charges of committing a war crime.

Travelling across the West Bank as the unrelenting construction of the wall continued, I found it difficult not to be overwhelmed by an all-pervasive impression of coloniser and colonised. Nowhere is this more apparent than in the slow obliteration of Arab East Jerusalem. It was in the tenth century that the great Arab geographer Mohammed ibn Ahmad al-Muqaddasi once boldly claimed that the city united the pleasures of this world with those of the next. These days, notions of unity in any shape or form are about as distant as those times in which Muqaddasi lived. Slowly, the wall is disconnecting East Jerusalem, and with it fades any hopes Palestinians had that one day it might be their capital in a state of their own. Perhaps Muqaddasi's other famous observation, that Jerusalem was also 'a golden basin filled with scorpions' more aptly catches the mood of Palestinians in the east of the city as their sense of community is eroded and their dislocation from the West Bank becomes complete.

As the wall slices through several districts separating children from their schools, shopkeepers from their stores and family members from each other, there is a new and growing rage among Palestinian Jerusalemites. Daniel Seidemann, an Israeli lawyer who specialises in relations between Palestinians and Israelis in Jerusalem, points out that there are almost a quarter of a million Palestinians living in the city and that most of them are going to find themselves on the Israeli side of the fence. 'It's the first time there has been a serious intent to build a wall around the city since the 16th century,' he says. 'It's certainly the biggest change to Jerusalem since 1967.' He also draws attention to the fact that over the past four years since 2001 there had been less than 200 individuals arrested for involvement in acts of terror. 'I don't make light of that; some of them acted with devastating effect, but 200 arrests is about the yield of two weeks in the West Bank,' Seidemann observes. The fact that the Palestinians of East Jerusalem have not participated in any significant numbers in the violent, deadly aspects of the intifada, says Seidemann, is 'not because they are Israelis,' but because in the east of the city there is what he calls a 'delicate ecosystem' of comparative coexistence. 'It is my fear that by building the fence the way we are, we are preventing suicide bombers from coming into the city at the expense of the radicalisation of the population of East Jerusalem. And if indeed my forecast is correct we will miss the placid days that we had in 2001 to 2004.'

Should Seidemann's worst-case scenario prevail, then it would also effectively put to rest the least convincing myth the Israeli government has peddled regarding the wall – the question of its 'permanence.' It's only temporary, they have frequently been heard to say; nothing more than a stopgap measure to help kickstart peace negotiations, which if they prove successful will enable Palestinians and Israelis to live alongside each other without the need for walls. Few ordinary Israelis buy this government line, happy in the certainty that their leaders will never sell them out on the issue of 'security.' Palestinians meanwhile understandably scoff at the idea that the Israelis would ever voluntarily dismantle the wall. The cost alone leads many to doubt the viability of such an undertaking, while historic precedent doesn't inspire confidence in the government's claims. Palestinians point out that they have been here before, when a similar procedure was used by Israel to take control of Palestinian land for a 'temporary' period to let them establish Jewish settlements. Most of those settlements still stand across the West Bank, and with the exception of Gaza where the myth of 'disengagement' there was widely seen as part of a longer-term political strategy, Israel shows little intention of giving up any of its appropriated land.

'Two things are certain about Israel,' said Muhammad Maraabi, the Deputy Mayor of Ras Atiya, a Palestinian village south of Qalqiliya. 'It never returns your land and it never pulls down walls it puts up.' If indeed the wall is ever to fall, then a political solution with or without the pressure of the intifada must be found. But as the shutters come down, many Palestinians are quick to point out that patience among a younger generation who have watched friends and families suffer at the hands of the Israelis is in seriously short supply.

Fearful of an intifada against the wall, at the core of which would lie even more violence and the devastating Israeli retribution that would undoubtedly follow, some Palestinians have advocated a different approach. Given the obviously emotive reaction the wall invokes, not to mention its undoubted illegality, isn't it the perfect issue on which once again world sympathy for their plight might be galvanized, they ask? To maximise this potential, some political elements within the Palestinian community have started advocating a new kind of intifada, a non-violent and mass civil disobedience campaign like the sort put forward by Arun Gandhi – grandson of India's illustrious freedom campaigner Mahatma. In recent years Arun Gandhi has visited the West Bank to witness for himself the conditions under which Palestinians live, the effects the wall is having in compounding their difficulties, and to discuss how any fightback campaign might be conducted. But, as Jonathan Cook wrote in a perceptive piece in *The Guardian* around that time, what Gandhi and his supporters failed to understand is that a non-violent struggle requires specific conditions that are not present in the current intifada. 'The first and most obvious condition is that non-violence should carry with it the moral weight that makes violent retaliation unconscionable. If the experience of the first and present al-Aqsa intifada proves anything, however, it is that non-violence by Palestinians is rarely reciprocated by the Israeli security forces.' Given this, most likely it will once again be a new generation of militant *shebab*, who will take the fight over the wall onto the streets.

If, as some Middle East observers suggest, the construction of the wall is a virtual death sentence for the Palestinians, then its creation also signals the defeat of hope for those Israelis who clung to the idea of a negotiated peace. 'You leave us no room to grow, you leave us no room to live,' argued Jamal Juma of the Palestinian Environment Association, in an impassioned interview with the Israeli newspaper *Yedioth Aharonoth* about the wall in May 2003.

> You want us to live like slaves. It won't work. If you had built the fence along the Green Line, there would be no problem. This way perhaps you'll have quiet for four/five years, but you will create only hatred. Instead of 20 percent Hamas, you'll have 60 per cent.

Juma's words were to prove prophetic, as the Palestinian people, their movement and intifada, moved to confront these latest challenges over their human rights and hopes of ending the occupation.

Standing on the hilltop at the Cliff Hotel that day when I visited the construction site of the wall there, it became clear that this razor cut across Palestinian land, hopes and collective psyche, was perhaps the biggest threat ever to those seeking to resist the juggernaut of Israeli political and military ambitions in the territories. Little did I or anyone else know then that an unpredictable new era was dawning that would see the Palestinian old guard decimated and the emergence of a very different kind of leadership.

9

THE DEMISE OF THE ENIGMA

'If Yasser Arafat didn't exist, you would
have to invent him.'

—Mohammed Sid-Ahmed, Egyptian journalist
Camp David summit, July 2000

Ramallah, October 29, 2004

It was just after daybreak, and the winter sky was full of sleety rain as the frail figure was loaded from the black Mercedes into a waiting Jordanian helicopter. Weak as he was, Yasser Arafat, ever the showman, still managed to blow kisses to the few hundred supporters that had turned out to say their good-byes. A little more than an hour after the helicopter took off, Arafat was out of the Middle East aboard a French presidential aircraft fitted out as an ambulance with life support systems, that whisked him from Amman to Paris and the Percy military hospital in the city's southern suburbs. After a 40-year career on the frontline of the Palestinian struggle against Israel – not to mention a few other adversaries – Yasser Arafat was embarking on the last battle of his life. It was a fight that a little over two weeks later he would lose, dying, as he had never wanted – in exile. To people around the world, he was the man in the chequered headscarf. For some, a great defender. For others, a corrupt dictator. Loved and loathed, he had been on the world stage longer than any other current leader, apart from Fidel Castro. And, like the charismatic Cuban, he had always been larger than life.

For all the years I had worked in Israel and the occupied territories, I only ever met Arafat once. It was back in 1996 and I was part of a small group of journalists who were given 20 minutes of interview time with the newly elected President of the Palestinian Authority. It was a fairly uninspiring and uneventful encounter, at which Arafat parried our questions about his 'overwhelming majority victory' in the election, and the reasons why Hamas and other opposition movements had not participated. Impossible as it was to form any real opinion of him in such a short time, my impressions that day were nevertheless of a man simply going through the motions. No doubt, given the endless interviews and press conferences Arafat had sat through, they had become a terrible chore to him. Doubtless too that he probably had more important things on his mind at the time.

Certainly it was about that time when rumours of his ill health had begun to circulate with talk of Parkinson's disease, a claim many Palestinians simply dismissed as propaganda disseminated by the Israeli security services. But putting all these things aside, there was something about 'Abu Ammar,' as he was affectionately nicknamed, that left me uninspired; something about him as a person that left me feeling that here was an individual almost constantly semi-detached from whatever was happening around him. He appeared to be a man preoccupied and lost in himself, who gave bizarre importance at our meeting to comparatively irrelevant things like where to sit, the quality of light in the room, or the whereabouts of some absent aide at that given moment. At first I thought the explanation for his behaviour could be put down to that wonderful but insistent Arab concern for the hospitality of their guests, but it was something more, a kind of strangeness that was quite discomfiting.

In the flashes of Arafat's personality that came through, never for a moment did I detect that wit or inspiration that singled out other political or guerrilla leaders I had met or interviewed in the past. This was no Nelson Mandela, who, when I was once given special access to photograph him during a visit to Scotland, would occasionally excuse himself for a few moments from a meeting to catch up on the progress of a championship boxing match involving one of his countrymen that was showing on television in the room next door. Nor did Arafat show the intelligence, curiosity and charm of Ahmed Shah Massoud, the Afghan guerrilla leader, who I met many times, before he was finally murdered by assassins dispatched by Osama bin Laden in Afghanistan two days before the 9/11 attacks in the United States. Certainly Arafat displayed nothing of the sharpness, dynamism and passion that some years later I would sense during my meeting with his younger Fatah protégé, Marwan Barghouti, who many had tipped as his possible successor.

Interestingly, when I later told a Palestinian acquaintance of my negative impressions of Arafat, I was to receive the sort of gentle rebuke that would become all too familiar whenever I let slip anything untoward about the great man. 'For an outsider to criticise him in the company of Palestinians is like intervening in a family dispute; even those with the best of intentions come off badly,' my friend reminded me only half jokingly.

He had a point. Over the years, I had met many Palestinians more than willing to sound off about Arafat. And as time passed and his political performance over the handling of the intifada and failed peace process began to frustrate many more, the critics became ever more vocal. Even then, time and again, I had always been conscious of how much they saw that criticism as their right, and their right alone, quickly rallying to the old warhorse whenever anyone else saw fit to take a political swipe in his direction. Quite simply, the more outsiders or enemies – especially the Israelis – found reason to attack or besiege Arafat, the more even those Palestinians sceptical of his abilities sought to defend him. It was an unfortunate attitude, not least as things became increasingly difficult for ordinary Palestinians as Israel clamped down on militancy within their communities, using tactics like Operation Defensive Shield and the drawing up of blueprints for the separation wall.

Just at precisely the moment when Palestinians were in dire need of real leadership, Arafat once again seemed to be found wanting. In turn his influence begun to wane badly, giving critics within his own ranks yet more ammunition, and the Israelis an additional lever with which to pressure him. There were of course those who had never liked him and never would. Over the years, such was the level of feeling that Arafat stirred up both at home and abroad, that it is probably fair to say that any biographer would have his work cut out writing an account of him that would be universally recognised as balanced and objective. Even for Middle East watchers who on the whole empathised with the Palestinian plight, Arafat was often a target. 'The Arafat mug was never going to find its way on to university walls like Guevara or even Castro,' wrote Robert Fisk just a day after the ailing Palestinian leader's helicopter had touched down in Paris. 'There was – and still is – a kind of seediness about it and maybe that's what the Israelis saw too, a man who could be relied on to police his people in their little Bantustans, another proxy to run the show when occupation became too tiresome,' Fisk continued, characteristically pulling no punches.

Many who did know Arafat well say they were amazed by the huge difference between the media personality and the man. On TV, Arafat could look fanatical, aggressive. In real life, they say he was warm and considerate. He was by all accounts a host who loved to pamper his guests at meals, offering them choice morsels with his fingers. He also liked to touch the people he talked with, to take them by the hand and conduct them along the corridors, to offer them small presents. While in the public eye Yasser Arafat's iconic status as the recognisable 'fighter' of the Palestinian cause was undeniable, his actual role and contribution during the course of the first uprising in the 1980s and the subsequent al-Aqsa intifada remains a vexed question. Even more contentious perhaps was the nature of the political legacy his death left behind, and how it contributed to the rise of a new guard, with a very different view of the way the occupation should be tackled and resisted. Arafat of course was no stranger to a fight. Here was a man who had been branded a terrorist and international public enemy number one while Osama bin Laden was still a boy; a man who, it is fair to say, probably never had a moment when a dozen or more intelligence services were not on his trail, or someone somewhere was planning to riddle him with bullets or blow him to pieces. Here too was a leader who had taken up responsibility for the destiny of his people while many of today's world statesmen like George Bush and Tony Blair were still trying to rally attention in nursery school.

As far as the Palestinian cause was concerned, perhaps there was some truth in the comment made by the Egyptian journalist Mohammed Sid-Ahmed during the early days of the first Camp David conference, when he said that 'if Yasser Arafat didn't exist, you would have to invent him.' Certainly Arafat himself was never in any doubt about how polarising his place in history would be. 'Choose your friends carefully. Your enemies will choose you,' he once advised.

Almost since the day he was born in Cairo on August 24, 1929 – although he has claimed he was born a 'son of Jerusalem' – Mohammed Abdel-Raouf Arafat al-Qudwa al-Hussaeini, to give him his full name, had been wedded to his adopted country's cause. Arafat's father was a Palestinian textile merchant with some Egyptian ancestry, while his mother came from an old Palestinian family in Jerusalem, then under British rule, which the Palestinians were opposing. After she died when he was five, Arafat was sent to live with his maternal uncle in Jerusalem, and though he revealed little about his childhood, one of his earliest memories was of British soldiers breaking into his uncle's house after midnight, beating members of the family and smashing furniture. In part, no doubt, as a result of such experiences, he took the name Yasser, a gesture believed to have been made to honour an Arab victim of the British mandate.

After four years in Jerusalem, his father brought him back to Cairo, where an older sister took care of him and his siblings. Arafat rarely mentioned his father, who was known as a strict disciplinarian. In 1952, when he died, Arafat was not at the funeral. As a young politician in Cairo, Arafat was a natural publicist. Intense, elusive, small at 5 ft. 4 inches, delicate and impulsive. Before he was 17 he was smuggling arms to Palestine to be used against the British and the Jews. The 1948 war with Israel and the Jewish state's takeover of Arab lands instilled in him a grim, lifelong cause, and at the age of 19 Arafat left his studies at the University of Faud I – later Cairo University – to fight against Jews in the Gaza area. By 1959, in Kuwait with the help of his comrades and friends Yahia Ghavani and Khalil al-Wazir, otherwise known as Abu Jihad, he founded al-Fatah, an underground network of secret cells, which began to publish a magazine advocating armed struggle against Israel. At the end of 1964, Arafat left Kuwait to become a full-time revolutionary, organising Fatah raids into Israel from Jordan.

A few years later in the Six Day War of 1967, Israel had crushed many of its Arab enemies and captured the West Bank and Gaza. Fatah remained its only credible force of opposition and, two years later, Arafat became the chairman of the Palestine Liberation Organisation (PLO). Quickly he developed the PLO into a state within the state of Jordan with its own military forces. King Hussein of Jordan, disturbed by its guerrilla attacks on Israel and other violent methods, eventually lost patience with the PLO and expelled it from his country. Regrouping in Beirut, Arafat sought to build a similar organisation in Lebanon, but the Israelis and the man who would become his life-long arch enemy – Ariel Sharon – had other ideas.

After the Israeli invasion of Lebanon in 1982, Sharon slowly tightened the noose around the Palestinian leader and his PLO fighters who were holed up in Beirut. During the siege of the city, which Arafat had dubbed the 'second Stalingrad,' Israeli soldiers were in constant pursuit of Arafat with snipers said to be ready to kill him. For almost 80 days Israeli warplanes pounded buildings in which the Palestinian leader was suspected of hiding, but Arafat refused to leave his besieged fighters. Back in 1982 during the terrible days of the battle for Beirut, the Israeli journalist and left-wing peace activist, Uri Avnery, who became one of Arafat's few Israeli confidants, asked him where he would go if he got out alive. Without hesitation, Arafat said, 'Home, of course.'

In the end, only after a long bloody battle and the intervention of the international community were Sharon's plans for Arafat's demise thwarted. Arafat – the great survivor – departed Beirut defiantly with his men, not for 'home' as he had hoped, but to the city of Tunis in an effort to keep the PLO alive.

Arafat's charmed life was rapidly becoming legendary. In 1986 Israeli fighter planes flew 3,000 miles from Tel Aviv to Tunis on a mission to blow him to pieces. Though Arafat's headquarters was reduced to rubble and most of those inside killed, Abu Ammar himself survived only because that day he had decided to delay his return to Tunis. Then there was the sandstorm in the Libyan desert in 1992, which brought down Arafat's personal plane in a crash landing. Though the pilot and several passengers including his bodyguards were killed, Arafat survived despite being badly smashed up. The injuries he suffered resulted less than a year later in internal haemorrhaging requiring an emergency operation to remove a blood clot. Some have speculated that the injury perhaps contributed to his continuing ill health in the period that followed, possibly accounting for the noticeable tremor of his lower lip in the last years of his life.

If the period after the expulsion from Lebanon was a low time for Arafat and the PLO, then the first Palestinian intifada in 1987 provided the chance to again seize the initiative against the Israelis. In reality of course the mass popular uprising of the war of the stones had stunned the PLO and likewise caught all the regional state powers off guard. Arafat was no exception, and he began to play a dual-purpose role in response to the intifada. Publicly at least, Arafat, often using PLO radio stations around the region, appeared to be urging those on the streets of Gaza and the occupied territories to increase the pressure on Israel. Behind the scenes it was a different story, with the PLO leader reluctant to give any real, material backing for fear of compounding his own recent failures.

Arafat's reaction to the outbreak of the intifada was typical of the way he handled so many crises and events. Rarely did he appear to be a leader with any cohesive plan, relying instead on a sort of instinct. While it might have been a sharply honed instinct borne out of his own and the PLO's personal survival, at best it invariably left the Palestinian people and their cause in political limbo, at worst hung out to dry. Many who had spent time with him in negotiations endorse this view of his approach. This was a man far from being a bookish intellectual, one who relied instead on gut intuition; a leader who had to make the most of the few means at his disposal – shrewdness, violence, diplomacy, propaganda.

Few will forget his famous debut on the international stage at the United Nations General Assembly of 1974, where he told delegates that he had come 'bearing an olive branch and a freedom-fighter's gun.' He then warned, 'Do not let the olive branch fall from my hand.' Such mistimed gestures all too often turned into catastrophic mistakes. As the first intifada gained momentum in those volatile days in 1987, Arafat almost missed the opportunity to capitalise on its potential. Palestinians in the occupied territories it seemed had lost their raw fear of the Israeli

state, but Arafat remained cautious and apprehensive. To Arafat's surprise, however, the intifada refused to go away, and he was left with few
options but to try and seize the initiative. For once Arafat made the right
call and appointed Khalil al-Wazir or Abu Jihad as its coordinator. As
the man responsible for the occupied territories within the PLO command, Abu Jihad had a detailed understanding of the conditions that
had led to the explosion of the uprising. As Arafat biographer Said K.
Aburish observed:

> When the intifada would not die and Arafat finally bowed to the
> inevitable, Abu Jihad ran after it with remarkable speed. Because he
> knew every village, school and large family in Gaza and the West
> Bank, he 'adopted' the intifada and provided it with the necessary
> financial backing and logistical support to keep it alive. Abu Jihad
> became the manager, the brain in exile of the spontaneous move-
> ment.

But, despite this astute appointment, Arafat's embracing of the
intifada also brought with it problems for the PLO leadership, problems
that would grow in the years ahead and ultimately lead to Arafat losing
any real control he might have had over the Palestinian 'street.'
    To begin with, those on the ground taking the fight to the Israelis
were often far removed from the rarefied circles of the Palestinian 'elite'
and rich benefactors on whose largesse Arafat greatly depended. What's
more, many of those groups out with Fatah who were leading the resistance – notably Hamas – had already very effectively connected the
intifada with social and welfare programmes in the occupied territories,
something Arafat and his closed circle had almost singularly neglected
to do. Arafat's problems with the Islamists were made worse by his
appeals to their regional supporters to stop supplying them with arms
and money. As ever when his survival was threatened, Abu Ammar
became less of an understanding 'man of the people' and ever more the
dictator. Not only did he promote and bolster the positions of those perceived to be loyal to him, but he used his substantial financial resources
to consolidate his friends and undermine his enemies whether within the
ranks of the intifada's Unified National Leadership (UNL), Fatah, the
PLO or his own numerous private security services. This money trail
and what remained of Arafat's 'fortune' after his death would become
the subject of intense speculation almost from the moment he drew his

last breath at the Percy military hospital in Paris. It was said his aides used to joke about him resembling 'a walking closet' so full were his pockets of the many notebooks in which he jotted down important memos, many of which were believed to detail his elaborate financial wheeling and dealing. Arafat was described as a 'micromanager,' often handing out no more than a few hundreds or thousands of dollars at a time. This 'backdoor' approach and the lack of transparency that came with it suited his way of working perfectly. 'Arafat never viewed money in a personal enrichment sense; you only have to see the way in which he lived,' says Alastair Crooke, a former British MI6 officer who was seconded to the European Union's mission to the Middle East.

> He was only interested in money as a political tool . . . he used it very much in the style of a last century tribal chieftain, handing out money to the centres of power and leaving it to them to hand it down to the bottom, provided the people at the bottom always had the option to come to him with a special plea.

With the PLO in the past having been expelled from both Jordan and Lebanon, Arafat was determined to ensure that should the organisation ever again find itself on the ropes, it would have something to fall back on. Indeed his concerns were to some extent borne out, when in the wake of the 1991 Gulf War and his terrible decision to side with Saddam Hussein, incoming funds from wealthy Palestinians and other Gulf providers almost dried up. So bad was the financial situation at the time that Arafat is said to have told a meeting of top PLO leaders in Tunis that the organisation barely had enough money to survive two or three years. Some say it was in part a result of this financial crisis that led Arafat to seek out peace negotiations with Israel. Certainly, after the end of the 1991 Gulf War, the United States was busy putting together an elaborate diplomatic initiative aimed at demonstrating its 'leadership' of the Middle East. It was in effect the beginning of the Oslo peace process. Arafat, keen to get involved, was offered the incentives of being the officially recognised Palestinian leader and the opportunity to negotiate with Israel for a 'state' in the West Bank and Gaza. As Arafat returned triumphantly after decades of exile to Gaza on July 1, 1994, at first glance it seemed like a victory born out of the intifada. Under the interim Oslo accords with Israel, the new Palestinian Authority had won a five-year period of self-rule over areas of the West Bank and Gaza

Strip. For Arafat this also meant a replenishment of badly needed cash,
with donor governments pledging $3 billion over that duration. The PA
would also be able to tap into lucrative monopolies that until then had
been run by the Israelis.

Some said a new era of hope for the Palestinian people had begun.
But in reality the only thing beginning was Yasser Arafat's distancing
from the very people whose uprising had enabled him to return to Gaza
at all. Arafat had been made a 'statesman' even if the price of his diplomatic acceptance was the neutering of the very same popular resistance
that had forced Israel and the United States to make him the offer in the
first place. If ever a moment revealed the differing strategies of Arafat
and his Tunis-based old guard, and those of the new generation of fighters against the occupation, this was it.

In Gaza and the West Bank at this time I watched and listened to the
first rumblings of disquiet; talk of sellouts, capitulation, even treachery.
'Why lift the pressure on the Israelis just when the intifada is making
them stop to think again about the occupation? Believe me, if Arafat
betrays the sacrifices people here in Gaza and those in the West Bank
have made over the last few years, he will never be forgiven,' one young
Fatah member I met in Gaza City warned at the height of the Oslo talks.
It seemed Arafat was in real danger of miscalculating the cost of climbing into bed politically with the likes of Bill Clinton and Ehud Barak.
Admittedly, Arafat did subsequently reject the terms offered by Clinton
and Barak that would have resulted in his people being confined to
walled-in ghettos even before the start of the separation wall. But he
would remain determined to consolidate the position of his Palestinian
Authority, which effectively eroded and in some cases made redundant
the political power of the popular committees that had been the back-
bone of the first intifada.

In Gaza meanwhile it was evident that unlike Arafat and his
Palestinian Authority, Hamas and the Islamists, far from distancing
themselves from the people within their constituency, were instead
working ever more closely with and through local committees. The con-
solidation of this network would allow Hamas especially to achieve
dominance in Gaza at the expense of Fatah, and would stoke up dangerous rivalries for the years ahead. These tensions were nothing new,
and Fatah leaders would have remembered well the remark made in the
early months of the intifada by Hamas spokesman Ibrahim Ghawsheh,
who declared that the primary aim of the intifada was to topple Arafat

himself. While the statement might have embarrassed many Hamas members who chose to distance themselves from it, it did hold a kernel of truth.

By the mid-1990s, at the point of his return to Gaza, there was already a sense that Arafat's era was coming to a close. 'Such feelings were motivated not by his old age or faltering health, nor by Israel's irrelevant designations of the man as a peace partner or otherwise,' commented Ramzy Baroud, the editor-in-chief of the *Palestine Chronicle*, looking back on Arafat's life in November 2004. 'It was just that the man who promised the moon failed to deliver a desolate refugee camp. The man who promised Jerusalem was in negotiations over the small neighbourhood of Abu Dis. The astute leader who spoke of the peace of the brave had little to say as the West Bank was once more overrun by the Israeli war machine.'

By the time Ariel Sharon went for his provocative walkabout on Haram al-Sharif in September 2000, Yasser Arafat was also a man well out of step with the sensibilities and desires of many Palestinians. As the *shebab* took to the streets once again, Arafat – despite some Israeli claims to the contrary – was not the orchestrator of the al-Aqsa intifada. Nor indeed was he simply a bystander, but in some ways its target, as Palestinian patience with his role as 'statesmen' finally ran out. Failure to reform his corrupt PA and deliver on peace lay at the root of his problems. Amid the poverty and squalor of the refugee camps in Gaza and the West Bank his acolytes flaunted their new wealth, angering many ordinary Palestinians and providing the best possible recruitment campaign for Islamist and other more militant groups. Put simply, the Palestinian people and the latest uprising had moved beyond Yasser Arafat.

Yet more trouble was just around the corner, as the al-Aqsa intifada gained momentum, and suicide bombers, along with Arafat's own failure to rein in militants, led to the Israeli onslaught that left him holed up inside a small airless room in his Ramallah compound in 2002. For Arafat it was the beginning of the end. It was back to that same compound where he had spent two and a half years penned in by the Israelis, that Egyptian helicopters brought his coffin on November 12, 2004, following a military ceremony in Cairo. His death in Paris the day before had left many questions still unanswered, not least why a string of doctors from Palestine, Jordan, Egypt, Tunisia and France, had been unable to come up with a definitive diagnosis. Had Arafat been the vic-

tim of poisoning as some had suggested, or at 75 had he simply succumbed to a long and debilitating illness?

Above the skies of Ramallah we watched as the helicopters circled.
Since early morning the streets had been packed with tens of thousands
of people. Mourners clambered over walls, climbed trees and broke
through the gates to get a look at their leader's final journey. As the helicopters touched down there was a massive surge towards them with the
crowds forming a solid mass in the square. Guards, gunmen and mourners fired Kalashnikovs into the air for a few minutes, before Arafat's coffin, draped in the Palestinian flag, was taken from one of the aircraft.
Most who surrounded Arafat's *cortège* that day knew his faults, but that
didn't seem to matter. A sea of people barely parted to allow a jeep bearing the coffin to pass, the crowd quickly closing back around the vehicle with many straining to touch the coffin and chanting 'Our blood,
our souls, we sacrifice for you, Yasser Arafat.'

His body was buried in a grave under soil brought from the al-Aqsa
compound in Jerusalem, the place where many Palestinians still hope
that one day his remains will be taken following the creation of a
Palestinian state. While the Israelis had moved quickly to seal off the
West Bank and Gaza on the day of the funeral, long before then, senior
Israeli security services officers had drawn up a document laying out
various scenarios and recommendations in the immediate aftermath of
Arafat's demise. 'The death of Yasser Arafat will cause chaos in the
zones controlled by the Palestinian authority and the revival of the
armed intifada,' the document stated. It then went on to acknowledge
that, 'Whatever the cause of Arafat's death, Israel will in any event be
singled out as being responsible.'

As it turned out few, apart from the most imaginative conspiracy
theorists, did hold Israel directly responsible when Arafat finally lost his
battle for life. Moreover, the intense speculation by both Israelis and
Palestinians alike over what would happen after his death, seemed to be
based on the false premise that it would somehow be a decisive factor
leading inevitably to an improvement in Palestinian–Israeli relations. To
say that such a premise was misguided would be an understatement. As
the passage of time has shown, Arafat's death was to make no difference
to the existence of settlements or the continuation of the occupation.
Nor did it make for any radical improvement in the human rights issues
most Palestinians face daily, nor indeed did it prevent the construction
of the separation barrier.

In his biography of Arafat, Said K. Aburish points out that one of the key strategic decisions he made as Palestinian leader was to resort to the armed struggle.

> The Palestinians were an unknown entity until they expressed themselves through the barrel of a gun. Decades of pleading their cause in international forums had produced less for them than the willingness of their young people to fight and die for it against staggering odds. It was the Palestinian fighter and his kin, the intifada child, who captured the imagination of the world. Their recognition by the world confirmed the existence of a Palestinian people with rights and aspirations.

Yasser Arafat's life was inextricably linked with the fate of the Palestinian people, his commitment to their cause undoubtedly total – if flawed. A European reporter curious about Arafat's personal life once asked the Israeli journalist and peace activist Uri Avnery, who was close to him, what the Palestinian leader did as a hobby when he was not busy with the Palestinian cause. 'He has no hobbies,' replied Avnery. 'There is not a single moment when he is not busy with the Palestinian cause. His identification with the Palestinian struggle is total. He has no other life.' This messianic zeal perhaps in part helps explain why Arafat's pursuit of his political ends meant that his means were often questionable. A revolutionary he might have been, a statesman he most certainly was not. Like many Arab heroes in history, Yasser Arafat was a man fond of gestures. It was typical of him that in 1953, when he sent a letter to an Egyptian leader, it was only three words long and said to have been written in his own blood. It stated simply, 'Don't forget Palestine.'

After years of hardship, the Palestinian people had grown sick and tired of gestures. What they wanted was real and tangible change. With Arafat's passing, the pressing question now was just who those leaders were, and who among them, if any, could be relied upon to deliver that change?

10

THE CHANGING OF
THE GUARD

'We eliminated all the terrorist squads except one.
The problem is that this one consists of 3.5 million Palestinians.'

—A high-ranking Israeli officer, January 2004

Jabaliya Refugee Camp, Gaza Strip, September 2004

'Days of Penitence' the Israeli army had called it. In many ways it was more than just a codename for the military assault the Israelis had launched into Gaza; it was a declaration of intent. Suffering pain for past sins was precisely what the Israeli high command had in mind for Hamas and Islamic Jihad, which it held responsible for the series of mortar and rocket attacks launched from the north of the Strip that had just killed a number of Israeli civilians including two children in the town of Sderot. For many Palestinians, certainly those in Gaza, this was a new intifada – the intifada of the Qassams. Those Palestinians imprisoned in the dusty camps and streets of the Strip, with no hope and no alternative means of political struggle, had decided to hit back with the only means at their disposal – the Qassam rockets. 'Why should we be the only ones who live in fear?' one student Muhammad Abu Oukal in Gaza asked. 'With these rockets, the Israelis feel fear, too. We have to live in peace together, or live in fear together.'

As far as the Israeli army was concerned these homemade missiles packed with explosives had now rained down on southern Israeli towns for far too long, and it was time to take action. The operation was also a sign of things to come in Gaza, the orders for its launch coming barely months after Ariel Sharon's plan for 'unilateral disengagement' from the Strip had been unveiled in late 2003. Once again it was Sharon up to his old tricks, exercising his belief that Israeli–Palestinian relations should be determined not by talks but by military superiority and the physical containment and control of any Palestinian resistance.

The 'penitence' had begun when a brigade of about 2,000 Israeli soldiers and hundreds of tanks and armoured vehicles rolled into northern Gaza, or 'Hamastan,' as certain Israeli military chiefs had taken to calling it. The focus of the attack would be centred on Beit Hanoun, Beit Lahia and the refugee camp of Jabaliya.

I had arrived in Jabaliya as the Israeli tanks were just beginning to mass on the Strip's northern fringes. The atmosphere was tense and intermittent gunfire could be heard echoing around the camp, occasionally punctuated by the colossal thump of Israeli tank shells and columns of dust rising from a number of locations. The camp was as I had always remembered it: a teeming tumbledown of cinder shanties with rag-curtained windows and sand-caked washing hanging from lines. Among the heaps of garbage and sand, I was introduced by my translator to 60-

year-old Nema Abu Wadi and her family, standing in the rubble of what had been their home. 'I live here with my two sons and their grandchildren. When the Israeli soldiers came they fired hundreds of bullets into the house, as we moved from room to room to try and avoid being shot,' Abu Wadi told me.

According to the Israelis, Hamas fighters had launched a number of Qassam rockets from the neighbourhood, but by the time the Israelis responded the Hamas men had vanished. 'There were many tanks just there on the road behind where you are standing,' Abu Wadi explained, pointing over my shoulder. 'Then they brought up the bulldozers and started knocking down our houses.' Inside what was left of Abu Wadi's house, large calibre bullets had taken chunks out of the walls, and as we spoke, the sharp crack of Israeli sniper fire was an uncomfortable reminder of how close the soldiers were still positioned.

Abu Wadi's neighbour, Mohammed Azam, hadn't managed to escape the hail of gunfire the day before. 'I was hit by two bullets in the right leg and two in the left, then I passed out, that's all I remember,' Azam told me. 'When I came round I was in hospital,' he added, leaning on a stick, the bandage on one foot wrapped in a carrier bag to protect the dressing from the soft brown sand the Israeli Merkava tanks had chewed up around his house.

In a little over two weeks, Operation Days of Penitence would take the lives of over 100 Palestinians, 42 of them civilians, and plunge the encircled, poverty-stricken Gaza Strip into scenes of anguish. I would watch mothers weep over their children's corpses, see tank fire rip through groups of fighters and bystanders, witness youngsters face-off with stones against the Israelis as tyres burned in the streets to obscure the Israeli surveillance drones overhead. On numerous occasions Hamas promised 'days of rage,' and the response from the *shebab* was ferocious.

For the Israelis on the other hand, Operation Days of Penitence was their most extensive incursion into the Gaza Strip since the beginning of the al-Aqsa intifada. It was also the largest offensive within the occupied territories since the 2002 reconquest of the West Bank during Operation Defensive Shield. There was no doubt about it, Ariel Sharon was clearly back in the political and military driving seat, and though we couldn't imagine it then, even more dramatic events were about to unfold in Gaza that would change irrevocably the face of the Palestinian–Israeli conflict.

Gaza Strip, August 14, 2005

It had been called many things. Among them, 'the moment of truth,' 'a test of unity' and 'the ultimate betrayal.' Depending on which side of the razor wire, checkpoint barriers or security fences you lived on, whether you were Arab or Jew, the start of the Israeli withdrawal from the Gaza Strip was seen as either the end of a dream, or the chance of a new beginning.

At midnight that Sunday, August 14, the Kissufim crossing at the entrance to the Israeli side of the Gaza Strip was to be closed to all civilian traffic, and early on Monday, a year and a half after Ariel Sharon announced his 'disengagement' plan, the pullout would finally begin. All 21 Jewish settlements in Gaza and four of 120 in the West Bank were to be removed.

For the last 18 years or so, I had witnessed the bitter struggle for Gaza. In a conflict of few compromises, the Strip had always been hardcore. Home to the toughest Palestinian resistance and the Israeli military's most punitive tactics, it had never surprised me that it was here that the first intifada had broken out. This long fought-over finger of land – one of the most densely populated places on the planet – had become not only the base for the most extreme Palestinian groups such as Islamic Jihad and Hamas, but home to the most stubborn and committed of Israeli settlers who regarded Gaza as part of a biblical greater Israel. In those tense days running up to the Israeli withdrawal I had decided to cross the frontlines that separated these two old enemies and talk to those whose lives – for better or worse – were about to be changed forever. What impact would it have on the intifada I wondered? Might it defuse Gaza's militancy, and give the chance of peace talks the kick start that many hoped it would? Or, was it just another ploy by a wily Ariel Sharon more determined than ever to divide and conquer his Palestinian foes?

It was not in Gaza itself, however, that I first met Issac Harel and his family. Just a few days before the withdrawal was due to begin, we found ourselves pushed shoulder to shoulder in a crush of over 100,000 opponents to the Gaza pullout, in the narrow cobbled alleyways that wind through Jerusalem's old city leading down from Damascus Gate to the Western or Wailing Wall. A settler in Gush Katif, one of the largest and most hardline settlements in Gaza, Harel had made the two-hour drive north to join the protest. 'See, look for yourself, so many of us, this is not something the Israeli people are taking lightly,' he shouted, as I helped him lift and pass the pushchair containing his baby son over a sea of heads in front of us, all wearing the Jewish *yarmulke*.

Issac Harel had lived and worked as a vegetable farmer in Gush Katif for more than ten years, and while he was totally opposed to being forced from his home, he rejected the idea of resisting the withdrawal using violence. 'Until the final moment I want to make it difficult for them. We will do everything possible to slow them down, but I will not use violence against our own soldiers,' he insisted, resigned to the fact that in the end he had no chance of winning. As we talked, the rabbi leading the prayers at the Western Wall, or HaKotel as it is known in Hebrew, cried out his grief at the coming loss of the sacred land in Gaza. All around us were ultra-orthodox Jews; men, women, the elderly and the very young, standing rapt in prayer or openly weeping at the rabbi's words of woe.

Nearby, a group of settlers wearing orange T-shirts – the colour that had come to symbolise opposition to the withdrawal – handed out leaflets calling on supporters to drive in convoys to the Kissufim crossing on Monday, in an effort to prevent security forces reaching Gush Katif. Across Israel, there were orange ribbons tied to car aerials, orange stickers plastered over Arabic road signs and even over old election posters showing the smiling face of Ariel Sharon, one-time hero of the settler movement, now the great betrayer. All were signs of the frustration and anger that was widely felt over the decision to leave Gaza. While Israeli Defence Minister Shaul Mofaz remained confident that most settlers would leave their homes peacefully, in the last few hours before the operation commenced, not everyone was so sure.

Twenty-year old Dan Amiel had lost his leg in a Palestinian rocket attack on the settlement of Kfar Darom ten months earlier. 'I already left my leg here. Now they want me to leave behind my life,' he complained bitterly. Walking with the aid of a prosthetic limb, he, his wife and son had returned to Kfar Darom just a week before to join 400 other settlers determined to defy the forced removal. Like many of the settlements in Gaza and elsewhere, Gush Katif and Kfar Darom were often only yards away but worlds apart from the Palestinians on the other side of the divide in slums like Khan Younis. On the settler side, it was a world of pretty red-roofed houses, scrubbed streets, glitzy shopping malls and children's playgrounds. On the side of the Palestinians, it was a ghetto of rundown refugee camps, decrepit concrete buildings almost half submerged by Gaza's drifting coastal sand and the heaps of rotting garbage that lay stinking in the fierce heat of the sun. Both lives may only have been a blink apart, but even for a reporter like myself able to go from one side to the other, it involved a round trip of a few hours.

If the Gaza Strip had been the harshest of frontlines in the fight against Israeli occupation, then Khan Younis had been its most frontline town. A maze of narrow streets, the town sits right alongside the Israeli settlement of Gush Katif, from where soldiers in watchtowers kept an eye open for Palestinian militants who might try to launch mortar or Qassam rocket attacks or slip across in incursion operations. The Israelis, via another crossing known as the Abu Huliq checkpoint, also controlled entry to and from central Khan Younis. 'Sometimes the shooting went on day and night. It was as if the bullets were free of charge,' said Abed el Nasser Abu Huliq, a legal advisor in the Khan Younis Ministry of Justice and the son of the man by whose name the checkpoint was now known. It was 1973 when Abu Huliq senior, along with an uncle, refused the Israelis permission to cut the road by setting up the checkpoint on land the family owned. For their dissent, both were subsequently arrested and imprisoned. 'Even during times of peace our family has had trouble with the Israelis because our land is so near to Gush Katif,' Abed el Nasser explained.

So what difference would the Israeli departure make to him and his family now? I asked. 'It will be a paradise again. We will not be demoralised any more. We will rehabilitate the land, see our children continue their education, learning computer skills instead of living with shooting. We will be able to speak with high spirits,' Abed el Nasser told me, smiling. Wonderful as the thought was, I knew – as I'm certain he did – it was no more than wishful thinking. For even with the Israelis gone, Gaza would be far from remotely comfortable for Palestinians. With a collapsed infrastructure, and next to nothing in the way of natural resources, the Strip had little to offer potential outside investors. Then there were the other far more pressing and serious problems facing Palestinians in the wake of the Israeli departure.

One morning during the course of my stay in Khan Younis, I woke to the sound of gunfire on the streets outside. Was it a battle between Islamic militants from Hamas and the security forces of the Palestinian Authority perhaps, or some other militia groups? 'Rival families, one shot a member of the other, and now they are sorting things out,' explained my fixer Zead Mostafa, who studied media and journalism, and hoped, despite serious concerns about what lay ahead, to continue his education. Like many Palestinians, Zead feared for the future, and he firmly believed that Gaza and towns such as Khan Younis would become potential free-fire zones where corrupt officials, rival militias, criminal gangs and adversarial families would use the rule of the Kalashnikov to ensure their power base remained intact. 'One big problem is that there are some people who have become very wealthy through the conditions the occupation has created, but most are unemployed or very poor. Change needs to come quickly or who knows what might happen,' warned Zead, expressing what many Gazans suspected, but which, after years of hardship and suffering, most were still reluctant to admit.

Some Palestinian leaders recognised the dangers, even if they could do little about them. 'This is a test. We need to convince the world we deserve a state that would be a stabilising factor in the region. If we fail, history will not forgive the Palestinians,' said Jibril al-Rajoub, security advisor to Palestinian President Mahmoud Abbas as the deadline for the Israeli withdrawal neared. With tensions running high, few at that precise moment were thinking quite so far ahead. Both sides, Palestinians and Israelis alike, had other more immediate problems to contend with. As the minutes and hours ticked away towards what would be a historic moment, everywhere across Israel and the occupied territories people became acutely aware of the dangers Sharon's 'disengagement' plan threw up.

Fears of unprecedented violence aimed at scuppering the withdrawal were a constant topic of conversation from the nightclubs of Tel Aviv to the ghettos of Gaza's forgotten refugee enclaves. It seemed impossible to imagine the whole operation being undertaken without some bombing or shooting outrage that could tip everything into the abyss. Israeli settler leaders upped the ante further by calls for mass protest actions. One of them, Tzvika Bar-Hai, told protesters that on the day the 'disengagement' was scheduled to begin (Monday), they should make their way to those Israeli towns closest to the Gaza Strip, by car, by bus and by foot, before then leaving en masse, to head for the numerous entrances into Gush Katif. The four main meeting points he told them would be the Negev towns of Ashkelon, Ofakim, Sderot, and Netivot. 'We will not be stopped at checkpoints, we will bypass them from the right and from the left,' Bar-Hai told supporters at a protest rally.

Some 55,000 Israeli security forces were to be deployed in response
to a range of potential threats. Combined teams of police and troops
fanned out into all the settlements in Gaza, to every street, every home,
making a record of houses already empty and making sure any remaining residents were told that they had 48 hours, taking them up to the
morning of August 17, to get out. While the official schedule called for
a four-week operation, unofficially Israeli planners hoped three weeks
would suffice. Until the Strip was sealed completely before dawn that
Monday, the only Israelis allowed in would be residents of the settlements and providers of essential services, including removers and rescue
services. Six rings of disengagement forces were also deployed around
the settlements. The first ring, combining army and police, was there to
deal with removing the settlers from their homes. The second ring, the
Israeli Defence Force, was charged with blocking the surrounding roads
to prevent anti-withdrawal activists from reaching the settlement. The
third and fourth rings would defend both civilian and security forces
from potential Palestinian attack, and the fifth ring would patrol the
Green Line and control roads near the Gaza border. Then there was the
ring nobody wanted to talk about – the zero ring. With Israeli security
services estimating that perhaps more than 3,000 right-wing activists
had already entered the Strip and infiltrated settlements to link up with
more hardline settlers, this zero ring of special forces and commandos
would be present to deal with any violent stand-off situation that could
arise. On both sides, people could only wait and watch. Each knowing
that the pullout had enormous implications for the future of
Israeli–Palestinian relations. For both peoples the risks and potential
rewards were as high as they had ever been.

As some Palestinians prepared to celebrate the settlers' departure,
others looked nervously to the future. For once, they had at least that
much in common with their Israeli adversaries.

Khan Younis, Gaza, August 21, 2005

Like many Palestinians in the town of Khan Younis during those
days, Salah Abu Wahab Najr simply had to venture on to his rooftop
and look down into the settlements of Morag and Neve Dekalim to witness scenes he never before would have dreamed possible. 'The Gaza
Strip is as small as this dish,' he told me, lifting the round silver tray on
the table in front of us. 'With one million people, we need space, we

need land.' Up until just a week before we talked, Salah, an unemployed labourer, refused to believe that Jewish settlers would actually ever leave the Gaza Strip. But by then, having personally watched Israeli troops chase a few settlers through the greenhouses of Morag – before bundling them aboard buses – he could scarcely disguise his glee. 'When you see something you enjoy, you will not forget it,' he said with a wry smile, gazing the few hundred yards towards the ten *dunams* of his land that ran along the perimeter of the small Morag settlement, sitting adjacent to the much larger Neve Dekalim. As long as the settlers had been there, Salah had been denied access to the land that was legally his.

Over those last few days, emotional scenes of Jewish settlers being forcibly removed had dominated the world's television headlines. Israeli Prime Minister Ariel Sharon had talked of how these had been the 'saddest days' of his life, and the words 'pogrom' and 'dispossessed' had slowly slipped into the language of many newspaper reports. Across Gaza and the West Bank, Palestinians were understandably bemused by this, puzzled by the level of world attention given to the plight of the settlers who had occupied their land illegally for almost 40 years. 'We know all about dispossession . . . what do you think this is?' said Naif Lahan, a bus driver, standing in the hills of rubble that lay at the Tufaha crossing. The junction – if the dirt roads that lead off it can be called that – sits just a few hundred yards from the 30-foot-high concrete wall that marked the perimeter of the Neve Dekalim settlement. In Arabic, the word *tufaha* means apple. Nobody quite seemed to know why the crossing was given this name. Perhaps there were orchards or fruit trees here once. There were certainly none there now, only mounds of compressed concrete and steel that were once homes, before the Israeli tanks and bulldozers moved in.

Those buildings still standing looked like a movie set from the final scenes of *Saving Private Ryan*. Here, every house had been peppered with bullet and shrapnel holes, the larger gaping chasms evidence of where tank shells had gone clean through, blowing people's lives away in an instant. Every surface was pitted with evidence of conflict. Around Tufaha, the electricity supply was erratic, and clean water had to be brought from a few blocks away. Yet, in these ruins, whole families, like moss in the crevices of a crack, still managed to grow and survive. When not bedded down on mattresses, they cooked, washed and ate in terrible squalor. Here and there children walked barefoot in the sandy earth strewn with shards of broken glass, old bullet casings and Gaza's endless discarded waste. Few families living right on the front line had a television set, and thus saw little of the dramatic close-up pictures of settlers wrestling with Israeli soldiers just a few hundred yards from where they lived. Those further back into the neighbourhood with access to television had complained over the past few days that continual overhead flying by Israeli unmanned surveillance drones had interfered with their digital reception. The 'camels,' as Gazans had inexplicably nicknamed the aircraft, had, they said, denied them the pleasure of seeing the settlers 'on the receiving end' for once. All night, every night, the buzz of the drones could be heard in the clear, starry sky, and many Palestinians were puzzled as to why, for the first time they could remember, the aircraft were lit up.

It was in March 2004 that the Israelis bulldozed the home of former geography teacher Abu Salah Shikir at the Tufaha crossing. Today, with the help of the Palestinian Authority, he, his wife and five children had been rehoused in a neighbouring district that still straddled the front line with Neve Dekalim. A tall man with receding hair and a heavy moustache, he liked to write love poems and songs in his spare time. 'To say the settlers have "lost" their homes is to use the wrong word. How can they come and occupy illegally and then lose anything?' he said, throwing my question back at me with irrefutable logic. On the wall above him was the room's only token decoration, a plaque with the words 'I love you' over the image of a single rose. 'I don't hate the Jews,' he continued. 'If another country came to Scotland and occupied it, would you give them a flower?' he asked in response to another of my questions.

By now Abu Salah Shikir found it painful to return to the ruins of his house at Tufaha crossing. 'In Gaza there is no gold, there is no oil, only sand and sadness. People eat their sadness daily,' he told me softly. I put it to him that the recent scenes – from Neve Dekalim and other settlements – of Jew fighting Jew could be repeated here in the future in a Gaza Strip packed with competing Palestinian militant groups and factions. 'Some people are blood merchants. They received benefits from the existence of the Israeli occupation; when the occupation ends, they will lose out,' he insisted. I hadn't the heart to disagree with him. To tell him that I thought Gaza and its long suffering people were in for even more unpredictable and potentially volatile times. Not that you would have guessed this looking around at the flag shops decked out with their special T-shirts celebrating the Israeli 'withdrawal' and 'victory of the intifada.' As someone said at the time it was as if Gaza was dressed up for a wedding but prepared for a funeral.

Flags were one of Gaza's few growth industries – not surprising really, given the range of political customers around. From almost every rooftop antenna, mast or pole flew the flags of Gaza's myriad Palestinian factions. The green of Hamas, yellow of Fatah, pale blue of the Abu Rish Brigades, white of the al-Aqsa Brigades, and the black of Islamic Jihad. Over the last few days as the Israeli withdrawal got into full swing, a giant banner showing a saluting Yasser Arafat had been strung across the Tuhafa crossing. Looking at the banner, I couldn't help wondering, what old Abu Ammar would have made of his nemesis Ariel Sharon's decision to withdraw from Gaza? More interestingly, perhaps, was how Arafat would have primed his Palestinian Authority to deal with the tussle for power that many Palestinians in Gaza now, like myself, believed was inevitable?

At rallies across Khan Younis all that week, the ominous first signs were already being expressed defiantly on the streets. 'My brothers, you are men of resistance, of bombs, mortars and rockets. Above all, you are men of victory,' reminded Abdullah Abu Sita, head of the Abu Rish Brigades, a militant offshoot of Fatah but with close links to the Islamic movement Hamas. Abu Sita's firebrand speech was full of the fighting talk sure to give Palestinian President Mahmoud Abbas a few sleepless nights – if he wasn't having them already. It was also the kind of Islamist sabre-rattling and clarion call guaranteed to send shivers down the spines of world leaders from Washington to Jerusalem, London to Cairo.

'We will continue in our jihad and resistance till we achieve full pull-out, not only from Palestine, but also from Baghdad, because the enemy is one,' Abu Sita bellowed into a microphone, surrounded by his masked holy warriors, carrying the ubiquitous Kalashnikovs and rocket propelled grenade launchers. 'We will attack the enemies of Islam, in Beit Hanoun, in Rafah, or in Fallujah,' insisted Abu Sita, in a clear indication that his idea of jihad was the exportable variety, ranging anywhere from north Gaza to Egypt and the towns of Iraq.

Held directly outside the Khan Younis municipality building, the rally was clearly aimed at throwing down the gauntlet to those within the PA, those whom the Abu Rish Brigades saw as appeasers of the Israelis. 'You are here now, but were home with your women when we were fighting the Israelis,' Abu Sita taunted Palestinian Authority police and soldiers, who shuffled nervously on guard outside the municipality building.

A few days later, it was the turn of Islamic Jihad to take to the streets. While their numbers were fewer than those mustered by Hamas, and their fighters less well equipped, they marched dangerously close to Tufaha crossing well within sight of the Israeli soldiers peering from watchtowers outside Neve Dekalim. It struck me then just how much of a tinderbox Gaza had become. Yes, it had always been a pressure cooker, but now there was an overwhelming sense that the coming months would be some of the most dangerous times this perennially perilous piece of land had ever had to face. Gaza had become a place where lawlessness was now the norm, where the total disregard of authority from even the youngest of street kids was a direct consequence of the violence of the intifada and Israeli occupation. For the foreseeable future at least, it was hard to see how its citizens could find themselves being anything more than at the political whims or beck and call of the Strip's many armed militant factions. Most of them bitterly resented the PA, and were keen to be seen as the true liberators when the Palestinian landrush for the former settlement areas got underway in the coming weeks.

Mahmoud el-Najar was a senior figure in the Palestinian Authority Mukhabarat or intelligence service in Gaza, though when we spoke he insisted that his duties were those of a human rights adviser to the police. 'Our main problem in the immediate future is stability and our economy,' he told me. 'The groups that pose a threat to peace in Gaza are from the smaller factions, many of whose members are disgruntled because they have not been given jobs or access to work within the authority.' A former student and Fatah member in Beirut during the time of the Israeli invasion in 1982, he said he was confident of the PA's ability to keep Gaza's factions in check, and of its capacity to quickly improve the area's economic lot. Mahmoud el-Najar was also adamant that Gazans would not pull up the ladder on their fellow Palestinians in the West Bank, who would remain under occupation despite the Gaza withdrawal.

There was no doubt that this was a troubling question and posed something of a dilemma for so many of the Palestinians in Gaza I spoke with during those uncertain days of the Israeli pullout. On the one hand, there was the desire and hope that the international community would invest financially in the Strip's economic resurrection. On the other, an insistence that they would continue to support their West Bank brothers and sisters in the intifada, and oppose Israeli settlement expansion there. For prospective foreign investors, such thoughts were simply not on. To them, the issues were fundamentally incompatible. Admittedly, it was very early days as yet, but reconciling these economic and political inconsistencies did not even seem to have registered on the awareness radar, except perhaps within President Abbas's closest circle. Then there was another question of political awareness that the Palestinians need-ed to consider quickly and respond to, one that revealed the real motives behind Ariel Sharon's grand disengagement scheme. As Dov Weisglass, Sharon's chief advisor had put it bluntly at the time, the disengagement process was about putting an end to the peace process and placing any possibility of having a Palestinian state in 'formaldehyde.' Formal-dehyde, as one Middle East commentator quickly pointed out, was what dead bodies were preserved with.

During those days that I spent in Gaza there was no denying the excitement many Palestinians felt at the prospect of the Israeli with-drawal and dismantling of the settlements there. After all, people here hadn't really had very much to smile about for many years. But the unpalatable fact remained that the Gaza disengagement would simply restructure Israel's occupation, so that instead of controlling the lives of the people of Gaza from within, it would do so from without. While Sharon's troops redeployed to the edges of the Gaza Strip, they would still continue to keep control over the air space, the sea space and the land borders. Despite claims from Washington that Gaza was just the start of the disengagement process, the reality was something quite dif-ferent. In withdrawing from Gaza, Sharon clearly intended to consoli-date his grip on the West Bank by holding on to four of its main settle-ment blocs, a move that had been publicly endorsed by President George W. Bush in a reversal of the US position since 1967. Palestinians in the West Bank continued to be reminded of this reality daily, as Israel's separation barrier snaked its way around their villages and towns, annexing their land and livelihoods in the process.

What's more, in order for Israel to consider future political negoti-ations with the Palestinians, Sharon made it clear that there had to be a total halt to violence, weapons had to be confiscated, and 'terror organ-isations' dismantled. Without absolute calm, 'the Palestinians would not be able to realise their national dream,' he insisted. In a nutshell, all the indications were that even after the Gaza withdrawal was complete, Sharon would not yield to the international community's desire for a two-state solution to the Arab–Israeli conflict. As ever he remained implacably opposed to the emergence of any independent and viable Palestinian state with its capital in East Jerusalem. Indeed, many Gazans themselves that I met at that time, optimistic as they tried to be, were clearly not convinced that they had seen the last of Israeli military might to match its political manoeuvrings. 'You know what will happen if Islamic Jihad or one of the other groups throws more rockets into Israel?' asked one elderly Palestinian man I spoke with. 'Sharon will send over his planes and bomb us, the Israelis will simply see such an attack from Gaza as an act of external aggression, and will then say they can respond as they wish,' was his worrying prediction. Unfortunately, it was one that would prove absolutely correct in the months ahead.

Looking back on those days of the Israeli withdrawal in Gaza, probably few Palestinians were under any real illusions about what lay ahead. All most wanted to do was for a few moments, at least, enjoy a sense of liberation, no matter how limited or deceptive it might prove to be. In Khan Younis one afternoon, as the last of the Israelis prepared to go, I'll always remember Salah Abu Wahab Najr making his way to the rooftop of his house. Not on this occasion to watch the forcible removal of any more settlers, but instead to hoist 38 Palestinian flags, one for each year of the occupation and separation from his land.

Jerusalem, January 26, 2006

'Today we woke up and the sky was a different colour. We have entered a new era,' was how Palestinian chief negotiator Saeb Erekat described it. A new era it most certainly was. In an election result ordinary Palestinians quickly dubbed the 'earthquake' and which stunned the world, the Islamic group Hamas had ended the four decade long domination of the ruling Fatah party, taking 76 seats in the 132-seat Palestinian parliament. The world could scarcely believe it. It was a long way from barely two years before when Hamas had virtually been decapitated, after two Israeli air strikes in the early months of 2004 assassinated its leader, Sheikh Ahmed Yassin, and his successor, Abdel Aziz Rantisi.

In Washington, George W. Bush, made the startling – if patently obvious – observation that the Hamas victory was clearly a sign that Palestinians were unhappy with the political status quo, but also that it showed democracy at work which was 'a positive thing for the Middle

East.' Bush seemed confused however by the full implications of a victory by an organisation both the US and the European Union had long since identified as a 'terrorist group.' 'I don't see how you can be a partner in peace if you advocate the destruction of a country as part of your platform,' he told reporters. 'You can't be a partner in peace . . . if your party has got an armed wing.'

In Israel too there was shock, even if journalist Bradley Burston in a *Ha'aretz* article entitled 'Does Hamas Want You Dead?' tried to leaven the questions in his piece about the Islamic group's future intentions with a touch of black humour.

> With the Islamic Jihad you know where you stand. They want you dead. It's part of a worldwide movement of wanting you dead. They take orders from people in Damascus who want you dead, people in Tehran who want you dead, people south of Beirut who want you dead. With Hamas, knowing where you stand is less cut and dried. . . . Now as Hamas prepares to enter the Palestinian parliament, and perhaps the cabinet, it's time to ask – will the real Hamas please stand up?

In a way Burston's piece caught succinctly the sense of bewilderment that confronted most Israelis on waking up that morning to hear that an organisation they had always regarded as one of the most deadly and uncompromising in the intifada had been given the seal of approval by most of the Palestinian population. Bad as it was, this latest blow also came while Israelis found themselves still reeling from the news that Prime Minister Ariel Sharon had slipped into a coma in the middle of Israel's own election campaign. 'We had a plan for every eventuality in the Middle East except for this one,' a senior Israeli security official was quoted as saying. Indeed, if truth were told, even Hamas themselves seemed momentarily dazed by the magnitude of their electoral success.

Across Gaza, the West Bank and in Syria, where Hamas had an office, suddenly their leaders were 'pitchforked peacefully' into office overnight with almost no transitional groundwork having been done for taking up the reins of power. The list of pressing issues and questions they faced was long and daunting to say the least. Suddenly, instead of clandestine meetings to discuss intifada tactics, strategy or attacks on Israel, its leaders faced new concerns. What would the group's legislative priorities be? Should its military commanders assume control over

Palestinian security forces at the risk of riling Fatah and the PA even further? Should Hamas recognise Israel and sit down with them at the negotiating table? For those long-term observers of the Palestinian movement and its intifada, few were truly surprised by the Hamas victory. The margin of their win, on the other hand, was something else.

All the signs had been there that a new Palestinian leadership was emerging after decades of control by the old guard. This new young guard was comprised not only of Hamas but those nationalist elements that included the likes of the Fatah's semi-militia Tanzim, and the armed wing, the al-Aqsa Brigades. For some years leading up to the elections, the intifada had consolidated into two vital trends within Palestinian politics and society. The first, a split between old and young within the nationalist movement, had greatly limited the PA leadership's capacity to manage the growing crisis and engage in any meaningful talks with Israel in the short term. The second was a broader decline in the power of the nationalists relative to the likes of Hamas, making it difficult for the nationalists to effectively lead the Palestinian people.

According to research carried out by Khalil Shikaki, Associate Professor of Political Science at Ber Zeit University, before the al-Aqsa intifada, Hamas had not significantly benefited from the decline of Arafat and Fatah. However, by July 2001, following the outbreak of the uprising, all that suddenly changed, and for the first time ever, support for Islamist and nationalist opposition groups combined 31 percent, surpassing the 30 per cent achieved by Fatah and its allies. The dramatic rise in popularity of Hamas in tandem with the al-Aqsa intifada was all the more significant given its slowness in joining the uprising. For many months, the tactics and pitch of the intifada had been dictated largely by Fatah, especially Marwan Barghouti's Tanzim.

Following Ariel Sharon's election as Prime Minister and his vow to bring security to Israel 'within 100 days,' Hamas finally threw in its lot with the uprising. Indeed, by the time the intifada was three years old Hamas' popularity had risen to 60 percent, confirming the group as a political player equal in power to Fatah in parts of the West Bank, and outstripping it in Gaza. While many people pointed to Hamas' election success as more to do with Palestinian disgruntlement, Arafat's decline and the Fatah old guard's failure to deliver on peace or tackle corruption, Hamas by 2006 had set its own winning agenda. Not only did it build on its reputation for being relatively corruption free, but it was also reaping the benefits from years of commitment to its elaborate welfare and support systems, especially in its Gaza stronghold. Almost inevitably, given such a radical shift in power within the Palestinian movement, trouble was quick to brew between Fatah and Hamas in the wake of the election. Many pointed to dangerous times ahead between the rival groups, while talk of a third intifada also began to go the rounds. While it's hard to imagine a Hamas leader and an American Christian right-winger having much in common, in May 2006 almost within weeks of each other a senior figure from each of these polar opposite camps voiced similar fears about the potentially dangerous times ahead.

First, Moussa Abu Marzouk, second in command of the Syrian-based leadership of Hamas, warned that Western attempts to isolate the new Hamas Palestinian government could trigger a violent third intifada against Israel. Then, almost simultaneously, it was the unlikely turn of Pat Buchanan, former Republican presidential hopeful and founder of the magazine *American Conservative*, to draw the same worrying conclusion in an article entitled 'Steering into a third intifada.'

Both men were not alone in their concern. From the tense impoverished refugee camps of Gaza to the cafés of the West Bank and Arab East Jerusalem, there were also increased rumblings of disquiet among ordinary Palestinians. Over rounds of Turkish coffee and Narghile pipe smoking, the troubled talk was of the gathering storm of another intifada brewing against Israeli repression, not to mention the possibility of an all-out civil war among Palestinians themselves. Those engaged in such discussions at the time had every reason to be worried, for ever since Hamas had taken office two months before there had been an escalating struggle for control of the Palestinian government, the security forces and the Palestinian streets. Around that period those who spent time in Gaza described it as a time bomb. Sometimes barely yards apart, rival militiamen from a newly formed Hamas force of 3,000 men and those of Palestinian President Mahmoud Abbas's Fatah had faced off in gun battles.

While Hamas insisted that their militia were deployed simply as a police force to help curtail the chaos and instability of Gaza, their Fatah rivals accused the Islamists of spearheading a *coup d'état* against President Abbas. 'This is the spark for Palestinian-on-Palestinian fighting, and from this spark . . . a civil war will break out,' warned Abdel Aziz Shaheen, a top Fatah official.

Perhaps sensing that the tipping point was fast approaching, Hamas eventually ordered its gunmen off Gaza's streets to ease tensions, but stopped short of disbanding the force that its Fatah rivals have dubbed the Black Militia. According to Youssef al-Zahar, one of the militia's leaders, his men at the height of the stand-off were ordered by the Hamas Interior Minister, Saeed Seyam, to withdraw, but 'concentrate in certain locations to be ready to rush to the scene when needed to confront chaos.' Within days, however, the Hamas men were already redeploying and tension was again rising.

The brinkmanship was further heightened after President Abbas gave Hamas ten days to back a plan for a Palestinian state alongside Israel, otherwise he would call a referendum on the proposal, effectively going over the government's head and setting the stage for a potentially lethal showdown. Predictably, the Hamas-led government said it would not make any political concession that would implicitly acknowledge Israel's right to exist. After all, the Islamist group has always said that it sought to destroy Israel, a position that triggered an international aid boycott and brought the Palestinian Authority economically to its knees. 'We will not recognise the legitimacy of the occupation, we will not renounce resistance and we will not recognise unjust [interim peace] agreements,' Prime Minister Ismail Haniyeh insisted while speaking at a Gaza mosque.

Meanwhile, alongside this tense on-off Hamas/Fatah stand-off, there was still the growing concern over an eruption of Palestinian anger into another intifada against Israel itself. Six years on since the start of that second intifada – which it's probably fair to say has never officially ended – little has changed for most Palestinians despite their efforts to make the world sit up and take notice by voting in Hamas. Humiliation, grinding poverty, curfews, movement controls and extrajudicial killings remain part of everyday life for most Palestinians. Their economic plight, especially, is dire. Barely 50 percent of men and one in nine women of working age are in a job. According to a report released by the International Labour Organisation (ILO) in May 2006, four out of ten Palestinians in the territories under Israeli military occupation or effective border control are now living below the international poverty line of $2.10 a day. It's a situation, says the ILO, that 'amounts to a daily affront to human dignity.'

In Gaza these terrible conditions were made even worse after Israel launched yet another large-scale military offensive into the Strip. Starting just before midnight on June 27, 2006, and continuing into the small hours of the following morning, Israeli warplanes carried out airstrikes on bridges and power plants in Gaza. With most of the Strip plunged into darkness, at around 2.30 a.m. on the morning of June 28, Israeli troops and tanks moved in to take control of the open areas east of Rafah. As ever with such deployments, the invasion was given a deceptively benign name and dubbed 'Operation Summer Rain.'

According to Israeli Prime Minister Ehud Olmert, the aim of the assault was 'not to mete out punishment' but rather to apply pressure so that an Israeli soldier, nineteen-year-old corporal, Gilad Shalit, would be freed. Shalit was captured after Hamas fighters infiltrated Israel from Gaza through a tunnel on June 25, in a raid that left two IDF soldiers dead, and corporal Shalit the first Israeli serviceman abducted since 1994.

'We want to create a new equation – freeing the abducted soldier in return for lessening the pressure on the Palestinians,' promised Olmert before Israeli forces unleashed their crushing onslaught across Gaza.

'Fight your enemies, who came to their deaths. Grab your rifles and resist,' urged Hamas leader Nizar Rayan over Palestinian radio, as Israeli tanks rumbled down Gaza's sandy streets, and helicopters and planes strafed whatever was deemed a threat.

As Operation Summer Rain once again threw Gaza into turmoil, I couldn't help think back to that day when along with Salah Abu Wahab Najr I stood on the roopftop of his home watching the settlers pack up and move out while the soldiers tore down the buildings they were leaving behind. How distant it now seemed. How quickly things had come full circle, bringing the days of rage back yet again.

Any hopes that might have sparked for Gazans during the Israeli pullout were now once again being blown away like the Gaza sand by Israeli tank and artillery shells as the IDF moved to consolidate their assault. As the sun rose on the first morning of the invasion, Palestinian families could be seen piling into cars or loading themselves onto horse drawn carts, fleeing before the advancing Israeli army that demolished greenhouses, olive trees and orange groves as part of a scorched-earth style advance. I felt a terrible sense of *déja vu* about Operation Summer Rain, the images of suffering that it threw up being so reminiscent of Operation Defensive Shield. And just like its bloody predecessor in the West Bank, the Israelis made clear their intentions in a series of broadcast messages and leaflets dropped across the Strip from Jabaliya to Khan Younis.

The IDF extends its operations to all areas of the Gaza Strip, and therefore conducts military activities in your area, for the time period that is required. . . . Anyone who interrupts IDF forces activities, conducted in order to complete their mission to bring the kidnapped soldier home safely will be in danger.

Keen as they were to bring home corporal Gilad Shalit, the Israeli mission also had as much to do with turning the screw on Gaza and the Palestinian resistance at precisely the moment when internal differences between Hamas and Fatah were coming to a head.

Watching ordinary Gazans try to cope with the hardships the fighting compounded, it was hard to imagine how their lives could become more difficult and dangerous.

It was a measure of how vulnerable Gaza already was that barely days after the Israeli invasion, Alvaro de Soto, United Nations Special Coordinator for the Middle East Peace Process, said that fuel would run out within two to three days, resulting in the collapse of the sewage system. Moreover, all 22 Gaza hospitals would lose electricity from spare generators within a week, meaning that some 200 surgical operations performed daily would have to be cancelled or postponed at precisely the moment the casualty numbers were escalating and hospitals would be overflowing with the wounded. Hundreds more Gazans living with the battles raging around them and suffering renal failure would face death due to the lack of electricity to run dialysis units.

'No-one can hide from us what they are doing, neither the Palestinian nor the Israeli side. We are appalled by seeing how they are playing with the future of defenceless civilians, including children,' observed UN relief coordinator Jan Egeland, warning that Gaza was just days away from a humanitarian crisis. One of the primary targets of the Israelis was the main water pumping stations, which supplied the central part of Gaza with all its water. In summer temperatures often exceeding 85 degrees, the shortage of water that resulted from these being put out of action was a virtual death sentence for the young, ill and elderly.

But while things were truly grim in Gaza, the situation in the West Bank was also deteriorating fast with the unrelenting imposition of Israel's controversial 420-mile long concrete separation barrier, or 'apartheid wall.' Everywhere it seemed that the sense of suffocation that so often in the past had given rise to an upsurge in Palestinian resistance was once again reaching critical levels.

In an article entitled 'Toward a third intifada,' published in May 2006 by the *Baltimore Sun*, Israeli writer Fred Schlomka pointed out how 'the Hebrew term "hafrada" which means "separation" or "apartheid",' has entered the mainstream lexicon in Israel and determined much of the government's policies since the Oslo process began in 1993.

Already, Palestinian access to Jerusalem has gone from being infrequent to almost impossible. The building of the barrier alone has left more than 22 Palestinian communities surrounded or stranded from the West Bank, and at least four of these without access to any health-care whatsoever.

According to a report published by the UN Office for Humanitarian Affairs (OCHA) in October 2006, the number of Israeli obstacles to free movement in the Palestinian territories had increased dramatically. As of September 2006, the West Bank closure system comprised 528 checkpoints and physical obstacles, almost a 40 percent rise from August of the previous year. While some Palestinians insist that the outbreak of another intifada is just a matter of time, others say that years of war have left people weary of conflict. Then there is the question of just who would lead any renewed intifada should it occur? And if the Palestinians once again take to the streets en masse, just how might Israel respond?

While Hamas and Fatah might yet face off against each other in the streets, within their ranks are fighters who only share a common enemy: Israel. Many of their leaders know that such a catastrophic course of action would only play into Israel's hands. It should also not be forgotten that Hamas was elected by an overwhelming majority of Palestinian citizens. While this might have had as much to do with a protest vote against the cronyism, corruption and political impotency of Arafat's long dominant Fatah and the PA, to freeze out Hamas now is also to fly in the face of an already disgruntled people. An isolated Hamas-led government, politically paralysed without economic aid and squeezed out of any negotiating process, could easily become the natural conduit for popular frustration, anger and violence. 'We tried the ballot box and where did it get us?' might quickly become the prevailing cry from the street.

Syrian-based Moussa Abu Marzouk, who is second in command of the Hamas leadership, put it quite bluntly in an interview early in 2006: 'We will try everything we can to make the government successful and serve the people, but if we're unable to do it, we'll go back to before.' This meant, he explained, a return to an intifada 'even more violent than in the past,' and the collapse of the Palestinian Authority itself.

Israel and the United States, meanwhile, have been drawing up their own go-it-alone contingency plans. Just weeks after the January election of Hamas, the *New York Times* reported that US and Israeli officials met at the "highest level" to plot the downfall of Hamas by "starving" the Palestinian Authority. This began with the US-EU aid cutoff and an escalation of military operations like 'Summer Rain in Gaza to further weaken the election victors. Meanwhile Prime Minister Ehud Olmert continued to insist that his government would not talk with the terrorist Hamas, providing a convenient pretext for Israel to continue its five-year policy of no negotiation and unilateral action. 'We cannot wait for the Palestinians forever,' Olmert told members of the US House of Representatives and Senate gathered in the House chamber in Washington during a visit. If the Palestinians 'ignore our outstretched hand for peace,' Olmert said, 'Israel will seek other alternatives to promote our future and the prospects of hope in the Middle East.'

The problem is that those alternatives almost certainly include repressive measures and border drawing, guaranteed to further stir the cauldron of Palestinian resentment. As a survey in September 2006 showed, Palestinians under occupation now are no more willing to submit to the Israeli occupation than they were before. Some 67 percent polled said they did not believe Hamas should recognise the state of Israel in order to meet international donor demands, even though 63 percent would support Palestinian recognition of Israel as a state for the Jewsish people after a peace agreement is reached and a Palestinian state is established. While the implications of a Palestinian civil war do not bear thinking about, some Middle East watchers believe that Israel is covering its bets by ensuring that President Abbas and his Fatah party are militarily prepared for any showdown with Hamas.

In May 2006, Israel quietly approved an arms transfer to enable Abbas to 'contend with Hamas.' 'I can't tell you the exact amount of weapons, but it is a limited amount intended for the purpose of securing Abbas's ability to protect himself on the backdrop of the important decisions he makes,' said Amos Gilad, a senior Israeli Defence Ministry official. Gilad was of course at the time referring to Abbas's earlier ultimatum to Hamas, in which he raised the notion of a referendum to back a plan for a Palestinian state alongside Israel. Meanwhile,

Abbas himself in turn is said to have already notified the US, Jordan and Egypt that he is preparing to take action against Hamas. This no doubt is music to Washington's ears. For some time now the United States too has quietly been working behind the scenes to ensure that things go its way and that Hamas – albeit a product of democratic elections – is effectively neutered.

In the months following Hamas's victory, Washington ploughed some $42 million into bolstering opponents to the Islamists. While such a sum might on the face of it not seem very much, in the cash-strapped Gaza Strip it would go a long way. Much of that cash is going towards helping Abbas strengthen his presidential guard by perhaps as much as 70 percent, as well as reinforcing Fatah militias and providing training and strategic advice to politicians and more secular parties opposed to Hamas. 'This project supports the objective to create democratic alternatives to authoritarian or radical Islamist political options,' one official US government document states. Not surprisingly, many seasoned Middle East watchers see such moves as ominous signs of an imminent attempt to overthrow the Hamas-led government in a political coup undertaken by local Fatah militias and supported by Israel and the United States.

'We don't operate with firecrackers and neon signs to attract attention to ourselves,' said one of the contractors working with Fatah on behalf of the US State Department. Even more worryingly, it seems that Washington's funds will also be used to encourage 'watchdog' groups and local journalists to investigate the activities of the Hamas-led government and parliament. All of which of course has the potential to ignite serious intra-Palestinian violence and even civil war.

'We are already at the beginning of a civil war, no doubt about it. They (Hamas) are accumulating weapons and a full-scale civil war can break out at any moment,' said Tawfiq Tirawi, the head of Palestinian Authority intelligence and a Fatah milita leader, in October 2006. While Hamas leaders including Prime Minister Ismail Haniyeh have stressed repeatedly that they will never be drawn into a civil war, in light of these moves against them, Hamas must feel it is being squeezed between a war with Israel and a war with its Palestinian brothers. For both Hamas and Fatah, the political stakes have never been higher. The pressure grows daily across the Palestinian leadership to ensure that they fulfil the hopes and aspirations of their people, but at the same time not bow to the terms and conditions of their Israeli occupiers.

'Let the Palestinian street speak,' threatened Yasser Arafat back in 2000 when the final round of US-sponsored peace talks with Israel collapsed. Shortly afterwards the al-Aqsa intifada spread like wildfire across the occupied territories. The Palestinian street may yet speak again. The troubling question is, just what might it deliver?

Afterword

'The long occupation has succeeded in changing us from children of Palestine to children of the idea of Palestine.'

—Mourid Barghouti

Bourj el-Barajneh Palestinian Refugee Camp, Beirut, July 2006

'Can you smell it?' asked Mohammed Ajami, my Lebanese translator, sniffing the humid air wafting through the open car window as we snaked our way through the bomb-blasted streets. 'It's that old time Beirut war stench; cordite, smoke and garbage.' All around us lay an eerie, apocalyptic landscape: rubble-strewn roads, severed electricity lines, and ripped apartment buildings with their windows blown out, curtains billowing like distress flags on a storm-stricken ship. For block after block, whole neighbourhoods lay smashed and deserted, save for a few people desperately rummaging through the shattered concrete, twisted steel and dust, salvaging what was left of their belongings and businesses. It was like travelling back through time, as if our driver had slipped into reverse gear, passing through 20 years or more to those dark days when the very word 'Beirut' first became a *leitmotif* for the worst possible hell-hole.

It was here in the city's southern suburbs, in the Palestinian refugee camp of Bourj el-Barajneh, that I came across 60-year-old Zakia Hammad, cowering along with other Palestinian women and children, in a dank, claustrophobic bunker. Like everyone else in the camp, Zakia was trying to escape the Israeli shells and bombs that thudded terrifyingly outside. Over the next hour or so, Zakia told me the story of how she had lost all her children to the previous wars that had wracked Beirut and Lebanon, including one daughter who was 12 years old when she was blown to pieces. 'I was two years old when the Israelis kicked my family out of Palestine,' she told me, before adding that she still dreamed of returning one day to the land of her birth. As we spoke, a little boy and girl came hurrying down the stairs into the bunker, breathlessly telling their mother how they had seen a woman cut and covered in blood from flying glass caused by the explosion of an incoming Israeli shell. I saw Zakai glance towards them. 'All my children are gone, dead, and now look at us,' she continued, tears glazing her eyes.

In the Middle East, it seems war is like a malevolent wind that blows, disappears then returns again. For so many Palestinians like Zakia Hammad and Ali Naji, a teacher in the Al-Bus refugee camp in the city of Tyre who I was to meet a few days later, war has cast a shadow over their lives for almost as long as they can remember. How will I ever get my book on the intifada finished, when events in Gaza or the West Bank constantly overtake what I write? I jokingly complained to Ali Naji one afternoon in the Al-Bus refugee camp during the recent war in Lebanon. 'The answer to that is simple,' he told me, smiling. 'There is no ending to your book until the Palestinians have a home of their own.' Most Palestinians – and Israelis – can scarcely begin to think of a day when their lives will be at peace. For those that continue the struggle against the Israeli occupation, the intifada is either ghost dancing or nation building, and sometimes it is both. At the very least, it has crystallised their sense of being a nation, but it is a phantom nation. Insubstantial perhaps, but incandescent yet.

Acknowledgments

I owe a lot of thanks, at home and overseas, professional and personal. Above all I am indebted to those Palestinians and Israelis who gave of their time to talk with me and allow a better understanding of the problems and traumas that afflict their daily lives. For their steadfast camaraderie in the field, my heartiest thanks to Mafouz Abu Turk, Steven Gordon, Ewan MacAskill, Q Sakamaki, Bob Tait, Martin Patience, Zead Mostafa and the late Rob Farn. I'm also grateful to Raja Shehadeh, a wonderful writer and lovely man.

This book would not have been possible without the unstinting support of a number of colleagues at the *Sunday Herald* and permission to use reports filed for the paper. I received tremendous encouragement from former *Sunday Herald* editor Andrew Jaspan, now editor-in-chief of *The Melbourne Age* newspaper in Australia. Current Editor Richard Walker and Deputy Editor David Milne have continued that commitment to reporting international stories from where they are happening. Diplomatic Editor Trevor Royle, a veteran of the book writing business, offered invaluable advice.

Former Deputy Foreign Editor Louise Shannon gets a special mention in dispatches. Not only did she hold the fort in my absence, but kindly took the time to let those I left behind at home know that I was safe and well. Neil 'Fingers' Mackay meanwhile was a constant source of inspiration – or maybe trepidation is a better word.

This book would never have seen the light of day had it not been for the commitment and enthusiasm of its publisher, Bob Smith, and the calm consummate professionalism of its editor Alison Rae. I'm also indebted to production manager Craig Brown, of Park Productions, as well as proofreader Cara Ellison and to the graphic endeavours of

John Henderson.

For her selfless support and putting up with the demands of a very selfish foreign correspondent, I can only say the biggest thank-you of all to Caron.

Notes

This is mainly a book of reporting. Over the years, countless Palestinians, Israelis and others allowed me to interview them, follow them around, and learn from them. There are too many to be named here and many would prefer not to be.

Other basic source material for this book falls into three categories: books, newspaper and magazine articles, and online sources. In particular I made extensive use of material published on the wonderful website 'Electronic Intifada' and the Israeli, Arab, UK and US press including: *Ha'aretz*, *Yedioth Ahronoth*, *Maariv*, *The Jerusalem Post*, *Palestine Report*, *Middle East International*, *Palestine Times*, *Al-Ahram*, *The Guardian*, *The Independent*, *The Daily Telegraph*, *Washington Post*, *New York Times*. News agency reports from Reuters, The Associated Press and Wafa were also useful for supporting eyewitness accounts.

Among the journalists whose work I found especially invaluable was the terrific reporting and piercing analysis of Suzanne Goldenberg, Jonathan Cook, Chris McGreal, Ewen MacAskill, Peter Beaumont, Robert Fisk, Jeremy Bowen, Orla Guerin, Zee'ev Schiff, Nigel Parry and Phil Reeves.

Vital background material, statistics and reports from human rights organisations were also used, and I am grateful to Amnesty International, Human Rights Watch, Palestine Human Rights Information Centre (PHRIC) and B'Tselem.

Foreword

'There is no truth in Beiruit, only versions', Bill Farrell quoted in *From Beiruit to Jerusalem*, Thomas Friedman, HarperCollins, 1990

'Israel's Intafada Victory', Charles Krauthammer, *Washington Post*, June 2004

'In the intifada the Palestinians discovered the power of their weakness and the Israelis the weakness of their power', Amos Elon, *A Blood-dimmed Tide: Dispatches from the Middle East*, Penguin, 2001

War of the stones

Definitions of intifada – 'Electronic Intifada'

Intidssar al-Atwar case, quoted in Noam Chomsky's *Fateful Triangle: The United States, Israel, and the Palestinians*, p. 474

Reference to 'enlightened occupation' and booklet issued by Israeli Civil Administration from *Intifada: The Palestinian Uprising – Israel's Third Front*, Zee'ev Schiff and Ehud Ya'Ari

Brigadier General Ya'acov Orr's account from Thomas Friedman's *From Beirut to Jerusalem*

Yigal Sarna, 'Uncle Ahmed's Cabin', article in *Yedioth Ahronoth*, July 3, 1987

Reference to Israel losing control over Palestinian population, Zeev Schiff and Ehud Ya'ari, *Intifada: The Palestinian Uprising – Israel's Third Front*

'The disturbances in the territories will not occur again', Defence Minister Yitzak Rabin quoted in Amos Elon's *A Blood-dimmed Tide: Dispatches from the Middle East*

'You can't imagine what's happening there ...', Israeli soldier originally quoted in *Davar*, December 22, 1987, then used in *The Intifada: An Overview: The First Two Years*, Jerusalem Media and Communications Centre Report, December 1989

Description of Ansar III camp first published in Hebrew-language magazine *Koteret Rashft*, 1989, then in 'How Israel Hides its Concentration Camps', Mitchell Kaidy, Washington Report on Middle East Affairs

First *communiqué* of the Unified National Leadership, 'No Voice Will Silence the Voice of the Intifada'

Account of Hebron activist from 'Intifada Diary', Nigel Parru, Electronic Intifada

'Don't worry, the army will assert control very quickly', Amos Elon, *A Blood-dimmed Tide: Dispatches from the Middle East*

'Force, power, beatings ...', John Kifner, *New York Times*, January 20,

1988; January 21, 1988; Glenn Frankel, *Washington Post*, January 23, 1988

'Our task now is to recreate the barrier of fear between Palestinians and the Israeli military ...', *Time*, February 8, 1988, p. 39

'The insurrection must be quelled immediately ...', Henry Kissinger quote, Robert D McFadden, *New York Times*, March 5, 1988

Account of Dr Raphael Wolden in Amos Elon, *A Blood-Dimmed Tide: Dispatches from the Middle East*

Account of Israeli novelist A B Yehoshua, *ibid*

'The Israeli government gave me a budget ... Israel gave major aid to Hamas', Richard Sale, terrorism correspondent, New York (UPI), February 24, 2001

'A direct attempt to divide and dilute support ...', *ibid*, Amos Elon

'The thing wrong with so many Israeli operations ...', *ibid*, Amos Elon

'The Israelis are like a guy who sets fire to his hair ...', *ibid*, Amos Elon

'The thinking on the part of some of the right wing ... Hamas history tied to Israel', Richard Sale, terrorism correspondent, New York (UPI), June 18, 2002

'Deeply entrenched state of mind ...', *ibid*, Amos Elon

'Ten months is too long a time ...', Rabin quoted in Noam Chomsky, *Fateful Triangle: The United States, Israel, and the Palestinians*

'Invisible transfers', *ibid*

'Nothing would stop it ... the effect was incredible', Intifada diary: Ten Years After, Nigel Parry, Electronic Intifada

'We will not finance the bullets ...', *The Intifada: An Overview: The First Two Years*, Jerusalem Media and Communications Centre (JMC), p. 52, December, 1989

Apocalypse tomorrow

'Iraq and Palestine represent a common will ...', *Al-Ahram*, 1991

'He was dressed in military clothes ...', Radio Islam, 1994

The bulldozer in the china shop

'How To Start An Uprising', Jeff Halper, Israeli Committee Against House Demolitions (ICAHD), November 15, 2000

'I can think of a lot of bad ideas ...', Dennis Ross quoted in 'Don't Let the Lights Go Out', Evan Goldstein, *Peace* Magazine, and Charles

Enderlin, *Shattered Dreams: The Failure of the Peace Process in the Middle East*, Other Press, 2003

'Murderer, murderer,' account of Sharon's visit to Harm al-Sharif, Suzanne Goldenberg, *The Guardian*, September 29, 2000

'Chairman Arafat, come try your best ... Quest for Middle East Peace: How And Why It Failed', Deborah Sontag, *New York Times*, July 26, 2001

'Act with courage and resourcefulness', address to the Knesset by PM Ehud Barak, Camp David Summit, July 10, 2000

'The Palestinians always complain that that we know ...' Phil Reeves, *The Independent*, September 10, 2000

'Do you want to attend my funeral?', Robert L Bartley, 'A Clarifying Moment', *The Wall Street Journal*, April 2, 2001

'Messianism: Targeting Haram al-Sharif', Jonathan Cook, *Al-Ahram*, July 31, 2003

'What provocation is there ...', 'Rioting as Sharon visits Islam holy site', Suzanne Goldenberg, *The Guardian*, September 29, 2000

'When we had seen a hundred bodies', *Pity the Nation*, Robert Fisk, Oxford University Press, 1992

'Pregnant women will give birth to terrorists', *ibid*, Fisk

'Blowing up of houses ...' and 'hitting the inhabitants', Israeli Defence Force orders in IDFA 644/56//207 cited in *Righteous Victims*, Vintage Books, New York, NY, 2001, p. 278 (Benny Morris)

'Like the Day of Judgement', account in *Peace Fire: Fragments from the Israel Palestine Story*, Ethan Casey and Paul Hilder, Free Association Books, 2002

'They have no right to the Haram ...', *ibid*

'The start of a "Six Year War"', *ibid*

'Must not forget the image of Mohammed al-Durra', *Blood Libel*, Clifford D May, Foundation for the Defence of Democracies, March 3, 2005

'When the people of Palestine are crying out against Israel ...', 'Making of a Martyr', Suzanne Goldenberg, *The Guardian*, October 3, 2000

'I went crazy. I was screaming and crying ...', quotes from Amal al-Durra and her husband, Nomi Morris, *The Age*, October 3, 2000

'First of all I am very, very sorry about this kid ...', *ibid*, Nomi Morris

'I came to the realisation that Palestinian cameramen ...', 'The Mysteries of an Iconic Video Frame', Doreen Carvajal, *International Herald Tribune*, February 7, 2005

'One gets the impression that instead of genuinely confronting this incident ...', 'Arab boy haunts army from grave', Suzanne Goldenberg, *The Guardian*, November 9, 2000

'All my children are disabled and Fares ...', Khalil Sakakini, Centre Ramallah, background material to 'The Hundred Martyrs' exhibition

'I somehow got into the building and found that the two Israelis were indeed inside', Ramallah's Chief of Police, Gideon Levy, *Ha'aretz* Magazine, October 20, 2000

'I just killed your husband', widows of Israeli soldiers tell of last, desperate phonecalls, Associated Press report, October 13, 2000

The resistance escalates

'There were body parts, flesh and blood', 'It can't continue like this', Ellis Shuman, *Israel Insider*, March 5, 2001.

'After the explosion ...', account of Police Assistant Commander Ahron Franco, Israel Radio, March 5, 2001

'Operations of this kind ...', *Israel Insider*, March 5, 2001

'There's a feeling of zero security', *Israel Insider*

'This intifada has laid down a new rule ...', Marwan Barghouti quoted in 'The intifada behind the al–Aqsa intifada', Gary C Gambill, Middle East Intelligence Bulletin, November 2000

'I knew that the end of September ...', Marwan Barghouti quoted in *Al-Hayat*, September, 2001

'While we were in the car ...', *ibid*

'Whoever thinks that this started ...', Imad Falouji quoted in *The Jerusalem Post*, March 2001

'We know very well that the most loyal forces of Arafat ...', Ariel Sharon quoted on BBC online, March 5, 2001

'We tried seven years of intifada without negotiations ...', Marwan Barghouti comment in November 2000 quoted in the *Christian Science Monitor*, 'The "Palestinian Napoleon" behind Mideast Ceasefire', July 3, 2003

'Fear, hate, anger, and frustration have risen on both sides ...', Mitchell Report, May, 2001

Testimony of Ra'ed Ahmad Salem al-Hamri, in report by Palestinian Human Rights Monitoring Group (PHRMG)

'Arafat refused to take notice of the impact that the intifada had on ...',

Shlomo Ben-Ami, *Scars of War, Wounds of Peace. The Israeli–Arab Tragedy*

'When the young survivors start looking ...', Ari Shavit, *Ha'aretz*, March 10, 2002

'It is very, very near – right in front of our eyes ...', 'An Arsenal of Believers', Nasra Hassan, *The New Yorker*

'And then I heard it ...', account of Netanya 'Passover' bombing by Naomi Ragen, *Peace Fire, Fragments from the Israel Palestine Story*, Ethan Casey & Paul Hilder

'I felt shock waves ...', account of Itai and Nechama Donenhirsch, *The Guardian*, March 28, 2002

'The sound I will never forget ...', Naomi Ragen in *Peace Fire, Fragments from the Israel Palestine Story*

'This is the time for Chairman Arafat to speak to his people ...', United States Secretary of State Colin Powell quoted in Israel Ministry of Foreign Affairs website, March 27, 2002

'I have a feeling this is going to be very bad.'

'In these wretched days, I've asked myself ...', 'Can repeat of Warsaw be stopped in Palestine?', Executive intelligence review, March 22, 2002

'Before searching a house ...', B'Tselem report, Operation Defensive Shield, 2002

'One, Arafat is a murderer', *Yediot Aharonot*, Alex Fishman, December 17, 2001

'All-out assault to smash the Palestinian Authority ...', Middle East Realities website, July 12, 2001

'Very clearly to Sharon about this issue and warned him ...', Middle East Realities website, July 13, 2001

'Coldbloodedly, with the patience of an old hunter ...', *Yediot Aharonot*, December 14, 2001

'Drinking from a very dangerous cup ...', *On the Frontline*, BBC documentary, Jeremy Bowen, January 2005

'Three had been shot in the head at close range ...', 'Three Days in Ramallah', Anthony Shadid, *Boston Globe*, April 1, 2002

'They were shot point-blank ...', *ibid*

'The town was under curfew ...', B'Tselem report, Operation Defensive Shield, 2002

'There were eight of us in the small room, including ...', B'Tselem report, Operation Defensive Shield, 2002

Rocket the casbah

'The camp was ready for war ...', Reuters, April 15, 2002

'The moment I drove the bulldozer into the camp ...', Moshe Nissim interview, *Yediot Aharonot*, May 31, 2002

'Not a massacre, but a brutal breach of war's rules ...', Peter Beaumont, *The Observer*, 2002

'So when does a bloodbath become an atrocity ...', Robert Fisk, *The Great War for Civilisation*, Fourth Estate, 2005

'Okay, so there wasn't a massacre ...', Arie Caspi, *Ha'aretz* magazine, 2002

'This war should be called the "war for the home" ...', Shaul Mofaz, Reuters

'Most of the people that founded the brigade ...', Tim Cornwall, *The Scotsman*, March 9, 2002

'I sat down on the step and grabbed the water pipe ...', B'Tselem report, Operation Defensive Shield, 2002

'The 78 martyrs in Nablus were kept in a refrigerated truck ...', Electronic intifada, 2002

'He kept moving from one place to another ...', *Al-Ahram*, 2002

'Though Israel could be said to have won tactically the war of the intifada ...', Shlomo Ben-Ami, *Scars of War*

Another brick in the wall

'This year will be the year that will shape the Palestinian struggle ...', *The Jerusalem Post*, 2004

'At first we all said it was terrible, it was inhuman ...', *Sydney Morning Herald*, Ross Dunn, June 15, 2002

'The first intifada destroyed the credibility of the greater Israel movement ...', interview on Radio Netherlands, January 29, 2005

'Who here cares about farmers like Nimr Ahmed ...', *A Wall in Their Heart*, Merron Rappaport Miftah, in *Yedioth Aharonoth*, June 3, 2003

'I don't think the fence will solve all the problems ...', *Ha'aretz*, 2003

'Two things are certain about Israel ...', *The Economist*, 2004

The demise of the enigma

'The Arafat mug was never ...', Robert Fisk, *The Independent*, 2004

'When the intifada would not die ...', Said K Aburush, *From Defender to Dictator*, Bloomsbury, 1999

'Arafat never viewed money in a personal enrichment sense ...', *The Financial Times*, 2004

'The death of Yasser Arafat ...', Israel news

'He ... has no hobbies,' replied Avnery ...', Gush Shalom, website interview with Uri Avnery, October 30, 2004

The changing of the guard

'This is a test. We need to convince the world ...', Israel News, August 11, 2005

'We will not be stopped at checkpoints ...', *Ha'aretz*, 2005

'Today we woke up and the sky was a different colour ...', BBC News, January 27, 2006

'I don't see how you can be a partner in peace', *Time*, February 6, 2006

'With the Islamic Jihad you know where you stand ...', Bradley Burston, *Ha'aretz*, 2006

'We had a plan for every eventuality in the Middle East ...', *Time*, February 6, 2006

'This is the spark for Palestinian-on-Palestinian fighting ...', Reuters, 2006

'We will not recognise the legitimacy of the occupation ...', Reuters, 2006

'I can't tell you the exact amount of weapons ...', *Israel Insider*, May 26, 2006

'Why should we be the only ones who live in fear?', *New York Times*, July 2006

'Formaldehyde', Dov Weisglass, Middle East Report Online, March 2005

'Not to mete out punishment', Ehud Olmert, Electronic Intifada, June 2006

'Some 67 per cent polled said they did not believe Hamas should recognise the state of Israel', Reuters/Zogby poll

'This project supports the objective to create democratic alternatives to authoritarian or radical Islamist political options,' one official US document states, Reuters, October 2006

'We don't operate with firecrackers and neon signs to attract attention to ourselves,' said one of the contractors working with Fatah on behalf of the US State Department, Reuters, October 2006

'We are already at the beginning of a civil war, no doubt about it. They (Hamas) are accumulating weapons and a full scale civil war can break out at any moment,' *Sunday Times*, October 8, 2006

Select Bibliography

Abbas, Mahmoud (Abu Mazen), *Through Secret Channels*, Garnett Publishing, 1995

Aburish, K Said, *Arafat, From Defender to Dictator*, Bloomsbury, 1998

Ashrawi, Hanan, *This Side of Peace*, Simon & Schuster, 1995

Ben-Ami, Shlomo, *Scars of War, Wounds of Peace: The Israeli–Arab Tragedy*, Weidenfeld & Nicolson, London, 2005

Bishara, Marwan, *Palestine/Israel: Peace or Apartheid*, Zed Books, 2001

Carey, Roane, *The New Intifada, Resisting Israel's Apartheid*, Verso, 2001

Casey, Ethan & Hilder, Paul, *Peace Fire, Fragments from the Israel Palestine Story*, Free Association Books, 2002

Chaliand, Gerard, *The Palestinian Resistance*, Pelican 1972

Chomsky, Noam, *Fateful Triangle, The United States, Israel & The Palestinians*, Pluto Press, 1999

Cobran, Helena, *The Palestinian Liberation Organisation, People, Power and Politics*, Columbia University Press, 1984

Di Giovanni, Janine, *Against the Stranger*, Penguin, 1994

Elon, Amos, *A Blood-dimmed Tide: Dispatches from the Middle East*, Penguin, 2001

Enderlin, Charles, *Shattered Dreams: The Failure of the Peace Process in the Middle East 1995–2002*, Other Press, 2003

Fisk, Robert, *Pity the Nation, Lebanon at War*, Oxford University Press, 1992

Fisk, Robert, *The Great War for Civilisation – The Conquest of the Middle East*, Fourth Estate, 2005

Gowers, Andrew & Walker, Tony, *Yasser Arafat and the Palestinian Revolution*, Corgi Books, 1991

Gresh, Alain, *The PLO: The Struggle Within*, Zed Books, 1989

Halevy, Efraim, *Man in the Shadows: Inside the Middle East Crisis with a Man who Led The Mossad*, Weidenfeld & Nicolson, London, 2006

Hiro, Dilip, *Sharing the Promised Land: An Interwoven Tale of Israelis and Palestinians*, Hodder & Stoughton, 1996

Hirst, David, *The Gun and the Olive Branch*, Faber, 1984

McDowell, David, *Palestine And Israel: The Uprising and Beyond*, I.B. Tauris, 1989

Said, Edward W, *The End of the Peace Process: Oslo and After*, Granta Books, 2000

Said, Edward W, *The Politics of Dispossession, the Struggle for Palestinian Self-determination 1969–1994*, Vintage, 1995

Said, Edward W, *Peace and Its Discontents*, Vintage, 1995

Shehadeh, Raja, *When The Bulbul Stopped Singing*, Profile, 2003

Shehadeh, Raja, *Strangers in the House*, Profile, 2002

Wasserstein, Bernard, *Israel and Palestine: Why They Fight and Can They Stop?*, Profile, 2003